Language,
Nation and
Development
in Southeast Asia

The **Institute of Southeast Asian Studies (ISEAS)** was established as an autonomous organization in 1968. It is a regional centre dedicated to the study of socio-political, security and economic trends and developments in Southeast Asia and its wider geostrategic and economic environment. The Institute's research programmes are the Regional Economic Studies (RES, including ASEAN and APEC), Regional Strategic and Political Studies (RSPS), and Regional Social and Cultural Studies (RSCS).

ISEAS Publishing, an established academic press, has issued almost 2,000 books and journals. It is the largest scholarly publisher of research about Southeast Asia from within the region. ISEAS Publishing works with many other academic and trade publishers and distributors to disseminate important research and analyses from and about Southeast Asia to the rest of the world.

Language, Nation and Development in Southeast Asia

EDITED BY

Lee Hock Guan
Leo Suryadinata

ISEAS

INSTITUTE OF SOUTHEAST ASIAN STUDIES
Singapore

First published in Singapore in 2007 by ISEAS Publishing
Institute of Southeast Asian Studies
30 Heng Mui Keng Terrace
Pasir Panjang, Singapore 119614
E-mail: publish@iseas.edu.sg
Website: http://bookshop.iseas.edu.sg

ISEAS Library Cataloguing-in-Publication Data

Language, nation and development in Southeast Asia / edited by Lee Hock Guan and Leo Suryadinata.
1. Language policy—Southeast Asia—Congresses.
2. Southeast Asia—Languages—Political aspects—Congresses.
I. Lee Hock Guan.
II. Suryadinata, Leo, 1941–
III. Institute of Southeast Asian Studies.
IV. Workshop on Language, Nation and Development in Southeast Asia (2003 : Singapore)
P119.32 A9L28   2007

ISBN 978-981-230-482-7 (hard cover)
ISBN 978-981-230-483-4 (PDF)

Cover Photo: Jelutong English School, Penang 1967. Photo courtesy of Lee Hock Guan.

Typeset by Superskill Graphics Pte Ltd
Printed in Singapore by Utopia Press Pte Ltd

Contents

Preface

In early 2003, the editors of this volume discussed the possibility of holding a workshop on "National Language Policy and Nation-Building in Southeast Asia". After a few meetings, we agreed that the workshop should add another dimension, i.e., economic development. This is particularly essential in an era of globalization where economic issues often take command. We then began to prepare the topics and identify a few individuals; some were to write papers, while others were to serve as commentators. We immediately discovered that it was difficult to get writers for some countries, and as a result, we decided to leave out Laos, Cambodia and Brunei Darussalam.

The preparation of the workshop was relatively smooth. All of the presenters, except one, came to the workshop and were enthusiastic in presenting their arguments. We were fortunate to have Professor Wang Gungwu who agreed to give a keynote speech. He raised some important issues which were later discussed during the workshop. At the end of the workshop, we agreed that the papers should be revised for publication. Due to unforeseen circumstances, the process was very slow. Some papers were dropped as writers did not have time to do the revisions. Meanwhile, both of us were also bogged down by other responsibilities. At last, the revised papers have been edited and published. We would like to offer our apologies to the writers included in this volume for the belated publication. However, the facts and arguments presented in the papers are still relevant to the current situation.

Finally, we would like to thank Ambassador Kesavapany, Director of the Institute of Southeast Asian Studies (ISEAS), for his support for the workshop and Dr Colin Durkorp of the Konrad Adenauer Stiftung, who kindly graced the opening of the workshop and financed both the workshop and this publication. Nevertheless, the views expressed in the various chapters are the responsibility of the paper-writers alone.

Lee Hock Guan
Leo Suryadinata

The Contributors

Melani Budianta is Professor and Head of Literary Studies Department, Faculty of Humanities, University of Indonesia.

Ashley Carruthers is Lecturer in the School of Archaeology and Anthropology at the Australian National University.

The late **Andrew Gonzalez** was Professor of English and Applied Linguistics at the De La Salle University, Manila.

Kyaw Yin Hlaing is Assistant Professor of Asian and International Studies at the City University of Hong Kong.

Lee Hock Guan is Senior Fellow at the Institute of Southeast Asian Studies, Singapore.

Theraphan Luangthongkum is Dean of the Faculty of Arts at Chulalongkorn University, Thailand.

Lucy R. Montolalu is Senior Lecturer of Linguistics at the University of Indonesia.

Leo Suryadinata is Director of the Chinese Heritage Centre at the Nanyang Technological University, Singapore.

Eugene K.B. Tan is Assistant Professor of Law at the Singapore Management University.

T. Ruanni F. Tupas is Lecturer in the Centre for English Language Communication at the National University of Singapore.

Wang Gungwu is Director of the East Asian Institute at the National University of Singapore.

Keynote Address

Wang Gungwu

I am delighted to have the opportunity to participate in this workshop. It was not difficult to get me to come because I have always had a soft spot for language. Of the three important words of your workshop — language, nation and development — my favourite is still language. However, the nature of language and the ways we use it have changed and I now have difficulty following recent language trends.[1] So I welcome this opportunity for me to think about it afresh. Several common and stimulating themes emerged from the workshop papers. Perhaps the most important point is the multiplicity of languages. We are fortunate in Southeast Asia to live in one of the regions where there are so many different languages and language families.[2] That diversity has enriched all of us.

Let me add a personal note. I was born in a place[3] where there were many different languages around me and grew up in another place[4] where a different set of languages prevailed. I was never able to master those languages, but the exposure to so many of them when young was very important to my life. It meant that I grew up being aware of the importance of language, the various ways people communicate, and the different nuances that surface when similar things are expressed in different languages. All these points I did not fully appreciate when I was young. Only later did I recognize how important they are to us as human beings, and that has left a strong impression on me. My experience was not unusual. Among the people I grew up with, most have had similar experiences. In addition, the people I have known professionally, in the universities and research institutes I have worked in, were also multilingual in one way or another. That confirmed for me that knowledge and sensitivity about language is something that we cannot do without.

Let me briefly discuss the three words, language, nation and development. It is not automatic or natural for us to link the three words together. It may seem obvious today to say language, nation, and development must be connected, but actually this is a very recent occurrence.[5] Of the three, language is the most basic. It has always been there, from the day we became humans, and probably even before that, when we began trying out utterances that marked the beginnings of language.[6] In a sense, we continue to develop such chains of sound and meaning as soon as we are born; and as our minds grow, so do our language skills. It is natural for us to want to communicate at the most fundamental level. Look at the way we build our own relationships, beginning with that between mother and child, among members of the family and with the community and the tribe when growing up.[7] The web of familial and communal relationships is something that no human being has been able to avoid, and language is the key to sealing those relationships.

This leads me to contrast language with the other two words, nation and development, because the other two are not basic to humans in the same way. The latter two concepts are very much constructs of the modern world and I think we should not forget that. We must not take for granted that nation has always been there. On the contrary, in this part of the world, especially in Southeast Asia, the idea of nation is so new that we still do not fully understand what it entails.[8] We know that the new nation in Southeast Asia was one of the products of our desire to free ourselves from colonial rule, so that we can have the independence to build up our own sense of national identity. But the fact remains that, in many countries, the leaders have been struggling for the past fifty years with the question of what a nation is, and in particular, with the question, "what is a nation-state"?

We know the history of how nationalism followed anti-colonialism and anti-imperialism. Knowing that, we cannot help but notice how recent its history is. Indeed, some of us can even remember when the word nation first came into our consciousness. In that context, we should stop and think about the difference between something that is basic to our lives and something that is a recent construct, a new project that would be difficult to realise in a few decades. Indeed, the more quickly we try to develop such a nation-state, the more threats there will probably be. Among those threats are problems associated with the language rights of the peoples that now live within the borders of the national territory. That is a consideration that we shall have to bear in mind. It is actually even more complicated than that. The world is changing so fast that, even as we are struggling with this concept of nation that we have borrowed from Western Europe and are still learning how to handle, we have to face the broader and equally demanding challenges of development.

Again we seem to assume that development is a natural thing.[9] Actually, it is not. Of course, in earlier times, societies that survived through the centuries did gradually develop, but that was not the kind of modern development that most people now expect. Today, when we use the word development, it involves strong and responsible states leading and guiding their peoples to make their nations prosperous through rapid economic development. In global terms, it involves keeping up with a world that is expanding at a very rapid rate, along an upward spiral of economic growth unknown in the human past. This process of globalization is now something that is beyond our control, so powerful and pervasive has it become. We have to respond to it whether we like it or not. Even nations and the nation-states themselves are under tremendous pressure from the fact that everyone is pursuing growth and the world is relentlessly developing. If states fail to respond and develop their countries, their citizens will not accept the leadership of these countries. Hence the tension that is growing between state and society because both the state and the communities that live within it are invariably linked to the capacity to develop together.

Wherever there is failure to develop, we talk about failed states. What do we mean by that? Essentially we mean that the leadership has failed to develop their country in ways that would satisfy the people, by raising their standards of living, and meeting the multiple expectations of modernization. As the people find their voice or voices, and as they are more articulate and speak up more, the states come under even greater pressure to deliver, to meet promises that their leaders had given when they were campaigning for support.[10] All political leaders are under great strain today, in a way that they never were in the past. In fact, if you look at rulers and their courtiers and functionaries in the past, most of them were self-indulgent and corrupt, at the expense of the majority of the people. That was what it used to be, but today most people would not allow that to happen without strenuous protest.

The modern world is putting different kinds of pressure on the political leadership everywhere. And one of the very powerful pressures in Southeast Asia comes from problems of nation-building and development. First, what should they do to build this new nation? Having inherited the bureaucratic state from the colonial power or built a revolutionary state against it, the people want their own nation. But how are they to build it?

Nation-building has been a very difficult task for all our leaders. In every country in Southeast Asia we find not just many languages and many national groups, but also many sub-languages and many sub-national groups, each demanding national recognition. On top of dealing with that, the political leaders find themselves also having to face pressures from outside. For example, the financial crisis of just a few years ago was an awakening experience for many of us in the region.[11] Suddenly, the whole region found itself utterly helpless in the face of unknown, intangible forces, affecting all of us. None of us quite anticipated the way it happened. The trigger was very sudden, and although it had been building up for sometime, not many people anticipated its coming. Even fewer expected the impact it had.

Let us return to the key word 'language' that lies behind the nation-state but also the process of development. We have had more than a couple of generations to see the kinds of challenges languages have posed to new nations. We have seen how nation-building pressures have strengthened certain languages and weakened others, in some cases, even destroying some languages. Thus one of the natural products of our need to maintain our human links have been so distorted by the pressures of nation-building that some languages have had to be sacrificed, so to speak, in the course of building up one dominant language as the national language. This is not to question the motives of the people who set down national policies. They have often done so for the best of reasons: to strengthen and prosper their countries, to enable their people to be united behind a strong sense of identity, and to enable their countries to be strong enough to defend themselves against their enemies. That is understandable, and indeed there was no way that the leaders who sought to harness the forces of nationalism and anti-colonialism could have avoided it. The damage to some languages was part of the high price that the country had to pay.

I am not talking only of the languages that came from elsewhere into the region — the ones from China or from India or even from the Middle East. Although the speakers of these languages have domiciled in, and identify with, the new nation-states, these languages might be considered alien to the region because they originated elsewhere. In fact, major languages like Chinese, Tamil, Arabic and others are not in any danger. What seem to me important are examples of languages within the region that are facing the pressures and contradictions that accompany the course of nation-building. For example, in a recent study of the census of Indonesia, we are reminded that, while the national language, Bahasa Indonesia, is vital to the nation-building process in Indonesia, the reality is that the vast majority of the Indonesian people do not speak it naturally.[12] It is striking to see how the people of Java, who make up more than half of the population of the country, speak different mother tongues and would not normally speak the Malay language that is the basis for Bahasa. Bahasa is the lingua franca they all use when speaking with people who are not natives of Java. Of course, this is understandable, but it emphasizes the ongoing contradictions within a nation where there is a national language as well as other languages used by large and powerful groups of people who want to keep and defend the use of their own native languages. The tensions created by the use of state power to treat other languages as secondary or inferior would ultimately be very disruptive to the nation-building process.

I am talking about state power here because this is what the nation-state means and because, in our region, states were established before nations. States set out to build nations using state power — all the bureaucratic modern power that states can wield today to try and forge a nation out of many different peoples and with many different cultures and languages. In the course of nation-building, it is to be expected that many of these languages and cultures would be under pressure, and some would disappear, or so weaken that they cannot survive on their own. In all Southeast Asian countries, the state apparatus and power has been used to deal with the sub-national languages, regional languages, tribal languages, community languages and foreign languages. State policy can be extremely beneficial, but it also can be destructive. I think we have to recognize that reality, and also that the need for this power is likely to remain for some time.

What really should get our full attention today is the pressure of development. This is the next stage. What does this mean? In fact, during the past few decades, the development demands are contrary to the nation-building pressures. This is largely because development requires something else, for example, the need to maintain a good standard of living or, better still, to improve standards of living so that people will be satisfied and not turn against the leadership. You have to accept that the linguistic skills needed to enable development are not necessarily the same as the linguistic needs for national solidarity. Indeed, the contradictions arise from the borderless nature of the economic situation today, seen for example, in the financial crisis that enveloped the region where economic forces rapidly and indiscriminately acted on every country. Thus the countries that are less prudent ended up hurting those that were more prudent. This was beyond the control of the leaders at the time. Given that experience, different attitudes towards change are now necessary, including that towards the uses of language.

In India, for example, private colleges are growing at a very fast rate by announcing and advertising the fact they are teaching in English. Even families from poor villages try to save money to send their children to these private colleges. The private colleges do not charge very high fees; in fact, their fees are low compared to elsewhere. The demand for private colleges is high because students prefer to go to private colleges teaching in English and not to state schools that teach in Hindi or in other regional languages. I remember travelling around Delhi seeing signs saying, "We teach in English" and being told what a strong selling point this is.[13] To actually forsake the public school system that teaches in your own language for the private one that teaches in English is an increasingly common phenomenon.

Not that many years ago, it was just the other way round. People gave up English so that students could learn in the national language. Everyone was encouraged to use the national language so that it could become a great and superior language. People were willing to give up a lot of to achieve that. We could look at what happened to the students in Ceylon (now Sri Lanka). In the 1950s, Sri Lanka had universities and schools with probably the best English standard of the non-English-speaking parts of the British Commonwealth in Asia and Africa. Yet, within a decade or two of changing its language policy to one of teaching everything in Singhalese, that position was lost. This was made clear to me when I interviewed a post-graduate student from Sri Lanka who wanted to do a research degree with me in the field of Chinese history. His Chinese was good, having studied the language in China, but his English was quite inadequate for an English-language university. What amazed me was that a Sri Lankan university graduate could have lost the ability to use English at that level just a decade or two after the switch to national language teaching. It was painful to see him struggle with a language that his fellow graduates a generation earlier had used with skill and eloquence. It is interesting, however, to see how, during the past decade, that position has been reversed, not just in Sri Lanka, but also almost everywhere in Asia.

One of the most remarkable developments observed in the last two decades is the way the People's Republic of China changed its language policies and the Chinese students have picked up English. It is simply incredible how language skills have changed. When I visited China in

1973, only a handful of Chinese could speak foreign languages, and the foreign language they knew best was Russian. English had virtually disappeared. But by 1980, second-hand bookshops were full of books in Russian that nobody wanted because everybody had switched to English. This came about because of the recognition that China needed to develop quickly out of the impoverished condition brought about by the decade of the Cultural Revolution. In order to do that, Deng Xiaoping, the country's new Communist leader, admitted that the Chinese had to learn from the outside world and that the best way to do so was through mastering the English language. Among the first things he did was to go to America and make his peace with the Americans. He also made English the foreign language that students needed to gain admission to the best universities. The four compulsory subjects for the examination to enter university were Chinese, English, and Mathematics and a fourth subject, usually Science.

It was a dramatic change to make English one of the compulsory subjects given that China had been ideologically anti-American for many years and forced everybody to learn Russian. The reason they switched was because of the pressure of rapid industrial development. Since the Chinese State put development ahead of everything else, they were willing to change their policies when they thought it would help accelerate that development. It is really staggering to see what they have done to transform the economic structure of the country. Today, every primary school child in China is starting on English. The Chinese have even reached the stage where, like the Indians, they are setting up private schools and colleges that allow the use of English as a medium of instruction, or at least teach much more English than is taught in the state institutions. The private schools are attracting parents who are prepared to pay higher fees in order for their child to learn English one or two years earlier. So within a generation, development has now almost superseded the question of linguistic nationalism in China. Indeed, many countries, including those like China which were once isolated, hostile, and almost xenophobic about foreigners, have in just one generation, completely turned around their language policies to favour a language that would support rapid development. We can now meet Chinese in Shanghai or Beijing who speak better English than people in Singapore.

I do not want to overstate this, but let me go back to the general point I made earlier. The three words — language, nation and development — are not equal. While they have different origins and histories, it is important to stress that only language is basic. But language can be sacrificed in the name of nation-building and, in turn, the national demands for development would put every person and institution under ever-greater pressure. What that could do to language use, and to the native languages themselves, is something of great interest. Many of the papers at this conference have touched on this aspect, and I do not need to say more. I would simply conclude in this way. Because the pressures facing us today are different, they require different strategies. National education systems need to adjust to meet some of these new demands. That is to be expected. There will be different rates of change in different countries, even within Southeast Asia, where you can see different countries responding differently to the challenges. I would be interested to find out how the different rates actually affect what the respective countries become in ten or twenty years' time. As for language policy, how much would that act as a kind of measure or index of how a country has moved from being nation-centred to development-centred? Language is a many splendid thing and its possibilities are great. We cannot underestimate the importance of language as a symbol that strikes deep chords in people. Hence, while states and their peoples are focused on some of the practical needs for development and globalization, it is still important that they do not lose the national and community languages that were there in the first place and that are so natural and so important for human development.

Notes

1. See for example the range of topics covered in the volume edited by Phillipson (2000).
2. Southeast Asia is a region of enormous linguistic diversity where hundreds, perhaps thousands, of languages are spoken. The classic work on this is still Norman H. Zide's *Studies in Comparative Austroasiatic Linguistics* (The Hague: Mouton, 1966).
3. Surabaya, Indonesia. Surabaya is a multilingual city in the eastern part of Java. The languages spoken in the city during my childhood were Indonesian/ Malay (as a lingua franca), Madurese, Dutch and various Chinese dialects (Hokkien, Hakka and Cantonese).
4. Ipoh, Malaysia. Besides Malay and English, there was Mandarin, Cantonese, Hokkien, Hakka and Teochew among the Chinese, and at least Tamil, Malayalam, Punjabi and Telugu among the Indian languages.
5. For a comprehensive discussion of nationalism and language, see Chapter 2 in May (2001). The global presence and role of English has led many countries to see that knowledge, if not mastery, of this language has become an important factor in helping most countries in their economic development.

6. There are two general theories of language. Noam Chomsky, the renowned linguist, proposed a naturalist theory of language which argues that linguistic capacities are already pre-wired into our brain as a result of natural selection. In contrast, a cognitive theory of language viewed human linguistic acquisition as a result of learning and cultural development.
7. As indicative of the importance of the mother-child dynamic we have the notion of 'mother tongue'. However, the mother-child dynamic today has become less fundamental in certain societies due to a variety of intervening agencies: television, maids, early childhood centres, and so on.
8. Experiences of nation-building in selected Southeast Asian countries can be found in Wang (2005).
9. Arndt (1987) and (1993).
10. The voice of the people has gained much mileage with the growing influence of democratic governance in the region; the most recent experience being that of Indonesia after the downfall of Soeharto.
11. Jomo (2004).
12. Suyardinata, Nurvidya, and Ananta (2003).
13. Command of English also enhances employment opportunities especially in jobs outsourced from Western countries.

References

Arndt, H.W. *Economic Development: The History of an Idea*. Chicago: University of Chicago Press, 1987.
——. *50 Years of Development Studies*. Canberra: National Centre for Development Studies, Research School of Pacific Studies, Australian National University, 1993.
Jomo, K.S., ed. *After the Storm: Crisis, Recovery and Sustaining Development in Four Asian Economies*. Singapore: Singapore University Press, 2004.
May, Stephen. *Language and Minority Rights: Ethnicity, Nationalism and the Politics of Language*. Essex, UK: Pearson Education Limited, 2001.
Phillipson, Robert, ed. *Rights to Language: Equity, Power and Education*. Mahwah, New Jersey: Lawrence Erlbaum Associates, Publishers, 2000.
Suryadinata, Leo, Evi Nurvidya, and Aris Ananta. *Indonesia's Population: Ethnicity and Religion in a Changing Political Landscape*. Singapore: Institute of Southeast Asian Studies, 2003.
Wang Gungwu, ed. *Nation-building: Five Southeast Asian Histories*. Singapore: Institute of Southeast Asian Studies, 2005.
Zide, Norman H., ed. *Studies in Comparative Austroasiatic Linguistics*. The Hague: Mouton, 1966.

Introduction

Lee Hock Guan
Leo Suryadinata

In the last two decades of the twentieth century, a surprising development in the Western European world was the emergence of spirited debates on the identity question. This rethinking of the identity question was propelled by two major transformations, one external and the other internal. The external transformation was in relation to the formation of the European Union, which aims to integrate the various European nation-states into a supranational state of sorts. In this supranational state, questions were raised about what will happen to the cultures and languages of the individual nation-state as it evolves. The internal transformation refers to the fact that many of the individual nation-states have over the years and with the arrival and settlement of non-European immigrants, become multiethnic societies.

Increasingly, the identity debates in Europe have revolved around the concept of "multiculturalism". According to Bhikhu Parekh, multiculturalist perspectives recognize the cultural embeddedness of human beings, the inescapability and desirability of cultural plurality, and the plural and multicultural constitution of each culture. It follows that a multicultural society values its cultural diversity and respects the rights of its members to their cultures and languages. The multicultural perspective is indeed a stark contrast to the traditional concept of the nation, also a European construct, which imagines a nation as a homogenous cultural entity. It is in fact the overwhelming dominance of this concept of nation that historically made and transformed the various Western European nation-states into largely culturally homogenous entities. Thus, in Europe now the move is to shift from the culturally homogenous nation to one that accommodates multiculturalism.

Ironically, in the post-colonial world, including Southeast Asia, the nation-building processes continue to be largely influenced by the prevalence of the traditional concept of the nation. In this regard, language was and remains a key site of contention. In the early years of nation-building, attempts to build a monolingual nation was the overriding policy in the Southeast Asian region even though the inhabitants in all the countries spoke a variety of languages. Efforts to build a monolingual nation in Southeast Asia were complicated by the recognition that as citizens, members of minority groups do have cultural rights, including the right to their language. The recognition of language rights, however, varied from country to country with some countries less tolerant than others. Even more importantly today is the minority groups' growing awareness of their cultural rights.

Besides the cultural aspect of language policies, globalization has also increased the awareness of the linkage between language and development, especially acquisition of scientific knowledge and for purposes of economic development. Indeed, this awareness, to a large extent, led the Singaporean leaders to adopt English as the medium of instruction since Independence. Similarly, in the latest move in 2003, the Malaysian Government has decided to re-introduce English as the medium of instruction for mathematics and science subjects. In general then, this linkage has forced the Southeast Asian countries to re-think their national language policy.

It will be pertinent to study the language policy of the Southeast Asian countries and issues in terms of nation-building and development. How was the national language chosen and pursued? Who made and what went into the policy? What are the positions of other non-national languages, both local/regional and foreign? How did the national language policy affect national integration and social cohesion, and national and ethnic identity formation? In light of the increasing recognition of a linkage between language and development, how has it influenced national language policies? What are the problems and prospects of the language policy in Southeast Asia?

CONTENTS OF THIS VOLUME

The two chapters on the Philippines demonstrate clearly the limits of the bilingual education policy in the country. On the one hand, Pilipino, which is largely Tagalog-based, is the national and official language which the majority of Filipinos accept as the national linguistic symbol of unity and identity and support teaching it in the educational system. Pilipino was indeed perceived to be essential to the construction of a national identity. On the other hand, English language competence continues to be regarded as an asset, in particular in relation to access to economic opportunities. Gonzalez shows that for a number of reasons "little investment" was devoted to developing Pilipino as a national language and this, in turn, has diminished its role as a symbol of unity and identity. A major problem was because of the growing dependence of the country on remittances from Filipinos working overseas, the preference for English as the main medium of instruction has further strengthened. This has led the State to put more emphasis and allocate more resources to "maintain and enhance competence in English among Filipinos".

From his analysis of the language debates since the 1970s, Tupas claims that the prominence of English in the educational system and society was kept because it was the "language of the rich". That is to say, since competency in English is linked to access to political and economic opportunities, the Filipino elite has a vested interest in preserving English as the main medium of instruction. It also helps that the educational system is structured such that children of the rich receive a superior English education while children of the disenfranchised are provided with an inferior English education. The perpetuation of the unequal quality of English education in the Philippines thus contributes to the reproduction of the existing class structure.

Indonesia is one of the few countries in the world where the ethnic majority's language, in this case Javanese, was not elevated to the status of official and national language after Independence. Montolalu and Suryadinata's chapter analyses the elevation and implementation of Malay, the vernacular language of the ethnic Malay minority, as the national language or Bahasa Indonesia. Historically, the status of Malay received a major boost when the Indonesian nationalist movement chose the language as a means to unify the multiethnic and multireligious population of the archipelago. For many decades after Independence, the post-colonial State has pursued a largely monolingual policy using Malay to promote nation-building such that vernacular languages and foreign languages have become marginalized. In recent years, however, the fortunes of the foreign languages, particularly English, and vernacular languages have experienced an upward swing; the former as a result of globalization, while the process of decentralization, since the fall of Soeharto in 1998, has revitalized the latter. Hence there are growing pressures on the Indonesian State to modify the national language policy.

Budianta's chapter examines the changing evaluation of what constitutes national literature in Indonesia, arguing that fixing the boundary of national literature invariably "involves power relations and subordination". When Malay was chosen as the national language, a hegemonic notion emerged and declared that national literature would include only works written in Malay, thus consigning works written in the other vernacular languages and foreign languages to the periphery. During the New Order era, the national literature boundary was further fixed to exclude works in Malay which the regime found ideologically unacceptable or did not fit with their imagined nation. Fortunately, the fall of the New Order has stirred up debates to revisit and redefine the concepts of national literature, in particular, "the decentralization movements and the regional awakenings in literature have strongly voiced the need to acknowledge literatures written in other languages as equal to that written in Bahasa Indonesia".

In multiethnic Singapore, the State regarded the function of language in nation-building in terms of constructing a Singaporean-Singapore identity that would avoid "setting off [the] centrifugal tendencies" in the society. National language and education policies were, however, in part dictated by a language ideological framework that: upheld a English-mother tongue bilingual strategy; assumed language as purveyor of ethnic cultures; aimed to create "a core of cultural elites for each race"; and adopted "a pragmatic approach to the learning of mother tongue languages and the fundamental of economic relevancy in language planning". Tan rightly noted that the competing objectives potentially could result in "governmental interventions in the language and cultural realm [that] do not always produce the convergence of goals much sought after". The changing Government policies toward the Chinese language since Independence captured very well the twists and turns of its language strategies. While initially politics and fears of Chinese chauvinism led the State to marginalize the Chinese element in the educational system, by the 1980s, policy-makers started to reverse somewhat the situation because they feared that Chinese Singaporeans were losing their cultural heritage and roots and becoming too "westernized". In the 1990s, the position of the Chinese language was considerably enhanced when the rise of China added an economic dimension to learning the language. This enhanced status of the Chinese language, however, potentially would have negative impacts on ethnic relations if it were not managed carefully.

The chapter on Malaysia shows that although Malay nationalism was influenced by the notion of a linguistically homogenous nation, various factors and circumstances hindered them from pursuing an unambiguously assimilationist policy. In particular, the prevailing "consociational politics", which give emphasis to inter-ethnic bargaining, effectively circumscribed the Malay-dominated state language and education policies. Implementation of the consociational elites' compromises on language and education, however, was marred by conflicting interpretations of the terms of the compromises, and encountered determined opposition from civil society groups who found the compromises unacceptable. The twists and turns in language and education issues and developments in Malaysia were also subjected to three central rationales: Malays' desire to consolidate their language as the sole official language and main medium of instruction; Chinese insistence on their citizen rights to be instructed in their mother tongue; and the ruling elites' perception that linked English competency to scientific and economic progress.

The chapter on Myanmar argues that Burman leaders were not single-minded in wanting to establish a monolingual nation precisely because they had "neither a clear nation-building discourse, nor a clear definition of Myanmarness". Thus, their real aim in promoting Burmese as the official language was more a strategy to perpetuate their rule than for the purposes of nation-building. Ethnic minorities hence were given the freedom to speak and write their own languages, provided such activities were not being used to undermine the legitimacy of, or attempt to topple, the Burman-dominated governments. Unsurprisingly, in recent years, the ethnic minority nationalists' growing grievance over the language question is not over the adoption of Burmese as the official language, but rather, over the diminishing status of their languages and cultures, as a result of neglect and negligible financial support by successive Burman-dominated governments.

The chapter on Vietnam focuses on why and how the Vietnamese State has changed its language and media policies so as to benefit from the opportunities brought about by globalization. Specifically, the Vietnamese State is keen to profit from the Vietnamese diaspora; there are about 2.7 million Vietnamese residing overseas. Thus, from the mid-1990s onwards, the Vietnamese State has reformulated its language and media policies from the past exclusive focus on "territorialized" nation-building to the current emphasis on "deterritorialized" nation-building, which "involve extending national belonging ... to those who have left, despite the fact they may have taken out citizenship in and undergone social and cultural integration into second nations". A variety of language and media initiatives have been employed for this purpose, such as: teaching Vietnamese language in overseas Vietnamese communities; Vietnamese newspapers and magazines, including using the Internet, and radio and television broadcasts. However, for a number of reasons, the State has managed only very limited success in its goal "to create a sense of connectedness and nationalist affect in overseas Vietnamese communities, and thus to sustain links to the homeland across diasporic generations".

Just like the other Southeast Asian countries, Thailand is both a linguistically and culturally diverse country. The author argues that initially, successive Thai governments had pursued a "hidden policy" that emphasized "assimilation". The then prevailing rationale was that national unity and security could only be realized on the basis of "one language and one culture in Thai society". Invariably, this was translated into the elevation of the language of the dominant group, the Thais, as the national language such that there is a language hierarchy, which is a mirror image of the social hierarchy: Standard Thai, regional Thai languages/dialects and minority languages (in descending order of importance). The author claims that "Thailand has never had serious racial problems that led to riots and wars", even though Southern Thailand has witnessed periodic armed confrontations, in part, due to the Malays' grievances against the "suppression" of their language and culture. Nevertheless, future ethnic relations, despite the recent violent conflicts in Southern Thailand, may benefit from a major shift in Government policy towards some sort of linguistic, and cultural, pluralism.

1

Language, Nation and Development in the Philippines

Andrew Gonzalez

Among the members of the Association of Southeast Asian Nations (ASEAN), the Philippines has been considered a laggard performer in socio-economic development. Although many development social scientists have often pointed out its vast potential (in terms of natural and human resources), the sad reality is that in the last thirty-years, the country has been described as on the verge of take-off but never quite taking off. Promise has not borne fruit in actual progress. The progress has been slow, erratic, and insufficient to make the economy match the better performers of the region.

Many explanations have been given for this poor performance. In James Fallows' article in the *Atlantic Monthly* (1987), he described the Philippines as "a damaged culture", an apt though hardly diplomatic remark, especially for a foreigner to make. It seems, to use the language of the Bible, that there was initial damage or "original sin" which was inflicted on the society which makes cultural cohesiveness very difficult to attain. A kinder remark has been made by a Japanese anthropologist (Kikuchi 1991) who characterizes Philippine culture as not having been sufficiently "crystallized" to make the necessary movement towards unity, nationhood and following this self-identity, rapid development.

Actually, Filipinos in this generation have been their own worst critics, blaming "politics" for the ills of society without quite defining what they mean by "politics". The euphoria following the dismantling of the Marcos dictatorship in 1986 was soon followed by disappointment and disenchantment, so much so, that many of the country's talented have been leaving in hundreds. In the 1950s and the 1960s, it was mostly members of the less affluent socioeconomic classes, who saw little opportunity for advancement, who left. The past twenty years, however, it has likewise been the affluent, some of the best and the brightest, who have migrated, seeing no future for the fulfillment of their talents in contemporary Philippine society.

LANGUAGE, NATION AND DEVELOPMENT IN THE PHILIPPINES

The per capita income of the Philippines is about US$1,020 (see World Bank 2003), less than that of Thailand, even after the 1997 currency crisis. Singapore, Taiwan, Hong Kong, and Malaysia are ahead of the Philippines with the per capita income of Singapore twenty times more than that of the Philippines, and the per capita income of Thailand more than two times that of the Philippines. The only countries behind the Philippines in the region are Indonesia, Vietnam, Myanmar, and Cambodia.

The image of the Philippines has suffered immensely as a possible tourist destination this past decade because of the terrorism and separatist movement in Mindanao, the continuing struggle with insurgents, and kidnappings. Investments have either been withdrawn or slowed down because of the unpredictable business climate, the inconsistency of policy, the frequent changes in laws, and the slow judicial and arbitration process to settle disagreements and disputes.

While English language competence continues to be an asset (the last national estimate for English speakers was 64.5 per cent of the population of 48,098,960 in 1980) (NCSO 1984), English language competence has likewise made it possible for the best and the brightest to migrate elsewhere. In fact, the educational system, which has gone down in quality the past twenty years, even in its best years has become both an asset and a liability: an asset because many Filipino graduates from the best schools in the country have been able to compete abroad; a liability, as in the process, they have been lost as assets to Philippine society.

In the Government's initiatives to maintain and enhance competence in English among Filipinos, it has unwittingly neglected the cultivation and the intellectualization of Tagalog-based Filipino, the national language. Hence, one of the manifestations of the non-crystallized culture described earlier is the lack of genuine adherence to and enthusiasm for Filipino even among today's youth. The failure to cultivate the national language as a language of intellectual discourse in universities is not the cause of non-crystallization, but one of its manifestations.

THE ETIOLOGY OF THE SLOW PACE OF CRYSTALLIZATION

The causes of the slow pace of socio-economic development are many and need to be understood fully to explain the present situation and perhaps to find ways of accelerating the process of cultural crystallization and hopefully its resultant effect of a more rapid socio-economic advancement. Indeed, the causes of the slow pace of crystallization are many and varied. No simplistic answer is acceptable. Moreover the interaction of these various causes is not easily quantifiable. A more intellectually satisfying explanatory model would be to state that it is a vector constituted by many multiple variables.

To begin with, the Philippines, while constituting an archipelago easily traversed by water, was slowly populated by a series of migrations from the South China mainland through Formosa (see Beyer 1935 and Jocano 1975, for migration patterns). Another subsequent series of migrations came from the Central Visayas in the Samar-Leyte region moving north, south and west. Scattered in different places were other ethnic groups which came in at different times from neighboring islands and settled in Mindanao.

The languages, placed at 120 mutually unintelligible varieties by McFarland (1993), have formed subgroups with clear characteristics (northern languages, central languages, and the varied language groups in Mindanao with genetic relationships to other scattered groups in Palawan, the Celebes, and Borneo).

Except for the Sultanate in Central Mindanao around the Iranun area, there was no larger government unit but small groups of kinship-bound families giving rise to a series of neighbouring ethnic groups, sometimes at war with each other. Nick Joaquin (1943, 1977), one of the national artists, asserts that prior to the arrival of the Spanish colonizers, we were not a nation but juxtaposed tribes which began to perceive themselves as Filipinos only in the last quarter of the nineteenth century (see Schumacher 1973). The culminating exemplar came in the person of Jose Rizal, whom essayist and translator Leon Ma. Guerrero (1963) called "the first Filipino".

In the eyes of the Spanish colonial administrators in 1896, the rebellion led by Andres Bonifacio was *una insurreción Tagala*, a rebellion of the Tagalogs (see Sastron 1897); even a nationalist such as Bonifacio referred to his country as Katagalugan (the region of the Tagalogs) rather than Pilipinas.

By the time of the Malolos Congress in 1897–1898, with Emilio Aguinaldo as leader, there was a clear consciousness that the people were no longer only Tagalogs, but Filipinos composed of many ethnic tribes. As revolutionary president, Aguinaldo mandated that the Filipinos be represented at the Assembly which drafted the Constitution and constituted the Malolos Republic. The representation included members from all over the archipelago and where there were none, individuals were assigned to represent an area dominated by an ethnic group.

However, even as early as that period, division set in in the rivalry for leadership between Aguinaldo and Bonifacio, both Tagalogs, which led to the execution of the latter. The Spanish colonial government paid off the revolutionaries camped at Biak-na-Bato in Bulacan with a settlement of 800,000 pesos (see Agoncillo 1990); they agreed to go into exile. However, there are still questions on how the sum which went with the revolutionaries to Hong Kong was actually spent; the remainder (the other half) was paid to leaders who had stayed in the Philippines. This latter sum has never been satisfactorily accounted for in our history books.

Unlike other wars of independence, the Philippine revolution was confined largely to the Tagalog area and its surroundings. The Filipino flag has eight rays of the sun to represent the first eight provinces which joined the revolution. There were small attempts, short-term, in the Visayas with the proclamation of the Republic of Negros, and skirmishes between Spanish colonial forces and local armies organized by ethnic leaders, but outside of the Luzon area, there was no unified local force which fought against the Spanish forces. When the American occupational forces under Admiral George Dewey and General Ellwell Otis met with the local Filipino leaders, the latter were not considered seriously. The American military forces reneged on the commitment of their Consul in Singapore that they were not merely another colonial force, but a friendly power willing to help the cause of independence of the Filipinos. Thus followed the Philippine American War which took place from 1898 to 1901. Soon after, many Filipino leaders organized a Federalista Party aimed at integrating the Philippines with the United States. The period of nationalistic fervor was thus short-lived, although the legislative movement towards independence from the United States began. Independence was carried out by legislation rather than by force, and through missions of representation to receptive democratic governments in Washington, D.C.

The strong personality of Manuel L. Quezon made him dominant as soon as he entered politics by becoming Senate President in 1916 under a bicameral system; the unicameral system under the Speaker, Sergio Osmeña, gave way to the new structure. Osmeña was a gentleman of the Old School, a genuine patriot; he refused to oppose Quezon and was content with second place. Although his integrity, talent, and patriotism were outstanding, perhaps he did not have sufficient forcefulness of character to pose serious opposition to Quezon, a Tagalog (Osmeña was

Cebuano). When finally Osmeña assumed the presidency upon the death of Quezon in 1944, it seems he did not campaign enough and lost to Manuel A. Roxas (another Visayan).

Other than political rivalry, the tutelage of legislation and experience of self-governance under the American Governor General was generally benign and without much incident. The focus of the country was towards independence through legal means. The unifying factor was the strong leadership of Manuel L. Quezon and the support of Sergio Osmeña and the sympathy of the American Democrats in Washington.

The urgency for a call to unity and nationhood beyond regional interests arose with the invasion by the Japanese Imperial State and the annexation of the Philippines and its pre-emption into the Greater East Asia Co-Prosperity Sphere. The majority of Filipinos never accepted Japanese rule; the Government of Jose P. Laurel cooperated with the Japanese Imperial Forces to protect Filipinos and to further the cause of democracy and nationalism. In the guerrilla struggle against the Japanese and in the initial struggle against Japanese invasion with the American forces in Bataan and Corregidor, the Filipinos emerged as one once more.

From the point of view of language, no consensus was possible in the 1935 constitutional convention, with the language provision ending up as a mandate to take steps towards the formation of a common national language under an academy. It was initially called the National Language Institute (by the 1936 law); later, after the selection of Tagalog as the basis of the national language, the institute was renamed the Institute of National Language (see Gonzalez 1980). The language became official in 1940, just before the outbreak of the Second World War, and was propagated as a subject in all colleges of education (normal schools) and in fourth year high school.

The Japanese Imperial Army discouraged the continuing use of English without much success. It mandated the teaching of Japanese as a foreign language, and during the 1943 Constitution, authored principally by Jose P. Laurel, Tagalog was confirmed as the national language and encouraged to flourish.

After the declaration of independence from the Americans in 1946, the national language was taught as a subject at every grade level, all other subjects continued to be taught in English, one of the requirements of the Tydings McDuffie Law which established the Commonwealth as a preparation for independence. The use of English as the main medium of instruction was supposed to continue only during the Commonwealth Period (1935–1946), but continued beyond 4 July 1946.

SOCIO-ECONOMIC DEVELOPMENT AND THE
LANGUAGE SITUATION AT PRESENT

The situation in the Philippines at present shows a society, already a state since 1898, but thereafter recolonized by another power and finally "granted" independence on 6 July 1946. Independence was officially "granted" in 1946, but the Philippines celebrated its centennial of independence on 12 June 1998.

Officially a state, and its official charter and public rhetoric declaring itself a unified nation, it has a national language (Filipino) spread out and spoken by 99 per cent of households (NSO 1990). Nevertheless, the country has not crystallized sufficiently as a nation to power its own development. There is continuing dependency for financial, military, and cultural purposes on the United States, confirmed recently by the reception accorded to President George W. Bush on his state visit to the Philippines on 18 October 2003. While Filipino is the national language, the official language, the language of linguistic symbol of unity and identity, little investment has been placed in developing it as a language of scholarly work at the universities. For basic education, a bilingual scheme of English and Filipino has been adopted, with English now more prominent than Filipino, since Filipino is used for only the Filipino Language Class and for some subjects in the curriculum, the rest being taught in English. Since the Ramos Administration, continuing to the present, there has been a re-emphasis on English and a concerted national effort now being made by the Department of Education to update teachers' skills in the use of English.

Surveys (Gonzalez and Bautista 1986, Gonzalez and Sibayan 1988) give evidence of the reality that for the Filipino, the notion of a national linguistic symbol of unity and identity has been accepted. But the notion that this means a monolingual use of English as the language of education in the schools would be totally unacceptable. The majority of Filipinos accept the principle that they must now grant a place to Filipino in the educational system under a bilingual scheme, but the continuing preference at present is that English should be the main medium of instruction. The imperative to improve English language teaching and learning stems from the fact that since the Estrada Administration, and now more than ever in the Macapagal-Arroyo Administration, overseas work for Filipinos has been officially encouraged, with one of their best assets being their competence in English.

The decision to re-orient Philippine education towards English dominance stems from economic necessity: the inability of the country to provide sufficient jobs for its thousands of graduates each year, because of a population growth rate of 2.3 per cent and a total population of 81.8 million in 2002 (see ADB 2003). In the face of China's cheap labour, the economic strategy of the Philippines is no longer heavy industrialization but once more agriculture, small businesses, tourism, the service industries (including the export of manpower and teachers of English), and English-speaking caregivers, domestic helpers, nurses and physical therapists. We now have more than seven million Filipinos living abroad as immigrants or as overseas workers, bringing an annual total of US$7.5 billion in 2002 to help the economy.

Thus, in a country which already has a problem of cohesion, recent world developments in the employment of English-speaking Filipinos have resulted in little cultivation of the national language, at least at the university level, and the continuing emphasis on the English language. As in Singapore and probably Switzerland, and in many Francophone and Anglophone countries in Africa, the national linguistic symbol of unity and identity does not transfer to the wider use of the national language other than for everyday communication and for ceremonial purposes. The language of the intellectuals is still the former colonial language; English is now considered as the almost universal language of wider communication or as an international auxiliary language.

The lack of reliance on the national language seems to be more a matter of utilitarian motivation and pragmatism. It may mean that the lack of expansion of domains of the language signals a lack of cohesion in society; it is not necessarily the main cause, but a manifestation as well as an international reinforcer of the lack of cohesion, in the sense that it has not helped towards the country's cohesive unity.

The causes of the lack of development in the country in terms of socio-economic progress have been cited, with language as a factor, but certainly not the main factor.

Presently, given the history of the country, agencies which should be helping towards cohesion and presumably more rapid development seem to be conspiring against speedier development. On a long-term basis, the almost exclusive reliance on English does not accelerate cohesion but in the minds of some worried nationalists, perpetuates a form of neocolonial cultural imperialism which, however, most Filipinos feel comfortable with. The educational system being in a non-native language relies heavily on English-language sources for its content and its derivative teaching materials. Most locally authored textbooks are based on foreign (American and British) sources and do not really take a nationalistic orientation in either Filipino or English (see UNESCO Philippines 2000).

The Catholic religion, because of its own stand on population control, has been a deterrent to any kind of population management programme which is immediately suspect as being a hidden movement towards expanded use of contraception and even worse, widespread practice of abortion. The cultural value placed on children, independent of Western religion but very much a part of indigenous culture and religion, continues to rely on children as potential sources of support in the parents' old age. But perhaps the largest stumbling block to rapid social development is the population itself and the quality of political life there is in the country. The Philippine structure of government was copied almost totally from the American structure of government, without the cultural presuppositions and values and experience of North America. What the Philippines has is the shadow, but not the substance of democracy, for while the structures are Western and are supposed to result in progress, they do not. The political leadership is corrupt and the family and cultural system of extended kinship and tribal loyalty (as opposed to national loyalty) reinforce favoritism and lack of professionalism in business and political life. The extended family system has made dynastic politics even worse with the Constitution of 1987, which was supposed to remedy the dynastic practice of the past by making elections limited to two terms for certain posts. What has happened is that when the husband can no longer run, his wife or son will run, and he himself will seek another political office. Thus, whole provinces are now dominated by different family members who play musical chairs when needed during elections. The system of justice faces grave difficulties because it is modeled on the American system of justice without the resources for making speedy legal processes possible. The investigative agencies supposedly handling the work do not have sufficient talent, manpower, training, and equipment to make crime-fighting viable. Also, the American system allowing several appeals, has become a way of delaying trials in the Philippines, so that it takes years to process any case, both administrative and civil.

CONCLUSION

This essay is descriptive, not prescriptive. It does not seek to suggest remedies, at least not as its primary objective. However, through analysis of the past and the present of the current state of language, nation and development in the country, the essay hopes to explain contemporary realities.

The point it tries to make is that the question of development is a multifactorial problem that goes beyond language and nationhood. The problem of development or lack of it has as its basis the social fabric of a society, its culture, traditions, values, language and ethnic composition, its common history, if any, that will explain why one state becomes a real nation and develops rapidly while another one does not, even if it has elements which have tremendous potential for rapid development. Not only the proper elements must be present in their proper combination, but a galvanizing principle is likewise needed to make the elements interact positively.

References

Asian Development Bank (ADB). *Key Indicators*, 2003.

Agoncillo, Teodoro. *History of the Filipino People*. Eighth Edition. Quezon City: GAROTECH Publishing, 1990.

Beyer, Otley. "The Philippine People of Pre-Spanish Times". *Philippine Magazine* 32: 476–77, 483, 515–17, 1935.

Fallows, James. "The Philippines: A Damaged Culture". *The Atlantic Monthly*, November 1987, pp. 49–52.

Gonzalez, Andrew FSC. *Language and Nationalism: The Philippine Experience Thus Far*. Quezon City: Ateneo de Manila University Press, 1980.

Gonzalez, Andrew FSC and MA. Lourdes S. Bautista. *Language Surveys in the Philippines* (1966–1984). Manila: DLSU Press, 1986.

——— and Bonifacio P. Sibayan, eds. *Evaluating Bilingual Education in the Philippines* (1974–1985). Manila: Linguistic Society of the Philippines, 1988.

Guerrero, Leon MA. *The First Filipino: A Biography of J.P. Rizal*, with an Introduction by Carlos Quirino. Manila: Jose Rizal National Centennial Commission, 1963.

Hayden, Joseph Ralston. *The Philippines. A Study in National Development*. New York: Macmillan, 1950.

Joaqin, Nick. "Our Usable Past". *Philipine Review* 1, no. 8 (1943): 42–48.

———. "History as Culture". *The Manila Review* 3, no. 2 (1977): 22–39.

Jocano, F. Landa. *Philippine Prehistory: An Anthropological Overview of the Beginnings of Filipino Society and Culture*. Quezon City: Philippine Center for Advanced Studies, University of the Philippines System, 1975.

Kikuchi, Yasushi. *Uncrystallized Philippine Society: A Social-anthropological Analysis*. Quezon City: New Day Publisher, 1991.

McFarland, Curtis D. "Subgrouping of Philippine Languages". In *Philippine*

Encyclopedia of the Social Sciences, Vol. 2, pp. 358–67. Manila: Philippine Social Science Council, 1993.

National Statistics Office (NSO). "Socio-economic and Demographic Characteristics". *Census of Population and Housing* Report No. 3. Philippines, Manila: National Statistics Office, 1990.

National Census and Statistics Office (NCSO). "National Summary". *Census of Population and Housing* 1980, Vol. II. Manila: National Census and Statistics Office, 1984.

"Remittances from Overseas Filipino Workers" 2002. <http://www.english.peopledaily.com.cn>.

Rubin, Joan and Bjorn Jernudd, eds. *Can Language be Planned?* Honolulu: The University of Hawaii Press, 1971.

Sastron, Manuel. *La Insurreccion en Filipinas y Guerra Hispano-americana en el Archipielago*. Madrid, Spain: Impr. De la sucesora de M. Minuesa de los Rios, 1901.

Schumacher, John N. *The Propaganda Movement: 1880–1895. The Creators of a Filipino Consciousness, the Makers of the Revolution*. Manila: Solidaridad Publishing House, 1973.

UNESCO (Philippines). Florentino H. Hornedo, Virginia A. Miralao and Felice P. Sta. Maria, eds. *The Social and Human Sciences in Philippine Basic Education*. Quezon City: Philippine Social Science Council, UNESCO National Commission of the Philippines (Social and Human Sciences Committee), 2000.

World Bank. *World Development Indicators*. Washington, D.C., 2003.

2

Go Back to Class: The Medium of Instruction Debate in the Philippines

T. Ruanni F. Tupas

INTRODUCTION

To understand the challenges faced by language policy-making and implementation in the Philippines, we need to examine the complex dynamics of "the coexistence of nationalist aspirations, sub-national group loyalties, and pragmatic concerns in a multilingual country" (Hau and Tinio 2003, p. 319). For the whole of the twentieth century, during which the search for a national language was deemed essential to the Filipinos' search for their own identity, these competing demands exposed both the various layers of power relations in the country, as well as the limiting and liberating conditions that created such relations. In a sense, all stakeholders to the problem of language in the country — no matter if this was a question of medium of instruction, official language, or national language — would configure their own positions out of these competing claims, either to defend their privileged positions or to demand more access to the various resources of power in society, such as quality education, economic mobility, and political representation.

The bitter debates on the national language that ensued during the writing of the Philippine Constitution in the early 1970s were a case in point. Region-based, ethno-linguistic animosity between rival elites appointed to write the constitution resurfaced; prior to this, from the 1930s onwards, Tagalog (renamed Pilipino in 1949)[1] became the national language mainly through the workings of a Tagalog-speaking national leadership. Gonzalez (1980) describes the event that revived such bitter animosity; it was the opening of the pre-Convention meeting originally meant to discuss the procedural rules for the Constitutional Convention:

The name tags and titles of the delegates, together with the districts were written in Pilipino; the opening procedural talk was given in Tagalog. When this happened, pandemonium reigned in the convention hall. The non-Tagalogs took exception to what they perceived as high-handedness and questioned, as a point of order, the use of Pilipino...(M)any asked for translations, and when non-Tagalogs were recognized, they began speaking in their own vernaculars, adding Babel to bedlam (p. 136).

From this "linguistic trivia turned to bedlam" (p. 135) followed intense debates centered on the issue of language. The language provision of the new constitution went through several revisions, with each draft crafting out differing structures of relations between available (and competing) languages. The first draft sought to do away with Pilipino in favour of English as the official language of the constitution and the country. The second draft sought to legislate "Filipino" and English as official languages, but this was an impossibility because it also defined "Filipino" as a national language that was yet to be developed by the National Assembly out of the many languages of the country. The third draft attempted to bring Pilipino back as an official language, although still secondary to English, but artfully referring to it as "Filipino" in the following section. The final draft demonstrated a cunning compromise among all competing positions: make English and Pilipino the official languages, with the English text of the constitution prevailing in cases where there were problems in interpretation. The National Assembly was to develop and adopt a national language called "Filipino" based on all existing local languages in the country (pp. 143–45). Pilipino became an official language but ceased to be a national language to give way to "Filipino", "a linguistic legal fiction" (p. 151), "a word with a sense but with no clear reference" (p. 147).

Interestingly, in 1974, a year after the new constitution was promulgated, the political compromise which resulted from the intense "language war" (pp. 98–122) that led to the language provision, set in motion a bilingual education policy through the National Board of Education (NBE) where English was to be used as a medium of instruction mainly in science and mathematics, and Pilipino in all other courses. For the first time since English was introduced by the United States at the start of the twentieth century, the power of the language in the educational system would now be seriously challenged by a local language. And true enough, from then on until now, the domains of Pilipino or Filipino have rapidly expanded

(Bautista 1988), with more and more Filipinos using the language, this time also helped by the Philippine media which started to vigorously use it to further reach out to the masses.

Before 1974, the term "bilingual education" was virtually unknown in Philippine education; not in use when the vernacular was allowed as an auxiliary medium of instruction in 1939, when Tagalog was first taught as a subject in 1940, nor when the vernacular was used as medium of instruction in the first two grades in 1957 (Sibayan 1984b, p. 125). What the NBE created was a purportedly rational education policy that helped address, at least theoretically and politically, the various agendas at play at the time. The justification for the bilingual education policy then, and for the next twenty-five years or so was: English for "access to economic opportunities" and Pilipino for "our search for identity" (Sibayan 1984a, p. 117).

The question we would like to ask in this paper, therefore, is: how were the unrelenting anti-Tagalog voices (read: sub-national group loyalties) of non-Tagalog speakers "silenced" or "appeased" by the implementation of the bilingual education policy? We must remember, as the quote from Sibayan above attests, that for much of the 1970s until today, the debate on language has been largely couched in the split between instrumentalist and identity positions (Tollefson 1991, 1986). However, I argue that such dichotomous treatment of the problem of language has largely impeded, more than clarified, the complex nature of the relation between language and society in the country on the one hand, and nationalism and development on the other hand. Tollefson and Tsui (2004) ask in relation to medium of instruction policies in the world: Which agenda? Whose agenda? The question we posed earlier will enable us to assess the underlying interests of both the pragmatist and nationalist positions on language. And in so doing we can make a case for medium-of-instruction policy as central to the study of socio-political processes in the country (see Tsui and Tollefson 2004).

THE "RETURN" OF ENGLISH: THE PROPONENTS

The trajectory from which we shall discuss the many issues that surround our question will be the most recent language debate in the Philippines.[2] On 29 January 2003, President Gloria Macapagal-Arroyo, in a keynote speech delivered during the seventy-fifth anniversary of Far Eastern University in Manila, ordered the "return" of English as the primary medium of instruction in the country. This speech, according to the leading

English-language newspaper, the Philippine Daily Inquirer (*The World's English*, 3 February 2003), "beat the drums for another cycle of the language wars". Based on 102 news articles, opinion columns, editorials and manifestos available in some of the major national newspapers in the country (75 in English and 27 in Filipino),[3] I will attempt to map out the ideological structure of the debate that ensued from the presidential directive, historicize it, as well as identify shifting theoretical and political grounds upon which the major positions are based. Thus, the brief historical sketch of the socio-political dynamics of the language problem in the Philippines given above is necessary to help locate this paper in a much larger perspective, where language issues are social issues, and where medium of instruction policies become the battleground for the preservation and/or reconstitution of power relations in the country.[4]

"We must continue our English literacy, which we are fast losing", declared President Macapagal-Arroyo in her speech (29 January 2003). English literacy, she argued, is needed to compete for high-paying jobs, especially information and communications technology or ICT. Between 30 January and 18 February, during which much of the debate was given prominent space in the papers, it is clear that the directive received broad support from the populace. The majority of the texts in consideration have been largely supportive of the presidential order or, at the very least, provided more space for the President's speech and various statements of support than the arguments against the directive. Among the titles, the President's order "gains support", "reaps praise", was "backed", "hailed", "lauded" and "welcomed". Linguistically, the social actors grammatically represented as taking the position of actively supporting the President include a wide range of people and institutions cutting across social classes, regional and political affiliations, and ages.[5] This wide-ranging support is hardly surprising as English, despite changes in the educational system in the country throughout the twentieth century, has generally been perceived positively by the people (Gonzalez and Bautista 1986). Amidst socio-political changes in the country, the symbolic power of English remained largely unscathed (Tupas 2001b; Sibayan and Gonzalez 1996).

The justifications given for the "return" of English as the primary medium of instruction are equally not surprising as they echo the similar reasons given for English in the country for more than three decades now. First, there is a case made for the deteriorating English language proficiency among Filipino students: "The decline of English in our society, even among schoolteachers, is nothing short of scandalous" (Puno

4 February 2003); and bilingual education, especially Filipino as medium of instruction, is largely to blame. This line of thought pervades both the official position of the Department of Education as well as the personal accounts of various column writers, including a number of editorials.

Second, because of the problem of English, we are now rapidly losing our edge in the international market, especially in the exportation of labour which has been the saving grace of the country's economy through billions of dollars of remittances from Filipino Overseas Workers or OFWs. The need to "arrest the declining proficiency of Filipino in the English language" by 'restoring' English as medium of instruction (*New Policy on English Lauded* 1 February 2003) is portrayed as a race against time in the midst of fierce competition in the so-called global village. China, Thailand, Korea, Japan and all other countries in the world are working double-time to teach their people the English language, and the decision to "return" English as primary medium of instruction in the Philippines puts the country back in the competitive mode. One popular columnist and TV personality who says the President has "the support of the people" writes: "We have lost too much time, we have lost our edge, and we must teach our young to think, read, write, talk and work in English" (Daza 4 February 2003). It is "a question of survival" (Puno 4 February 2003).

Thirdly, anticipating nationalist criticisms of the directive, many supporters of the "return" of English argue that nationalism cannot be equated with language. Filipinos can be nationalistic with English and those who insist that using the Filipino language makes one nationalistic are "misguided" and engaged in myopic nationalism that is, in fact, anti-poor. Historically, most Filipinos' support of English has always been grounded in this argument (Gonzalez 1999; Gonzalez and Sibayan 1988), a positioning that is clearly in response to the nationalist politics of the 1960s and 1970s which correlated English with (neo)colonial power and the "miseducation of the Filipino people" (Constantino 1970), and which asserted the use of a national language as a symbol of unity and national identity, and as a means to close the gap between the elite and the Filipino masses (Tollefson 1986). The bilingual education policy of 1974 was a response to this kind of "activism on the use of Filipino for education in the 1960s and especially in the 1970s" (Sibayan 1988, p. 49). The "silent majority", however, "which is about 70 to 80 per cent of our people, think that they can be nationalists without speaking Filipino" (p. 51).

The interrelatedness of these three arguments for the "return" of English as medium of instruction — deteriorating English language proficiency,

global competitiveness, and nationalism without the national language —
is perhaps best captured in the following statement by another columnist
and political scientist, Alex Magno (11 February 2003):

> One of the greatest crimes inflicted by parochial nationalism on
> our people was to diminish our competence in a universal language
> in the name of uncovering our 'nationhood'. The net result of
> misplaced nationalism has been to make our graduates less
> functional and, therefore, less productive, in the new environment.
> The ultimate outcome of that is wider poverty due to lessened
> competitiveness.

THE CRITICS

The discursive representation of the opposition to the presidential directive
on English may be deemed as aggressive, non-confrontational, and
defensive. For example, critics "insist" and "slam" the new directive
while they also "clarify" and "explain"[6] the policy.[7] The critics are also
put on the defensive as they contradict the belief that it is bilingual
education, thus the Filipino language, that is to blame for the deteriorating
proficiency of Filipinos in English. Unlike the supporters of the policy,
however, the social actors represented linguistically to take the cudgels
for the national language as medium of instruction have a much narrower
socio-political base.[8] While Filipino has successfully spread across much
of the Philippines (Nical, Smolicz and Secombe 2004; Bautista 1988),
and while there is some evidence of gradual acceptance of the language
as a national language even among non-Tagalog speakers (Espiritu 1999;
Kobari 1999),[9] this group of academics and militant students and teachers
remains "the vocal minority" in Philippine society (Gonzalez 1994,
p. 264), thus still much maligned and disparaged like their political
predecessors in the 1960s and 1970s (Tupas 2003). In the recent debate,
they are the "noisy leftists who call themselves nationalists when they
are in fact communists" (Voices on INQ.net 7 February 2003);[10] in the
past, they were "certain scattered militant groups of our population"
(Yabes 1970, p. 16).

However, the argument that language is directly equated with national
identity and nationalism — the subject of much criticism and derision —
is absent in the discourse of the critics of the directive. The ideological
structure upon which the arguments are based has very little use of
"nationalist" or "nationalism" as a political rallying point. This does not

mean that proponents of the national language have dropped their nationalist stance, but this may demonstrate how the widening theoretical, educational and political basis of the nationalist discourse has been largely ignored by those who argue for the primary use of English in the educational system, in favour of the more limiting nationalist discourse of the 1960s and 1970s. Opposition to the presidential order, in other words, continues to be perceived as ideologically anchored in the linguistic nationalism of the 1960s and 1970s, even if none of those who oppose the recent directive use it as the focal point of the debate.

First, opposition to the directive argues that it is unconstitutional. Article 14, Section 6 of the 1987 Constitution states that: "Subject to provisions of law and as the Congress may deem appropriate, the Government shall take steps to initiate and sustain the use of Filipino as a medium of official communication and as language of instruction in the educational system." Due to the inactivity of Congress, the President defends her directive with the following statement: "Unless Congress enacts a law mandating Filipino as the language of instruction, I am directing the Department of Education to return English as the primary medium of instruction, provided some subject will still be taught in Filipino" (Macapagal-Arroyo 29 January 2003). The critics argue that this is a misreading of the Constitution. Instead of helping initiate and sustain the use of the national language as the primary medium of instruction, the President instead has moved to ease out Filipino from the educational system. It is English, they say, that needs abolition as medium of instruction, until such time that Filipino has attained the recognition and role as national language.

Second, the "return" of English is not a factual statement since English actually never really left the schools. The speech of the President qualifies the word with the use of "primary" which, of course, assumes that English has been a secondary medium of instruction. But even under the bilingual education programme, English has been the language in the teaching of science, mathematics, and technology, thus making sure that despite Filipino's expanding domains in Philippine life, English remained the language of prestige and economic mobility. Thus, the use of quotation marks in "return" of English signifies the contentious discourse that goes with it.

And third, the critics argue that the directive is very much at odds with past and recent scientific and modern education principles which stipulate that children learn a second language more efficiently if they are already literate in their first language. To this end, they refer to past studies both

in the Philippines and abroad, before and after the institutionalization of
the bilingual education policy in 1974 (e.g., Congressional Commission
on Education 1991; UNESCO 1953).

Put together, opposition to the directive contends that the ultimate
aim of the President was to further align the educational system with
a (neoliberal) economic structure that serves foreign interests rather
than the interests of the Filipino people (Tupas 2001b). While eschewing
the language-identity or language-nationalism argument in favour of
empirically-driven and educationally sound rationalizations, these critics
continue to push for nationalist economics that is geared towards a
restructuring of needs and priorities which put Filipino interests above
the interests of multinational companies. They hope — consciously or
unconsciously — to avoid the political pitfalls of rallying around the
much maligned discourse of linguistic nationalism, and instead operate
with less ideologized, more cogent argumentation. In fact, their counter-
proposal includes the use of Filipino as medium of instruction in basic
literacy and elementary education, and English as medium of instruction
at the intermediate or secondary level — definitely a far cry from past
nationalist proposals to make Filipino the sole medium of instruction in
all levels. This strategy, they argue, will fulfill in an effective and
democratic way, the true spirit of bilingual education. Nevertheless, as
we have noted earlier, the critics' more nuanced deployment of a
nationalist language politics has been largely ignored, with the
proponents of English as primary medium of instruction choosing to
debate with past arguments rather than present ones. Among our sources,
very little word attributed to the advocates of English has refuted the
claim that the directive is either unconstitutional or educationally
contentious.[11]

THE POSITION OF NON-TAGALOG SPEAKERS[12]

Indisputably, the response from non-Tagalog speakers in the newspapers
has been swift and triumphant: they fully support the President's directive.
In a sense, their position is not very different from those who favour the
use of English as primary medium of instruction — deteriorating English
language proficiency, global competitiveness, and nationalism without
the national language. This position, however, is not always clearly
articulated and must always be situated within this group's poignant
resistance to Filipino as the national language which they claim is still
99.9 per cent Tagalog. One columnist from Cebu in the Visayas, for

example, wholeheartedly supports the 'return' to English "to improve the student's proficiency in the language and make them more globally competitive!" (Avila 2 February 2003). He then justifies this position with a regionally-marked response:

> Indeed, having a National Language based on one ethnic group has only given us a distorted sense of nationalism. The Tagalog think that they are God's greatest gift to this archipelago, hence everyone should speak their language, even if it is unintelligible to Cebuano, Ilocano or Chavacano. Thus, thanks to politics, Tagalog is being forced upon us... and to many of us Cebuanos, this is nothing but another form of ethnic cleansing, something we found out was also being done in Croatia, Serbia or Bosnia.

Exaggerations apart, such strong sentiments, if historically viewed, go far back to the 1930s when "ethnic rivalry" based on language emerged as a result of the choice of Tagalog as the national language (Gonzalez 1991) and the 1970s when such animosity re-emerged during the writing of the 1973 Constitution (Gonzalez 1980). Already in the 1930s, the mention of Tagalog as one of the official languages of the country along with English and Spanish was deemed divisive. Another columnist, this time from Mindanao, echoes this view as she asserts that "at the risk of being tarred and feathered by so-called 'nationalists' it is really much easier for us non-Tagalog speakers to love our country by learning about it in English" (Mustafa 3 February 2003):

> Perhaps very few among Tagalog-speaking people realized that the constitutional provision imposing Pilipino or Filipino as the medium of instruction in schools was seen by us non-Tagalogs as a rather oppressive, divisive and alienating law.
>
> The more extreme view saw it as another attempt of the "Christian government" at "neo-colonization" with the corollary intent of pushing ethnic and tribal communities... further down the pit of illiteracy and ignorance, from which the possibility of social mobility would be next to impossible.

Again exaggerations apart, there is some educational and theoretical support for these powerful statements. In Sibayan's (1984*b*) typology of language use among Filipino students under the bilingual education scheme, he rightly notes that those from rural non-Tagalog speaking areas would be the most educationally disadvantaged, and those from urban Tagalog-speaking places the most advantaged. For the former, learning Tagalog-based Filipino and English would entail learning two second languages, as opposed to the latter who had to learn only one new second language, English. On "ethnic" grounds, English could at least serve as a "neutral" language.

Politically, there is also a tendency among the proponents of Filipino as the national language to ignore the important distinction between Filipino and other vernacular languages in the country. They rightly argue, for example, that it is the mother tongue, not second languages, that facilitates most effective learning especially in the early years of primary education when basic literacy is of utmost importance. However, this mother tongue or native language is almost always the Filipino language as can be gleaned from their pronouncements on the latest language debate. Such discursive conflation of first language or native language and Filipino, for example, may be gleaned through the following excerpt from a news article which centers around the argument that Filipino should be used as sole medium of instruction in grade school (*Use Filipino to Teach*) 1 February 2003:

> The country's more successful Asian neighbors such as Malaysia, Thailand and South Korea, have also done very well, even though they give priority to their own language and culture, he [Zafra][13] added.
>
> "Such a system that emphasizes the role of the *first language* will produce students who are literate in *Filipino* and are very ready to learn English and in English," Zafra said.
>
> Zafra also said that the effective way to teach students, particularly preschoolers, is to use *Filipino* since experts discovered that children learn faster and better in their *native language* (italics added for emphasis).

Interestingly, despite the highly-charged emotional language that usually accompanies regional sentiments against Filipino as the national language or medium of instruction, arguments usually gravitate towards English and not the vernacular languages. Gonzalez (1980, p. 44) notes, for example, that despite regionalistic animosity among members of the Philippine Assembly on the question of the national language in the 1930s, the only local language ever put forward and seriously considered was Tagalog. In a much more recent study by Nical, Smolicz and Secombe (2004) on language attitudes, language use and language proficiency among high school students, teachers and parents in the island of Leyte in the Visayas, it is noteworthy to note "the low-attitude means for regional languages in school, indicating that respondents generally were unsure of the relevance and/or appropriateness of these languages in formal education" (p. 170). At the same time, they do not see the need for Filipino since English will always be used vis-à-vis their own languages (p. 171). English is valued most among all languages available in the communities and schools. Considering the fact that English for much of the twentieth century was never the language of unity and the language of the great majority (Constantino 1970; Tollefson 1986; Gonzalez and Sibayan 1996; Tupas 2001b; Hau and Tinio 2003), we therefore need to ask why regional sentiments, fearful of Tagalog imperialism, for the most part choose to rally around English and everything that it stands for in the country.

A SUMMARY OF ARGUMENTS

At this point, let me now summarize and comment on the ideological structure underpinning the most recent debate in the Philippines. The official justification for the "return" of English as primary medium of instruction is the perceived deterioration of English language proficiency among Filipino students. Considering the fact that proficiency in the language is necessary to capture high-paying jobs in the global market such as information and communications technology or ICT, the decision to make English medium of instruction "again" is imperative. This decision of the President has received broad support from the general population. There is wide agreement that English language proficiency has deteriorated, a gloomy reality that needs to be arrested through the use of English as primary medium of instruction in order to be competitive again in the global market, especially the exportation of labor. Support for this decision demonstrates an enlightened nationalism since proficiency in English does not in any way mean Filipinos are not nationalistic.

Critics, however, argue that the presidential directive is unconstitutional and educationally flawed. They also contend that the "return" of English as primary medium of instruction is not true because the language for the whole of the twentieth century, even during the period of bilingual education, has always been the primary and powerful medium of instruction. In this way, the critics deflect attention away from Filipino as the cause of the deterioration of English language proficiency among Filipinos, and blame the problem on the entire education system itself, which lacks adequate support from the national government. Contrary to expectations, as has been in the past, the critics refuse to rally around the need for a national language as a symbol of nationalism, and instead deal with the issue on educational and legal grounds. Based on these grounds, they propose a bilingual structure of education where Filipino is used as the medium of instruction in the primary level and English in the secondary level.

It is unfortunate that supporters of the directive have not listened to the finer points of the criticism and instead have chosen to challenge the critics on grounds associated with the more problematic nationalist language politics of the 1960s and 1970s. They continue to malign the opposition — as has always been the case — calling them "ideologues" when, in fact, it is they who approach the debate largely on ideological grounds. Amidst all the ferocity and passion of their support for the directive, they take it as a given that making English the primary medium of instruction will solve the problem of English language proficiency among the students. No evidence or study throughout the debate in the papers has been used to justify this very important assumption.

The position of non-Tagalog speakers, on the other hand, is best represented by English-language column writers. They generally support the directive, arguing that Filipino as the national language is divisive and unproductive. It has also put most non-Tagalog speakers at a disadvantage in the educational system. The "return" of English, therefore, will address this problem, especially now that English is needed by the country to be globally competitive. However, this position does not advance the cause of the vernacular languages; it is simply against the imposition of Filipino as a national language and, more especially, as medium of instruction. In its stead, English should be installed as the sole medium of instruction because this is, at least, a "neutral" language.

THE LANGUAGE DEBATE AS A CLASS ISSUE

We are therefore now at the crux of the debate: while English in the country may indeed be "ethnic-free", it has never been "class-free" (c.f. Annamalai 2004). The problem of class in the recent debate is curiously absent even if it is this dimension that largely galvanized nationalist calls in the 1960s for a revamp of the educational system. The English language, Constantino (1970) wrote, created the wedge between the small Filipino elite and the great majority of the Filipino masses. Sibayan and Gonzalez (1996) describe the Philippine social structure as constitutive of a hierarchy of English language proficiencies, with the economic and intellectual elite deploying the best English due mainly to access to quality education and cultural and technological support within the family and community. Most Filipinos, however, are poor, unable to attend good schools and, therefore, at best, they have passive competence of the English language which is just enough to qualify them for low-paying jobs or placements as domestic helpers abroad.[14] In short, socio-economic class is the major indicator of educational and professional achievement. In addition, Tollefson (1991), Ordoñez (1997), Tupas (2001) and Lorente and Tupas (2002) show how the socio-economic structure of the country, created to a large extent by an export-driven economy and a system of class relations which date back to colonial times (Anderson 1988; Ileto 1999), yields conditions where the poor, like everyone else, clamour for English, with the hope that it will save them from their wretchedness. But precisely because they are poor and are unable to afford good education, they only get the kind of English that perpetuates their present conditions.[15]

It is from this perspective, therefore, that we can make sense of the ethnically-marked resistance to Filipino as the national language and medium of instruction. When an English-language columnist from Mindanao, therefore, vehemently resists Filipino and applauds the President on behalf of "the youth of Sulu and all non-Tagalog-speaking students" (Mustafa 3 February 2003), she fails to include in the equation the fact that the social structure itself, and the educational system in particular, as it has always been the case in the Philippines throughout the twentieth century, will continue to distribute society's wealth unequally, much of it of course will be available only among the country's minority elite. Given the same social conditions that create a highly unequal access to education, a "return" to English as primary medium of instruction is unlikely to help the majority of those this writer from Mindanao hopes to represent. As Hau and Tinio (2003) rightly argue, the sub-national dimensions of the debate over Filipino actually reflect "intra-elite rivalry and internecine battles over resource allocations that happened to be parcelled out by region" (p. 342). The recent debate on language, therefore, is essentially a class issue:

> In the Philippines, language issues are part of a social structure
> that evolved in colonial times and persist in the postcolonial era.
> Framing language-policy debates in simple "ethnic" terms therefore

> misses an important historical point: Languages in the Philippines
> exist in a hierarchy (or hierarchies) influenced to an enormous
> degree by the relative status of the colonial language — English
> (p. 338).

Going back now to the question we posed at the start of this paper on how sub-national groups, despite vociferous resistance in Congress against Pilipino as the national language, were "silenced" or "appeased" by a bilingual education policy which largely disenfranchised the vernacular languages in the educational system — a view of the situation from the point of view of class, not ethnicity, will allow us to see how indeed bilingual education was a political compromise between competing elites: the Tagalog-speaking elites who nevertheless were conversant in English and who took up the fight for Pilipino as the national language, and the non-Tagalog elites who were likewise conversant in English, but who feared that the imposition of Pilipino as the national language would put them at a disadvantage with regard to resources necessitating competence in Pilipino. This does not preclude the likelihood that regionalistic animosity is deep-seated among the people themselves (as the study of Nical, Smolicz, and Secombe (2004) shows), but like Tsui and Tollefson (2004), we also need to ask why such well-entrenched regionalisms in the country have not followed the direction taken by many other societies with similar issues: to demand minority language rights (May 2001; Tollefson and Tsui 2004). In the Philippines, sub-national loyalties gravitate towards English and the symbolic power it represents despite — or because of — its history of being the language of the rich.[16]

CONCLUSION: THE WAY(S) TO GO

The foregoing discussion, therefore, demolishes the analytical ideological dichotomy between instrumentalist and identity positions in relation to (dominant) language debate in the Philippines. With this analytical framework, instrumentalist views rally around an international language — English — as the logical choice to be an official language and medium of instruction. Identity proponents advocate the establishment, spread, and maintenance of a national language with which all Filipinos are supposed to identify as "Filipinos". This analytical framework is not only simplistic in the sense that it marginalizes important dimensions of the debate, but it also fails to capture the underlying social tensions and fissures which are themselves constitutive of the complex dynamics of power relations in the Philippines.

By bringing the problem of class back to the discussion, we see that the socio-political picture becomes more realistic. The instrumentalist position, powerful as it is, gains even more leverage through class-induced, but nevertheless justifiable regionalistic distrust of the national language. The identity position, on the other hand, in response to the essentializing excesses of linguistic nationalism, has broadened its ideological and educational ground to construct a more ideologically palatable nationalist language politics. Therefore, given the centrality of class in the issue of language in the Philippines, this paper affirms the following conceptualization of medium of instruction policy by Tsui and Tollefson (2004, p. 2):

> Medium-of-instruction policy determines which social and linguistic groups have access to political and economic opportunities, and which groups are disenfranchised. It is therefore a key means of power (re)distribution and social (re)construction, as well as a key arena in which political conflicts among countries and ethnolinguistic, social and political groups are realized.

What, then, is the way to go? For Hau and Tinio (2003), it should be the use of Filipino as the primary language of instruction, with the vernacular languages allowed to flourish by making them auxiliary media of instruction, and English taught as a second language. For the critics of the most recent presidential directive, it should be Filipino as medium of instruction in the elementary level, then English in the secondary level. For Canieso-Doronila (1998), who has worked in literacy development programs in several rural Filipino communities, it should be the vernacular languages (Filipino if it is the first language) at the basic literacy level, then Filipino at the intermediate level until high school, but English in high school if students choose it. Though with fine distinctions between them, two things are clear: first, the current structure of bilingual education as well as the most recent presidential directive cannot address the widening disparity between the Filipino elite and the great majority of Filipinos; and second, no one is saying that English is not important in today's world.

The issue, of course, is "not just a question of replacing English with Filipino. Just as English creates linguistic hierarchies that separate those who speak the language from those who do not, Filipino has the potential to be as exclusionary as English (Hau and Tinio 2003, p. 347). It is for this same reason that the discursive conflation of "mother tongue" and "Filipino" needs to be redressed by making sure that the fine distinctions are made in a much more inclusive nationalist discourse and by promoting the vernacular languages as, at the very least, the languages of basic literacy or as auxiliary media of instruction. At any rate,

> There is a compelling need in the Philippines to create linguistic public spaces where different classes and groups can meet on a common linguistic ground. English was supposed to play this role, but it only succeeded in reinforcing class differences. Filipino appears to stand a better chance.

Sociolinguistically and realistically speaking, Filipino is the lingua franca of the Philippines; despite claims that it is incomprehensible to most non-Tagalog speakers, it currently serves as the major language of inter-ethnic communication. For some non-Tagalog speakers of Filipino like me (who speaks two Visayan languages: Aklanon, my first language, and Ilonggo, my regional language), it is now more an issue of attitudes, not inability to speak the national language.

It is true that the relationship between language and nationalism is never straightforward. Nationalism without a national language is conceivable. But given the enduring problem of language in the Philippines, a successful nationalist politics would mean galvanizing the whole nation into accepting, promoting, and taking pride in the national language as a medium of instruction. This can possibly happen if such politics and most Filipinos together redirect language debates towards socio-economic and political issues besieging the country, in which case the language issue in the Philippines is inescapably a social issue as well. This goes without saying that, while their linkages are not transparent as this paper has shown, nationalist politics, the national language, and medium of instruction policy as they have been and are currently deployed across unequal structures of relations in the country together must gravitate towards — and build upon — a much more equitable Philippine society. The success, or lack of it, of Filipino as the national language and as a medium of instruction to a large extent depends on — and helps determine — the kind of socio-economic and political transformation Philippine society will undertake in the future.

Notes

1. Mainly to de-ethnicize the name of the national language.
2. Between the implementation of bilingual education in 1974 and this recent debate, the 1987 Philippine Constitution during the term of Cory Aquino brought back "Filipino" as the national language of the Philippines.

3. This paper does not deal with the possibility that content of the debate may slightly differ between English- and Filipino-language newspapers. It may be observed, for example, that the content in Filipino-language newspapers is oriented towards a critical stance towards English and its use as medium of instruction, rather than towards a support for the status quo in education which is more likely available in English-language broadsheets. Nevertheless, this possibility does not affect this paper since its job is mainly to map the ideological structure of the debate which is something shared by both kinds of newspapers.

4. It may be argued that the discourses on language that I am analyzing are themselves already mediated by the media and therefore may not be reliable in providing an adequate picture of the debate; after all, writers and editors choose which statements to quote and ignore. This is a valid concern, but this can easily be addressed by referring to complete versions of important documents, especially the President's speech and the manifesto (both in English and Filipino) of a number of educational institutions and teachers' groups declaring opposition to the directive. Moreover, as the purpose of this paper, as earlier mentioned, is to identify ideologies in the debate, the paper does not aim to provide empirical evidence for the amount of support given to English and/or Filipino as this has been done many times over the past three decades since the bilingual education policy was set in place in the 1970s (e.g., Gonzalez and Bautista 1986).

5. Education Secretary Edilberto de Jesus, Presidential Spokesman Ignacio Bunye a staunch critic of the President Sen. Teresa Aquino-Oreta, Foundation for Upgrading the Standard of Education (FUSE), Rep. Edmundo Reyes, Chair of the House Committee on Basic Education and Culture, Professor Maria Celeste Gonzalez, Head of Ateneo de Manila's Department of Education, academic and business leaders, top executives, businessman Lucio Tan, the head of a recruitment agency based in Dubai, a French diplomat who was an official resident in Manila, *Times* readers in many parts of the world, and so on.

6. For example: "Isyu ng balik-Ingles, niliwanag" or roughly, "*Issue of return-to-English, explained*" (Espiritu, 7 February 2003).

7. It is interesting to note that the depiction of a combative opposition to the directive appears in English-language newspapers, while the portrayal of a sober, unruffled opposition occurs in Filipino-language dailies.

8. Alliance of Concerned Teachers, Antonio Tinio, Alliance Chairman, National Union of Students of the Philippines, militant teachers' group, a group of academics, Galileo Zafra of UP's Sentro ng Wikang Filipino, University of the Philippines, Ateneo de Manila University, De La Salle University, and other universities and colleges, Teresita Inciong, Director of the Bureau of Elementary Education, Filipino departments of three universities, writers' groups, Filipino teachers' association.

9. In a recent study of Cebuano students, for example, Kobari (1999) finds that "some changes in Cebuano students' attitudes towards Filipino have taken place. Their perceived proficiency in Filipino has greatly improved and their perceptions and attitudes towards Filipino and learning Filipino have become more positive" (p. 64).

10. They are also referred to as "super-duper nationalists" (Cruz 4 February 2003), "the usual objectors" (Ng 1 February 2003), the "ideologues " (Puno 4 February 2003), and "those deranged, misguided UP and Ateneo professors" (Garcia 6 February 2003).

11. Only one columnist in English who is supportive of the President's directive has noted the educational rationale for the use of Filipino as medium of instruction, especially in the elementary grades. But she does not refute this; in fact, she believes in it. The only problem, she says, is that the teaching of Filipino has also been neglected: "We have neglected the development of a dynamic language — one that is spoken and used throughout our 7,100 islands, one that is not rejected by those with regional sentiments" (Pamintuan 3 February 2003). But this is hardly a case against Filipino as medium of instruction, nor a case for English as primary medium of instruction. This is a problem of the failure of the educational system as a whole.

12. In this paper, "non-Tagalog speakers" refers to Filipinos who do not speak Tagalog as a first language. This does not mean they do not speak the language. Historically, however, its reference was never clear, since it could refer to those who spoke vernacular languages either with or without competence in Tagalog.

13. Galileo Zafra, Director of the University of the Philippines' Sentro ng Wikang Filipino or Filipino Language Centre.

14. There is much literature investigating the complex dynamics of the enduring relations between the Philippine elite and the masses. Classic works include Agoncillo (1956), Constantino (1975; 1970), Ileto (1979), Schirmer and Shalom (1987), Anderson (1988) and Canieso-Doronila (1989).

15. This social structure, of course, is not a completely closed structure. It also generates similar conditions as well as possibilities of changing such conditions. For comparable analyses of the role of English in other societies, see Annamalai (2004) for India, Rahman (1999) for Pakistan, and Lin (1999) for Hong Kong.

16. This should not mislead us into believing that English is a monolithic entity, thus simplistically drawing up a fight between languages per se. According to Sibayan and Gonzalez (1996), there is a range of English language proficiencies available in the Philippines, with the highest level of proficiency available mainly among those who are highly educated and/or brought up in an English-speaking, thus rich, community (see also Tupas 2001a). Most Filipinos have access to English as well, but what kind of English and how much "good English" depend on their proximity to the highly exclusive

quality education. Thus, the notion of English as the language of the rich cannot be invalidated simply by referring to the number of Filipinos who have access to English, because only those few who have acquired "good" English could possibly have achieved the promises of the English language (e.g., social mobility, prestige, high-paying jobs, economic power).

References

Agoncillo, Teodoro A. *The Revolt of the Masses — The Story of Bonifacio and the Katipunan.* Quezon City: University of the Philippines, 1956.

Anderson, Benedict. "Cacique Democracy in the Philippines: Origins and Dreams". *New Left Review* (1988): 3–31.

Annamalai, E. "Medium of Power: The Question of English in Education in India". In *Medium of Instruction Policies — Which Agenda? Whose Agenda?*, edited by James W. Tollefson, & Amy B.M. Tsui, pp. 177–94. Mahwah, New Jersey & London: Lawrence Erlbaum Associates, 2004.

Avila, Bobit S. "Kudos to GMA for the Return of English". *The Philippine Star*, 2 February 2003, p. 22.

Bautista, Maria Lourdes S. "Domains of English in the 21st Century". In *The Role of English and its Maintenance in the Philippines — The Transcript, Consensus and Papers of the Solidarity Seminar on Language and Development*, edited by Andrew B. Gonzalez, pp. 71–80. Manila, Philippines: Solidaridad Publishing House, 1988.

Canieso-Doronila, Maria Luisa. *The Limits of Educational Change — National Identity Formation in a Philippine Public Elementary School.* Philippines: University of the Philippines, 1989.

Congressional Commission on Education (EDCOM). *Making Education Work: Agenda for Reform.* Quezon City: Congress of the Republic of the Philippines, 1991.

Constantino, Renato. *A History of the Philippines: From the Spanish Colonization to the Second World War* (with the collaboration of Letizia Constantino). New York & London: Monthly Review Press, 1975.

——. "The Mis-education of the Filipino". *Journal of Contemporary Asia* 1, no. 1 (1970): 20–36.

Cruz, Neal H. "Gun Ban, Return-to-English Policies Hailed". *Philippine Daily Inquirer*, 4 February 2003, p. A8.

Daza, Julie Yap. "Easier Said than Done". *Manila Standard*, 4 February 2003, p. 15.

Espiritu, Clemencia C. "Isyu ng balik-Ingles, niliwanag". *Kabayan*, 7 February 2003, p. 7.

——. "The Cebuano Response to the Language Controversy in the Philippines: Implications for the Intellectualization of Filipino". In *The Filipino Bilingual: A Multidisciplinary Perspective (Festschrift in Honor of Emy M. Pascasio)*, edited by M.L.S. Bautista and G.O. Tan, pp. 65–69. Manila: De La Salle University Press, 1999.

Garcia, Syke. "Let the Profs do 'Balagtasan' ". *Manila Times*, 6 February 2003, p. A7.

Gonzalez, Andrew B. "Philippine Bilingual Education Revisited". In *The Filipino Bilingual: A Multidisciplinary Perspective (Festschrift in Honor of Emy M. Pascasio)*, edited by M.L.S. Bautista & G.O Tan, pp. 11–15. Manila, Philippines: Linguistic Society of the Philippines, 1999.

———. "Language and Nationalism in the Philippines: An Update". In *Language Planning in Southeast Asia*, compiled by A. Hassan, pp. 253–67. Malaysia: Ministry of Education, 1994.

———. "Cebuano and Tagalog: Ethnic Rivalry Redivivus. In *Language and Ethnicity (Festschrift in honor of Joshua A. Fishman on the occasion of his 65th birthday)*, edited by J.R. Dow, (vol. II), pp. 111–29. Amsterdam/ Philadelphia: John Benjamins Publishing Company, 1991.

———. *Language and Nationalism: The Philippine Experience Thus Far*. Quezon City, Metro Manila: Ateneo de Manila University Press, 1980.

Gonzalez, Andrew & Maria Lourdes S. Bautista. *Language Surveys in the Philippines (1966–1984)*. Philippines: De La Salle University Press, 1986.

Gonzalez, Andrew B. & Bonifacio P. Sibayan, eds. *Evaluating Bilingual Education in the Philippines (1974–1985)*. Manila: Linguistic Society of the Philippines, 1988.

Hau, Caroline S. and Victoria L. Tinio. "Language Policy and Ethnic Relations in the Philippines". In *Fighting Words: Language Policy and Ethnic Relations in Asia*, edited by Michael E. Brown & Sumit Ganguly, pp. 319–49. Cambridge & London: The MIT Press, 2003.

Ileto, Reynaldo C. *Knowing America's Colony — A Hundred Years from the Philippine War* (Philippine Studies Occasional Papers Series No. 13). Hawai'i: Center for Philippine Studies, School of Hawaiian, Asian and Pacific Studies, University of Hawai'i at Manoa, 1999.

———. *Payson and Revolution: Popular Movements in the Philippines, 1840–1910*. Quezon City, Matro Manila: Ateneo de Manila University Press, 1979.

Kobari, Yoshihiro. "Reassessment after 15 Years: Attitudes of the Students of Cebu Institute of Technology towards Filipino in Tertiary Education". In *The Filipino Bilingual: A Multidisciplinary Perspective (Festschrift in honor of Emy M. Pascasio)*, edited by M.L.S. Bautista and G.O. Tan, pp. 56–64. Manila: De La Salle University Press, 1999.

Lin, Angel M. Y. "Doing-English-Lessons in the Reproduction or Transformation of Social Worlds?" *TESOL Quarterly* 33, no. 3 (1999): 393–412.

Lorente, Beatriz P. & T. Ruanni F. Tupas. *The ACELT Journal* 6, no. 2 (2002): 20–32.

Macapagal-Arroyo, Gloria. "Return English as the Medium of Instruction". Speech delivered during the 75th anniversary of the Far Eastern University, Manila, 29 January 2003.

Magno, Alex. "A Mountain of a Problem". *Manila Standard*, 11 February 2003, p. 14.

May, Stephen. *Language and Minority Rights — Ethnicity, Nationalism and the Politics of Language.* England: Pearson Education Limited, 2001.

Mustafa, Noralyn. "Back to the Future". *Philippine Daily Inquirer*, 3 February 2003, p. A9.

"New Policy on English Lauded". *Manila Bulletin*, 1 February 2003, p. B-10.

Ng, Willie. "It May Take Time But Back-to-English is Fine". *Manila Bulletin*, 1 February 2003, p. 10.

Nical, Iluminado, Jerzy J. Smolicz & Margaret J. Secombe. "Rural Students and the Philippine Bilingual Education Program on the Island of Leyte". In *Medium of Instruction Policies — Which Agenda? Whose Agenda?*, edited by James W. Tollefson, & Amy B. M. Tsui, pp. 153–76. Mahwah, New Jersey & London: Lawrence Erlbaum Associates, 2004.

Ordoñez, Elmer. "English and Decolonization". *Journal of Asian English Studies* 2, nos. 1 & 2 (1997): 17–21

Pamintuan, Ana Marie. "Blind Leading the Blind". *Philippine Star*, 3 February 2003, p. 10.

Puno, Ricardo V. Jr. "Potshots". *Manila Times*, 4 February 2003, p. A6.

Rahman, Tariq. *Language, Education, and Culture.* Oxford: Oxford University Press, 1999.

Schirmer, Daniel B. and Stephen Rosskam Shalom, eds. *The Philippines Reader — A History of Colonialism, Neocolonialism, Dictatorship, and Resistance.* Quezon City, Philippines: KEN incorporated, 1987.

Sibayan, Bonifacio P. "Transcript of the Discussion". In *The Role of English and its Maintenance in the Philippines – The Transcript, Consensus and Papers of the Solidarity Seminar on Language and Development*, edited by Andrew B. Gonzalez, pp. 19–69. Manila, Philippines: Solidaridad Publishing House, 1988.

————. "A Tentative Typology of Philippine Bilingualism". In *Language, Identity and Socioeconomic Development*, edited by Bonifacio P. Sibayan & Lorna Z. Segovia (Occasional papers No. 32), pp. 116–23. Singapore: SEAMEO Regional Language Centre, 1984*a*.

————. "Bilingual Education in the Philippines: Strategy and Structures". In *Language, Identity and Socioeconomic Development*, edited by Bonifacio P. Sibayan & Lorna Z. Segovia (Occasional papers No. 32), pp. 124–49. Singapore: SEAMEO Regional Language Centre, 1984*b*.

Sibayan, Bonifacio P. & Andrew Gonzalez. "Post-imperial English in the Philippines". In *Post-imperial English — Status Changes in Former British and American Colonies, 1940–1990*, edited by Joshua A. Fishman, Andrew W. Conrad & Alma Rubal-Lopez, pp. 139–72. Berlin & New York: Mouton de Gruyter, 1996.

"The World's English". *Philippine Daily Inquirer*, 3 February 2003, p. A8.

Tollefson, James W. *Planning Language, Planning Inequality — Language Policy in the Community.* London & New York: Longman, 1991.

———. "Language Policy and the Radical Left in the Philippines: The New People's Army and its Antecedents". *Language Problems & Language Planning* 10, no. 2 (1986): 177–89.

Tollefson, James W. & Amy B.M. Tsui, eds. *Medium of Instruction Policies — Which Agenda? Whose Agenda?*. Mahwah, New Jersey & London: Lawrence Erlbaum Associates, 2004.

Tsui, Amy B.M. & James W. Tollefson. "The Centrality of Medium-of-Instruction Policy in Sociopolitical Processes". In *Medium of Instruction Policies — Which Agenda? Whose Agenda?*, edited by James W. Tollefson & Amy B.M. Tsui, pp. 1–18. Mahwah, New Jersey & London: Lawrence Erlbaum Associates, 2004.

Tupas, T. Ruanni F. "Global Politics and the Englishes of the World". In *Language Across Boundaries*, edited by Janet Cotterill & Anne Ife (Selected papers from the Annual Meeting of the British Association for Applied Linguistics held at Anglia Polytechnic University, Cambridge September 2000), pp. 81–98. London & New York: British Association for Applied Linguistics with Continuum, 2001*a*.

———. "History, Language Planners, and Strategies of Forgetting: The Problem of Consciousness in the Philippines". *Language Problems & Language Planning* 27, no. 1 (2003): 1–25.

———. "Linguistic Imperialism in the Philippines: Reflections of an English Language Teacher of Filipino Overseas Workers". *The Asia-Pacific Education Researcher* 10, no. 1 (2001*b*): 1–40.

UNESCO. *The Use of Vernacular Language in Education.* Paris: UNESCO, 1953.

"Use Filipino to Teach, Academics Insist". *Manila Times*, 1 February 2003, p. A3.

"Voices on INQ7.net". *Philippine Daily Inquirer*, 7 February 2003, p. A10.

Yabes, Leopoldo. "The English Program in the University". *Education Quarterly* 8, nos. 1 & 2 (1970): 15–33.

3

National Language and Nation-Building: The Case of Bahasa Indonesia

Lucy R. Montolalu and Leo Suryadinata

INTRODUCTION

The national language of Indonesia is originally called Malay, which is a minority language in the Indonesian archipelago. Why was this minority language eventually chosen as the national language of Indonesia? This chapter deals with the origin of the Indonesian national language and its development from 1928 to the *Reformasi* (Reform) period. It also examines Indonesian policy towards the national language and its relationships with nation-building. However, globalization and revival of ethnicity are two factors which may serve as challenges to the national language policy. This paper will therefore also discuss problems and prospects of such a policy.

THE ROLE OF THE MALAY LANGUAGE PRIOR TO INDONESIA'S INDEPENDENCE

Indonesia is a multiethnic and multilingual society, of which the largest ethnic group is Javanese (47 per cent according to the 1930 population census). Nevertheless, the Javanese language was not selected as the national language of Indonesia. One of the reasons was that Javanese is a complicated language which has also been used only by the Javanese. Besides, the language is hierarchical; it is divided into high Javanese and low Javanese, which should be used in accordance with the position of the person in society, therefore it is non-democratic. The languages of other ethnic groups, for instance, the Sundanese (14.5 per cent according to the 1930 population census) and Madurese (7 per cent according to the 1930 population census),

were not used by others either. Only the language of the Malays, who
constituted about 1.6 per cent according to the 1930 census (see Table
3.1), was used as a lingua franca in the Indonesian archipelago.[1] Different
ethnic groups when they met used this language to communicate.[2]

Because of the above reasons, during the nationalist movement of
Indonesia, which started in the first decade of the twentieth century, the
language used among the nationalists was Malay. All the newspapers
read by Indonesian political public were published in this language rather
than in vernacular languages (often known in Indonesian as *bahasa daerah,*
or regional languages). Indonesian youths have always been in the forefront
of Indonesian politics as well as the Indonesian nationalist movement. It
was the youth who held the first Indonesian youth congress in 1926.
However, the first congress was unable to produce a pledge which could
unite the Dutch East Indies — or "Indonesia" as Indonesian nationalists
called it. Only at the second Indonesian youth congress were the secular
nationalist youths able to get together and they pledged as follows:

> We, the sons and daughters of Indonesia, recognize one
> motherland: Indonesia; We, the sons and daughters of Indonesia,
> recognize one nation: the Indonesian nation; We, the sons and
> daughters of Indonesia, hold in high esteem a unifying language
> (*Bahasa Persatoean*): the Indonesian language!

TABLE 3.1
Language Speakers in 1930 Census

No.	Language/Ethnic group	Percentage
1.	Javanese	47.02%
2.	Sundanese	14.53%
3.	Madurese	7.28%
4.	Minangkabau	3.36%
5.	Buginese	2.59%
6.	Batak	2.04%
7.	Balinese	1.88%
8.	Batavians	1.66%
9.	Malay	1.61%
10.	Banjarese	1.52%
11.	Achenese	1.41%

Source: Leo Suryadinata, Aris Ananta and Evi Nurvidya Arifin,
*Indonesia's Population: Ethnicity and Religion in a Changing Political
Landscape*, p. 12 (Singapore: Institute of Southeast Asian Studies,
2003. (Please note that the numbers indicate ethnic groups but we
assume that they also reflect the ethnic languages that they speak.)

The unifying language mentioned in the pledge was the Malay language (*Bahasa Melayu*) which was then called the Indonesian language (*Bahasa Indonesia*) for the first time. The congress recognized the unifying role of the Malay language in the Indonesian nationalist movement. Although it was called the Indonesian language, it was not called the national language of Indonesia. It was only after Indonesia achieved independence that Malay — then officially called the Indonesian language — became the national language of Indonesia (*bahasa nasional*).

It appears that the selection of the Malay language as the Indonesian national language was quite smooth as other languages, as stated earlier, were not widely used by other ethnic groups. In other words, no other regional or vernacular language would have been able to be accepted by other ethnic groups.

It is also important to note that the Malay language is the language of a minority group. The largest ethnic group, the Javanese, has not been able to gain advantages. All ethnic groups (with the exception of the Malay) are in the same position — they have to learn the language. The majority ethnic group, the Javanese, was wise enough to accept this minority language as the national language. This explains why the national language policy of Indonesia has been relatively successful. There has never been any opposition to the language.

As noted earlier, Indonesia is a multiethnic and multilingual society, and the Indonesian nationalist leaders of Javanese origin were wise enough not to insist on having Javanese as the national language of Indonesia; otherwise, it would have not been possible for the nationalists to get together and oppose Dutch colonialism. Nevertheless, other vernacular languages did not disappear.

The Japanese occupation of Indonesia contributed to the further spread of Bahasa Indonesia; the Japanese prohibited Dutch education and use of the Dutch language in schools; they were fully aware that it would take time to teach the Indonesian people the Japanese language, and as a result, they encouraged the teaching of Malay as the medium of instruction in all Indonesian schools.

THE DEVELOPMENT OF NATIONAL LANGUAGE POLICY

Soon after the Japanese surrender, Sukarno proclaimed Indonesia's independence on 17 August 1945. The Dutch did not recognize the new republic and attempted to reoccupy Indonesia. This led to armed conflict between the Indonesians and the Dutch which lasted for at least four years. Through both armed struggle and diplomacy, in December 1949 the Dutch were forced to transfer power to the Indonesians. In the view of many Indonesian nationalists, because Indonesia's independence was won through armed struggle rather than diplomacy, there was a deep resentment against everything that had to do with the Dutch, including the Dutch language, Dutch culture, and Dutch education. That is why soon after Independence, the Dutch language was immediately replaced by Bahasa Indonesia as stipulated in article 36 of the 1945 Constitution: "The language of the State shall be the Indonesian language." This article shows a constitutional foundation and a political will in the language domain. All other languages in Indonesia were regulated to sub-national status, and the Indonesian Government adopted a policy of not developing the sub-national language. Bahasa Indonesia became the national language in Indonesia.

Throughout the country all official, administrative and government businesses have to be conducted in Bahasa Indonesia. The medium of instruction in all schools were supposed to be in Bahasa Indonesia, except for the first three years in primary schools, when regional languages were allowed. This national language policy aimed at "Indonesianizing" school children of different ethnic groups. National ideas were being transmitted through the national language education, and national feelings were being inculcated.

However, the national language policy in Indonesia is not without problems. Its development is often seen as at the expense of regional languages (vernacular languages). It is true that the Indonesian language has been enriched by vernacular languages; for instance, its vocabulary has often been taken from that of vernacular languages, but vernacular languages were left alone. The national language itself also has problems of standardization and further developments. Indeed the 1975 and 1999 National Language Congresses aimed at addressing these issues.

Indonesia is a nation based on a common language, which is Bahasa Indonesia. Indonesian nation-building appeared to have been closely linked with the national language. The Indonesian language has become the most important identity for the Indonesians of various ethnic groups. The Indonesian national values such as *Pancasila* and *bhinneka tunggal ika* (unity in diversity) were also transmitted to the people via the national language. It is therefore understandable that the Indonesian language has occupied a prominent position among Indonesian vernacular languages. Despite this prominent position, the Indonesian language has to face competition from the other languages: vernacular languages and foreign languages.

NATIONAL LANGUAGE, VERNACULAR LANGUAGE
AND FOREIGN LANGUAGE

Using position as a criterion, there are three groups of languages in Indonesia: the national language, the vernacular language, and the foreign language. The position of the national language is occupied by Bahasa Indonesia since 1928. It is closely related to the Indonesian group identity. The vernacular languages are used by people in the regions for daily conversation among the members of the same ethnic groups, and foreign languages are used in communication with foreigners.

According to its social function, these three languages are used as (1) formal language, (2) language in a wider relationship, (3) language in educational systems, and (4) language in art, science and technology. Bahasa Indonesia performs its function as the State's formal language. This means that in all formal affairs of the State, Bahasa Indonesia is used. In fact, Bahasa Indonesia also performs a wider function; it is used for communication between different Indonesian ethnic groups, even with some neighboring countries where Malay is used.

Bahasa Indonesia also functions as the medium of instruction in a formal educational system; this function has a close relationship with policies in determining language as a medium and/or as a subject of study, as mentioned in the Education Act No. 30, 1989.

Indonesia as a multiracial society faces not only the problem of the national language, but also vernacular languages and foreign languages. How to strike a balance between the national language and mother tongue? Vernacular languages are still alive and used by the ethnic group concerned. Arts, literature, movies and songs can be easily expressed in the national language, and in vernacular languages as well. In fact, the shadow plays or puppet shows are still performed in the ethnic language rather than the national language.

In the modern world, especially in an era of globalization, the national language of Indonesia and vernacular languages are not sufficient to catch up with the rapidly developing world. Foreign languages, especially English, are keys to the gate of the scientific and modern technological world and other world civilizations. The English language has been taught in Indonesian secondary schools, but the standard has not been high. However, with globalization, universities have started paying attention to this foreign language. At the University of Indonesia, for instance, during the 1996–97 academic year, it conducted a university-wide English proficiency test for all its new students. Those who passed the test did not have to take the English language course, but those who failed were required to take an English course.[3] Generally, the English standard of Indonesian students is still low.

Nevertheless, Indonesian nationalism is still strong. Indonesian educationists who are mainly nationalists, have also been concerned with the student's command of the national language, as not every student is well versed in standard Bahasa Indonesia.

EFFORTS TO DEVELOP THE INDONESIAN LANGUAGE

One of the decisions of the Indonesian Language Congress was the establishment of a language centre. In 1947, the Faculty of Letters and Philosophy, University of Indonesia, set up an institute for language and cultural studies. This institute became the *Lembaga Bahasa* dan *Budaya* in 1952. It later changed its name several times and in 1975 it became the *Pusat Pembinaan dan Pengembangan Bahasa*. This language centre has five divisions: (1) division of administration, (2) division of Bahasa Indonesia and regional languages, (3) division of literature and regional literature, (4) division of dictionaries and technical terms, and (5) division of the development of Indonesian language and literature. With those divisions, Pusat Bahasa's responsibility is extended to cover Javanese, Sundanese, Madurese, and other regional languages.

The main responsibility of this centre is to ensure that Bahasa Indonesia becomes a national language in its true sense. One of the domains that has received such attention is the spelling reform, known as the Soewandi spelling, which was proposed and adopted. This spelling system lasted for twenty years. In 1967 a new spelling committee was officially established and a draft of the new spelling system was proposed. Nevertheless, it was only in 1972 that the Soewandi spelling was replaced by the New Spelling System of Indonesia, which is known as *Ejaan Bahasa Indonesia yang Disempurnakan* (The perfected spelling system of Bahasa Indonesia). This spelling system, which is currently used in Indonesia, tended to make Indonesian closer to Malaysian Malay, at least in their spellings, if not in vocabulary.

One serious national language problem was its lack of new vocabulary. In scientific terms and modern technology Bahasa Indonesia turns for help to foreign languages, because the vernacular languages cannot contribute much to it. The lexical items in Bahasa Indonesia got much help from the Javanese vernacular language. In 1938, the first congress on the national language, recommended the compilation of a vocabulary which contains international terms side by side with the Indonesian terms. During the Japanese occupation, the *Indonesia Go Seibu Iinkai* or committee to develop Bahasa Indonesia published a book entitled *Istilah Bahasa Indonesia,* which consists of 1,861 terms in Dutch with their Indonesian equivalents. In 1945, the committee in Jakarta compiled 7,000 terms. After Independence, the Bahasa Indonesia commission produced another dictionary entitled *Kamus Istilah* (1951). In 1966, this commission "created" 321,719 terms for 23 branches of science. In 1958, the same committee published another document. This document, entitled *Pedoman Umum Pembentukan Istilah,* offers guidelines for "creating" new terms.

"Borrowing" cannot be avoided. There are many Indonesian words that are borrowed from foreign languages such as *kafe, servis mobil.* The words *kafe* and *servis* are borrowed from English. Besides, Bahasa Indonesia takes over new concepts and inventions in science and technology from English, *komputer, televisi, telefon, faksimili,* and *e-mail* are English loan words.

To anticipate the need of scientific and technical terms and the fast inflow of foreign words and concepts, Pusat Bahasa published two kinds of books: (1) technical terms for scientific branches, and (2) booklets of foreign words which have been taken in. Pusat Bahasa provides official recognition and codification of borrowed words, from foreign as well as from vernacular languages. Several dictionaries were published, first a dictionary called *Kamus Umum Bahasa Indonesia* by WJS Poerwadarminta, secondly a dictionary called *Kamus Umum Bahasa Indonesia* by Adiwimarta (1983). Pusat Bahasa published in 1988 a dictionary called *Kamus Besar Bahasa Indonesia* by Adiwimarta et al. This dictionary contains 62,000 entries; a revision was made in 1991 with approximately 72,000 entries under the same title. Beside this dictionary, some private dictionaries appeared, like *Kamus Indonesia* by Harahap (1951), *Kamus Besar bahasa* by Arifin (1951) and *Kamus Modern Bahasa Indonesia* by Zain (1954).

Another important decision made by the Indonesian Language Congress II in 1954 was the need for a good national language grammar. This idea came into reality in 1988 at the fifth Indonesian Language Congress. The grammar was entitled *Tatabahasa Baku Bahasa Indonesia* edited by Moeliono and Darjowidjojo. This grammar was revised and expanded three times. The second was edited by Alwi, Darjowidjojo and Lapoliwa in 1993 and the third one was edited by Alwi, Dardjowidjojo, Lapoliwa and Moeliono in 2000.

Since 1978, Pusat Bahasa has held six Indonesian language congresses. The third congress was held in Jakarta in 1978, after twenty-four years Pusat Bahasa felt it was necessary to hold a congress again. In this congress, scholars discussed various problems faced by the development of the Indonesian language and made suggestions for possible solutions. Since then, the Pusat Bahasa has held a national language congress every five years. The last congress was held in October 2003. At every congress the Pusat Bahasa reported its past activities and progress.

To consolidate the status of the national language, Pusat Bahasa provided weekly television series, lectures and courses for various agencies (both governmental as well as private) to upgrade the standard of the national language. Pusat Bahasa also gave information through a hotline telephone service to the public. Besides, it promoted research on both national language and vernacular languages. They work together with domestic as well as foreign agencies; domestic agencies include the National Defense Council, the National Law Council, the State Electric Company, while foreign agencies include the Ford Foundation, the Summer Institute of Linguistics, and Language Development Project (ILDEP).

HOW SUCCESSFUL IS THE PROMOTION OF BAHASA INDONESIA?

Since Indonesia attained independence, the Government has popularized the Indonesian national language. A question can be posed here as to how popular the Indonesian language is among various ethnic groups over a period of time. The census data will be able to give us some indication. With regard to the usage of Bahasa Indonesia, Indonesians can be divided into three groups: The first group consists of people who use Bahasa Indonesia as their daily language, the second group comprises those who do not use Bahasa Indonesia as their daily language, and the third group consists of those who do not understand Bahasa Indonesia. A comparison of those three groups is shown below.

In 1980 (see Table 3.2), only 11.93 per cent of Indonesians used Bahasa Indonesia as their daily language, while 39.18 per cent did not understand Bahasa Indonesia at all. However, by 1990 (see Table 3.3), the number of Indonesians who used Bahasa Indonesia daily increased slightly from 11.9 per cent to 15.19 per cent, while the number of those who did not

TABLE 3.2
Speakers of Bahasa Indonesia in Daily Use in 1980

No.	Specification	Amount	Percentage
1.	People who use Bahasa Indonesia daily	17,505,303	11.93%
2.	People who do not use Bahasa Indonesia daily	71,758,926	48.89%
3.	People who do not understand Bahasa Indonesia	57,512,244	39.18%

Source: Cited and calculated from Central Bureau of Statistics, *Penduduk Indonesia: Hasil Sensus Penduduk 1980* (Jakarta: 1983).

TABLE 3.3
Speakers of Bahasa Indonesia in Daily Use in 1990

No.	Specification	Amount	Percentage
1.	People who use Bahasa Indonesia daily	24,042,010	15.19%
2.	People who do not use Bahasa Indonesia daily	107,066,136	67.65%
3.	People who do not understand Bahasa Indonesia	27,055,488	17.16%

Source: Cited and calculated from Central Bureau of Statistics, *Penduduk Indonesia: Hasil Sensus Penduduk 1990* (Jakarta: 1992).

understand Bahasa Indonesia reduced significantly, from 39.18 per cent to 17.16 per cent. An equally significant increase in 1990 was in the second category, which is the people who do not use Bahasa Indonesia daily. In 1980, the number was 48.89 per cent while in 1990, it increased to 67.65 per cent. This is the majority group among the Indonesian population which indicates that Indonesians are mainly bilingual.

The above tables show that a significant number of Indonesians still do not understand the national language.

If we look at Table 3.4 which shows the number of vernacular language speakers, it is clear that they are still the majority. In 2000, 34 per cent of Indonesians are Indonesian language speakers. While there is an increase in the number of national language speakers, there is a small decrease in the vernacular language speakers.

If the above trends continue, Indonesian language speakers will increase gradually while vernacular language speakers will decrease slowly. However, the implementation of the 1999 Autonomy Law, which offers local governments more authority in developing their own culture and

TABLE 3.4
Vernacular Language Speakers in 1980, 1990, 2000

No.	Language	1980	1990	2000
1.	Javanese	40.44%	38.08%	34.70%
2.	Sundanese	15.06%	15.26%	13.86%
3.	Madurese	4.71%	4.29 %	3.78%
4.	Batak	2.12%	1.97%	1.91%
5.	Minangkabau	2.42%	2.23%	2.06%
6.	Balinese	1.69%	1.64%	1.42%
7.	Buginese	2.26%	2.04%	1.91%
8.	Indonesian	11.93%	15.19%	34.00%
9.	Others	17.48%	17.11%	4.57%
10.	No answer	0.76%	0.45%	0.31%

Sources: Compiled from various census and survey data.

language, may affect the continuing development of the national language of Indonesia.

Nevertheless, it should be noted that in the past, there was no opposition to the Indonesian language among Indonesian ethnic groups. It is a fact that all major dailies and an absolute majority of local magazines have been published in Bahasa Indonesia.[4] Only in the 1970s, some Sundanese suggested to the Government that government servants posted to the Sundanese areas should pass the proficiency test in Sundanese.[5] With the regional autonomy law, this kind of demand may be revived.

CONCLUSION

From the forgoing discussion, it is clear that the Indonesian national language was a product of the Indonesian nationalist movement. It was selected by the young Indonesian nationalists in order to unify multiethnic and multi-religious Indonesians. It has also become the tool of Indonesian nation-building since Independence. In the last sixty years or so, Bahasa Indonesia has become the main language of education, culture, science, technology, administration, religion and economics.

The largely monolingual policy, which emphasizes the Indonesian language, often ignores vernacular languages and foreign languages. The challenges of globalization pressurize Indonesians to pay more attention to foreign languages but it appears that the Government is not yet ready to change the current language policy. Nevertheless, since the fall of

Soeharto resulted in democratization of Indonesian politics, foreign languages are encouraged, yet it is more an ad hoc rather than a well thought out policy. Regional autonomy laws and the revival of ethnicity have given rise to vernacular culture and languages which may hinder the further development of the Indonesian national language. However, since the national language is based on a language of a minority group and it has a history of acceptance for more than half a century, it is very likely that it will remain as the national language of Indonesia in the years to come.

Notes

1. According to the 2000 population census, the Malay ethnic group constitutes 3.45 per cent of the total Indonesian population. But the percentage of Javanese and Madurese decrease to 41.71 per cent and 3.45 per cent. See Leo Suryadinata, Evi Nurvidya Arifin, and Aris Ananta, *Indonesia's Population: Ethnicity and Religion in a Changing Political Landscape* (Singapore: Institute of Southeast Asian Studies, 2003), p. 7.
2. The most important ethnic marker for indigenous Indonesians is the language they use.
3. *Suara Pembaruan*, 2 September 1996.
4. Roger Paget. "Indonesian newspapers 1965–1967", *Indonesia*, no. 4 (October 1967): 170–210. The three newspapers published in Indonesian ethnic languages were *Sipatahoenan* (Sundanese daily in Bandung), *Minggoean Sipatahoenan* (Sundanese weekly, also in Bandung) and *Kalawarti Merdika* (Javanese weekly in Jakarta).
5. Leo Suryadinata, "Ethnicity and National Integration in Indonesia: An Analysis", *Asia Quarterly* (Belgium), no. 3 (1976).

Select Bibliography

Alwi, Hasan. *Bahasa Indonesia Pemakai dan Pemakaiannya*. Jakarta: Departemen Pendidikan Nasional, 2000*a*.
——— et al. *Politik Bahasa*. Jakarta, Departemen Pendidikan Nasional, 2000*b*.
Dardjowidjojo, Soenjono. "Strategies for a Successful National Language Policy: The Indonesian Case." *International Congress of Sociology*. Germany: University of Bielefeld, 1994.
Halim, Amran. "Fungsi Politik Bahasa Nasional". *Bahasa dan Sastra* I/1/75. Jakarta: Pusat Pembinaan dan Pengembangan Bahasa, 1975.
Kridalaksana, Harimurti. "Sejarah Peristilahan Dalam Bahasa Indonesia". *Dalam Masa Lampau Bahasa Indonesia: Sebuah Bunga Rampai*, 1991.

————. "Undang-undang Bahasa sebagai Sarana Pemantapan Politik Bahasa Nasional". *Kongres Bahasa Indonesia VIII*. Jakarta: Pusat Pebinaan dan Pengembangan Bahasa, 2003.

Suryadinata, Leo. "Indonesian Nationalism and the Pre-war Youth Movement: A Revisit". *Journal Southeast Asian Studies* 9, no. 1 (March 1978): 99–114.

Tan Ta Sen. *Language Policies in Insular Southeast Asia: A Comparative Study*. Singapore: Southeast Asian Studies Programme, Nanyang University, 1978.

4

Diverse Voices: Indonesian Literature and Nation-Building

Melani Budianta

INTRODUCTION

In *Rethinking Nation*, Wong (2002) criticizes "literary workshops, conferences, seminars, [that] continue to trot out the theme 'Literature and Nation-Building' as if the idea of 'Nation' is fixed, indeed, sacrosanct and thus not open to debate."[1] Writing about literatures written in English in the Malay-oriented cultural/national politics, Wong is challenging "the belief that cultural identity is similarly fixed and unchanging, and that there is a pristine, pure origin to this identity."

This paper will seriously consider the concern that Wong raises. Looking retrospectively towards the past runs the risk of committing anachronism, of imposing our contemporary, taken-for-granted notions that was then still nonexistent or in the making. Furthermore, what Wong suggests here is the need for scholars to critically position themselves vis-à-vis national myth-making, defined by Elias (1970) as follows:

> [the creation of] the national past with which present generations can identify themselves, which gives them a feeling of pride in their own national identity and which can serve as a catalyst in a nation-building process that usually includes the integration of disparate regional groups and different social strata around certain dominant core groups...

This national self image usually masks not only internal power-relations but also the complicated, heterogeneous, and conflict-ridden processes that continue throughout processes of nation-building. This paper will start by looking at the formative history of Indonesian literature, precisely as the site of these myth-making processes, and by identifying the diverse voices that are being subordinated. Secondly, using a constructivist perspective, the paper will read three texts of pre-Independence literatures as illustrations of the roles these diverse voices play in nation-building. The paper will end by looking at the continuities as well as disruption of Indonesian literary history in the perspective of the contemporary scene in the continued processes of nation-building in Indonesia.

LITERARY HISTORY AND COLONIAL LEGACY

The perennial question that haunts scholars of Indonesian literary history is, "when Indonesian literature begins" (Damono 2003, p. 1). Tracing birth and origin cannot be separated from a more fundamental task of defining what Indonesian literature actually is. As Wahyudi (2000) shows in his comprehensive overview of the polemics on that subject, the quest cannot but be related to the understanding of what a nation is, thus to ask "when it all begins" is a crucially charged question. In defining Indonesian literature, it is important to note that the existence of oral and written literatures in the archipelago that later became the Dutch Indies precede the birth of a nation-state called Indonesia. As early as the ninth century, handwritten manuscripts were found in the islands. As contacts with outsiders intensify, especially with the spread of Islam — after earlier adoption of Hinduism and Buddhism — literatures written in Arabic script appeared in the archipelago as early as the twelfth century. The definition of national literature to date, however, does not cover literatures written in all those languages, but rests on those written in Malay, one vernacular language that emerged as a lingua franca and market language in the region from the seventeenth century, and developed into what was later called Bahasa Indonesia.

One significant milestone that marks the adoption of Malay as the national language is the Pledge of Youth on 28 October 1928. On that occasion, various indigenous youth organizations in the Dutch Indies took a vow that they belonged to one nation, one homeland, and supported the language that united them all, that is, Bahasa Indonesia. That historic moment has since been remembered as another pledge of commitment for uniting diverse population in the process of nation-building, a process which historians claimed to have started in 1908. With Bahasa Indonesia as a crucial site for nationalism, literary historians had the reason to trace the "origin" of national literature in texts written in Malay. As Indonesian literature grew, the definition of modern Indonesian literature was further restricted to cover only printed materials using Latin alphabets, because the use of prints "marks the divide between old and modern literatures" (Damono 2003, p. 1).

On the basis of language and script, Wahyudi (2000) supported Sapardi Djoko Damono's argument that " Indonesian literature started to exist when literature in the Malay language is spread all over Indonesia… not for the interest of a certain group, but for inhabitants of Nusantara or the Dutch Indies" (Wahyudi 2000, p. 8). Both do not differentiate between low or high dialects, as "there has never been any distinction between low and high language in any [history of] modern literature" (Damono 2003, p. 9).

With that argument, Damono traces the earliest poems amongst those printed in *Bianglala*, a publication for Catholic communities in Indonesia, published in Batavia in the 1870s. Further development of Indonesian literature in the early twentieth century was closely tied to the publishing industries, first owned by the Dutch or Indo-Dutch, and many of which were later owned and run by *Peranakan* Chinese. It is not surprising, therefore, that the language used widely in the mass media was interchangeably called the low Malay, market Malay or Chinese Malay. Scholars have noted that the first Malay grammar book by non-Dutch scholars was written by Lie Kim Hok in 1884 (Suryadinata 1996; Lombard 1996). Damono (2003) made a significant observation of the contribution of Chinese Malay poets in creatively experimenting and making alive traditional poetic forms, such as *pantun* and *syair*. He contrasted this with the western orientation of the established poets of the *Pujangga Baru* magazine (appearing in the 1930s) in embracing the sonnet as their poetic form.

The works of today's Indonesian literary historians (Damono 2003; Wahyudi 2000; Sumardjo 1999) followed the groundbreaking research done earlier by scholars mentioned by Suryadinata (1996). Yet the more dominant mode of Indonesian literary scholarship before the dawn of the twenty-first century had preferred high Malay, and thus overlooked the Chinese Malay literature. Both A. Teeuw and H.B. Jassin, two founding literary critics of Indonesian literature, had concentrated on works published by Balai Pustaka, a publisher originally founded by the colonial government to provide reading materials for the larger public.[2] This is a colonial legacy, since it was a conscious policy by the colonial government to closely guard the boundary of good literature within the confines of high Malay, "the language of a particular group, which can be described as elitist" (Damono 1979). Most writers of Balai Pustaka were educated young men from Sumatra, who had more access and cultural affinity to the high Malay language (Damono 1979).[3]

What we have seen in the formative years of Indonesian literary history is the selection among existing diverse literatures of what qualifies as national literature. The process of selection involves power relations and subordination. The colonial government promoted this language in schools and through the Balai Pustaka publications. Literatures written in low Malay, on the other hand, were labelled as "wild literatures", suggesting low and unsophisticated quality as well as unsanctioned political orientation that they may nurture towards colonial authority. Besides Malay Chinese literature, literatures outside the Balai Pustaka circle also include those published by political organizations, such as PKI (Indonesian Communist Party), churches and religious organizations, such as Serikat Islam, and other social organizations, like women's groups. Besides the Peranakan Chinese, writers of popular literatures written in low Malay came from diverse backgrounds, including Dutch, Indo-Dutch, Javanese, and Menadonese, whose original novels dated back as early as the 1890s. In fact, Wahyudi (2000) argued that the earliest drama was *Lelakon Raden Beij Soerio Retno* by F. Wiggers (1901), while the earliest novel was *Njai Dasima* by G. Francis (1896).

By calling those works "wild literature", the colonial policy betrayed a security interest in keeping the unwanted elements from the confines of "good literature" for their colonial subjects. Post-colonial Indonesian literary establishment inherited this cultural policy by overlooking the existing diversity, and by fixing the boundary of national literature.

A legalistic approach to define Indonesian literature is Slamet Mulyana's insistence that "all literary works before 1945 could not be included as Indonesian literature" (in Wahyudi 2000, p. 5). Ayip Rosidi marks the birth of Indonesian literature in 1922, with the publication of Muhamad Yamin's nationalistic poetry collection, *Tanah Air*. He based his reasoning on the grounds of nationalism. In the section to follow, we will look at three examples of those marginalized texts, in order to reconsider their contribution to the processes of nation-building. In order to do that, we need to first unpack some conceptual underpinnings that entail such analysis.

SOME THEORETICAL CONSIDERATIONS

In *Adakah Bangsa dalam Sastra* (Zaidan and Senggono 2003), scholars of Indonesian literature disagree about the relations between literature and the processes of nation-building.[4] First is the argument that "literature is an effect, not a cause" of social, political phenomena, as raised by Budi Darma. In Budi Darma's metaphor, literature is only "one coach, not the locomotive of social change" (p. 22).

Indonesian literary history has witnessed instances in which social and political conditions moulded and shaped literary production. One historic turning point is the 1965–1966 bloody upheaval, where the number of people killed has remained undocumented. There are many theories of what occurred on that fateful day 30 September 1965; for example, internal power struggle within the army, the CIA plot to overthrow President Sukarno). The official explanation held the Indonesian Communist Party (PKI) and its affiliate organizations responsible for plotting to take over power. This scapegoating justified the massive persecution of those suspected to be "leftist", including writers and artists, and the banning of their works. This era also sees the closing down of Chinese language schools, and an assimilation policy towards Indonesians of Chinese background, such as changing Chinese names, and banning Chinese rituals, dance and music. Peranakan Chinese intellectuals who supported the assimilation policy later explained that a cultural break with mainland China was necessary to "save" Indonesians with Chinese background from being persecuted as communists.[5]

The New Order era (1966–1998) gives shape to its literary and cultural esthetics. Yet, the 1965 event was a culmination of intricate and complicated processes on the ground, which involved not only political activists, but also writers and artists. Novels imbued with Marxist ideology had appeared as early as the 1920s (see the discussion of *Hikajat Kadiroen* below). The polarization of the leftist and right-wing groups (i.e. Lekra and Lesbumi) resulted in the Cultural Manifesto (1963) that underlined the right-wing *l'art pour l'art* philosophy as a response to the leftist aesthetics.

These examples suggest that the relationship between social change and literature cannot be simply reduced to a linear cause and effect formula. The mimetic approach that sees literature as a mere reflection of reality has been questioned by a constructivist approach that considers literature, as well as other media of verbal expressions, as means for constructing reality. Saini K.M. (in Zaidan and Sugono 2003) for example, acknowledges that in the period of 1900–1942, "literature is not merely pointing to the growth and formation of the Indonesian sensibility, but is also a part of it" (p. 84). Another fitting example is the life and work of Muhammad Yamin, the leader of Jong Sumatra (a regional youth organization), who became the motor of the nationalist movement. He was among the organizers of the Youth Pledge of 1928. His patriotic poems, translations, and books help construct national myths and symbols (e.g. the historic origin of the national flag, and the legend of Gajah Mada, a warrior from a Hindu Kingdom in the fourteenth century that swore to unite the archipelago).

Another rebuttal of the relations between literature and nation-building comes from Nirwan Dewanto (in Zaidan and Senggono 2003), who separates the discourse on politics that poets and writers actively engaged during all periods of Indonesian literary history, and "the contents" of their literary works. "Nationalism in Indonesian literature is not expressed by the content (or quality) of the literary works but by the belief (credo) of the writers, and by the efforts of literary historian in writing a national literary history" (ibid., p. 48). Dewanto further differentiates between conscious literary politics, which is tied up with identity-politics, and the content of the writers' work, which he characterizes with "artistic modernism". This artistic modernism, according to Dewanto, is not a direct reaction against tradition, "but an effort in associating with a changing world", an effort that finds its voice in "emptiness, alienation, and even madness" (ibid., p. 47). Yet by this very example, Dewanto is actually affirming the ties between the changing world and the writers' effort in deflecting it in certain artistic forms.

Implied in Dewanto's reasoning is the inside-outside, internal-external dichotomy that informs modernist orientation. The discussion of *Hikajat Kadiroen* below will show how the form and content of novels and fiction not only reflect, but also constitute the political discourse itself. To reverse the logic, political and ideological discourses exist in its textual manifestation, in the form of narratives, metaphors and symbols. As Bhabha (1990) puts it, narratives play roles in the "wide dissemination through which we construct the field of meanings and symbols associated with national life" (p. 3). Benedict Anderson (1983) has explained how nation-state, as a political, social and cultural entity, needs to be imagined by its subjects who are separated in geography. Continuous textual reinforcement of that imagination, in the form of maps, census statistics, monuments, novels and fictions, determines the existence of the nation-state. As indicated by Wong (2003) and Elias (1970), nation-states also need a sense of origin that requires narration.

As citizens need a sense of belonging or being a member of the large entity of the nation-state, nation-building entails not only "military and legal penetration of specific territory" but also "the cultural standardization of the population, and the extension of political citizenship and participation" (Hagen 2003). Saini (in Zaidan and Senggono 2003) calls this cultural standardization the inculcation of "Indonesian sensibility" through language, mass media, national curriculum, and national ideologies. According to Anderson (1983), print capitalism provides a space for creating this sense of participation and membership in a community: "These fellow-readers, to whom they were connected through print, formed, in their secular, particular, visible invisibility, the embryo of nationally-imagined communities" (p. 47).

The process of nation-building, however, is not as linear and singular as a national myth tends to produce, especially as it involves the integration of a heterogeneous society into one political entity. It can involve "long term processes of integration and disintegration in the course of which tensions and struggles between centrifugal and centripetal tendencies and between established and outsider groups occur as a regular feature characteristic of the structure of these developments" (Elias 1970). Precisely as a means for constructing a sense of community, literature of such a heterogeneous society can serve as the sites of competing and conflicting visions.

In a previous work, I have shown how literature engages in cross-cultural interaction (Budianta 2002). First, in imagining one's community, literature helps to situate its location vis-à-vis others, in local-national-global spheres. Secondly, as Edward Said and feminist scholars have shown, literature functions as a representation of one's identity as well as a representation of otherness, in a positive as well as negative or critical manner. Such representation could support or resist hegemonic or dominant ideologies, or shown to have ambivalent, conflicting tendencies. It can voice empathy, solidarity and cross-cultural understanding, or a rejection of others. It can envision an exclusive, essentialist notion of the imagined community, or a hybrid identity and borderless and fluid diversity.

The three texts below illustrate different ways, at times conflicting and competing, for constructing cultural sensibilities and political consciousness of a nation yet in the making.

ILLUSTRATIONS FROM PRE-INDEPENDENCE LITERATURE

Tadi saya sudah berichtiar mengajak rayat menjadi pinter dan kuat, supaya akhirnya kita bisa merdika mengurus negeri kita sendiri. Na, ini hal sungguhlah perkara kebangsa'an.
Semaoen, *Hikayat Kadiroen,* 1920

I have tried to persuade the people to be smart and strong, so that they finally could have the freedom to manage our own country. Now, this is really a matter of nationalism.

Marti,
Do'akanlah aku dapat bekerja dengan penuh cita-cita. Kau masih ingat, bahwa pertalian persaudaraan antara kau dan aku harus mengekalkan kesetiaan kita akan sumpah kita berdua: bekerja bagi mereka yang tertindas dan untuk Indonesia, tanah air kita bersama,

Lastri

Soewarsih Djojopuspito, *Manusia Bebas*, 1940–1975

Marti,
Please pray that I could work aspiringly. Please be reminded that our blood ties should seal our loyalty to the oath we have taken together: to work for those who are oppressed and for Indonesia, our mother land.

Lastri

Kau saksiken sekarang, Raden Adipati, itu tanda-tanda yang diramalkan oleh orang dulu, sudah mulai kaliatan. Antero Pulo Jawa sudah dililit oleh besi rail dari kreta pi: itu autobus, vrachtauto dan automobiel yang macemnya sagagi rumah, satiap hari muncang mancing dari satu ka lain termpat. Masin-masin terbang bukan saja bisa diliat, tapi juga bisa disewa dan dinaekin oleh penduduk yang brani membayar. Kalu ini semua ditambah lagi dengen pergolakan antara rahayat yang mengandung angen-angen ingin merdika, maka saya percaya dalam bebrapa pulu taon lagi ini pulo Jawa aken menampak perobahan yang sanget penting, hingga itu ramalan terbukti.
Kwe Tek Hoay, *Drama Dari Krakatau* 1929, p. 581

You see now, Prince Regent, these are the signs foretold by our forefathers, signs that now become visible. The whole Java island is already wound up by iron railways: those buses, trucks and cars, in variety of kinds, moving daily from one place to another. Those flying machines not only can be seen, but can be rent and ridden by citizens who pay. If all of these are accompanied by the upheavals among the people who demand independence, I believe

in the coming years the Javanese island will show an apparent
and significant change to realize the prophecy.

These three quotes above, taken from three novels written in the pre-
Independence era, suggest that literatures written in the East Indies had
since early on touched upon the issues of nationalism (*perkara
kebangsaan*). More importantly, *Hikayat Kadiroen* by Semaoen (1920),
Drama Dari Krakatau (1929) by Kwee Tek Hoay, and *Manusia Bebas* by
Suwarsih Djojopuspito (1940 in Dutch edition; 1975 in Indonesian), where
the quotes come from, were not part of the the mainstream culture of
East Indies, which was represented by the State-sponsored Balai Pustaka.
It was common to trace seeds of nationalism from books published by
the Balai Pustaka, because, as indicated earlier, this publishing house was
for a long time considered to be the birthplace of Indonesian literature.
This paper argues that literatures written outside the Balai Pustaka played
no less crucial roles in the processes of nation-building. These three
works do not represent the overall diversity of literature of the pre-
Independence Indonesia, but serve as illustrations of that diversity. Through
these three novels we could see the varying visions of becoming or living
in a common space in the pre-Independence, colonial world. Occupying
different locations, the three texts construct different esthetic as well as
ideological strategies in imagining their national communities.

Hikajat Kadiroen

Hikajat Kadiroen was written by Semaoen while he was incarcerated for
four months in 1919 after translating and publishing a pamphlet written
by Sneevliet, a Dutch leftist activist, in *Sinar Hindia* magazine. This
story of Kadiroen was first serialized as *fuilleton* in the same magazine
and was later published in a book form by Kantoor PKI (The Indonesian
Communist Party Bureau) in 1920. The novel could be seen as a narrative
version of Semaoen's judicial defence (which was published separately
by Sarikat Islam Semarang, March 1919). In this case, *Hikajat Kadiroen*
represents literatures written under the wings of political organizations
with specific ideological or cultural/social orientation, which were
mushrooming in the decades preceding Independence.[6] Another leading
figure or leftist writer of the same period was Mas Marco Kartodikromo.
In his judicial defence, Semaoen justifies his actions in the framework of
a general *hikajat* (or tale), which is Karl Marx's Communist Manifesto:
"The only *hikajat* in the community of one's society is the *hikajat* of ...

class conflict." Both in this judicial as well as in his literary text, Semaoen uses the term from the genre of Malay literature (which mixes fiction with legends and history) to refer to Marxist theory, thus aptly and precociously using the concept of the grand narrative.

Hikajat Kadiroen is an entertaining read that uses popular narrative techniques: comedy of situation, play of language, slapstick humour, suspense, plus the plots of both a thriller and a detective novel. The novel contrasts the capitalist and feudal villains to Kadiroen, a low-profile hero who fights for small people, including a character named Soeket (Javanese word for grass, a direct personification of the grassroots). In and out his narrative, the novel weaves an intense intellectual debate that leads readers to the prescribed grand narrative. Like the Puritan conversion narrative in the eighteenth century American literature, the protagonist was gradually converted to communism and was granted a romantic happy ending. Here we see the superimposition of two kinds of narrative, Marxist and Kadiroen's *hikajat*, inseparable one from another.

Through this novel, Marxist ideology not only gets a concrete form, but is also translated culturally. The ideological message in this novel is fused with religious discourse. Marxist historical determinism is translated into "God's providence (*Kodrat Toean Allah*) for mankind". In any instance, the characters are encouraged to pray, confess, and thank God. Socialism is considered in tune with all kinds of religions (igama-igama apa saja), including Christianity, Islam, Hinduism and Buddhism. By posing God's providence as the answer, the novel freely criticizes unjust cultural practices, including those made in the name of religion. In this way the novel achieves two conflicting goals, i.e. explaining Marxism in more culturally acceptable religious terms, as well as attacking religious practice on the basis of Marxist terms.

Hikajat Kadiroen also functions as a direct model for behaviour, a book of ethics. Each chapter is a litany of all kinds of corruption and power abuse, contrasted with a model character of high integrity, who passes through different professions (policeman, government official, journalist), covering his public as well as private life (equal job division at home, without servants). Kadiroen's childhood self-learning is a model of personal edification, covering physics, geography, civics, law, religion or metaphysics, agriculture, biology, etc. Kadiroen's daily schedule reminds us of the similar part in *The Autobiography of Benjamin Franklin*. If Franklin's autobiography provides the American readers with the blueprint for socializing capitalist ethos (the concept of a self-made man that changes his social status from rags to riches, thanks to his thrift and hard work in a free competitive world), *Hikajat Kadiroen* provides an educational model for the Indonesian communist, using a tight yardstick of moral integrity, in order to free his people from the colonialization of the "moneyed groups" (*kaum wang*).

Manusia Bebas

Manusia Bebas occupies a more complicated and disadvantaged position in Indonesian literature before and as well as after Independence. Within or outside Balai Pustaka publications, women writers were scarcely found in literatures of pre-Independence. Suwarsih Djojopuspito, the author of this novel, was among the few. Yet she told of her difficulty in getting through the publishing world in the 1930s. Her first novel, *Marjanah,* written in Sundanese, was refused by the Balai Pustaka. With the help of Edi du Peron, an Indo-Dutch writer who became a popular literary protégée in the literary circles of the Dutch Indies in the 1930s, Suwarsih wrote and published her second novel in Dutch. *Buiten Het Gareel,* with an introduction by Peron, was published in the Netherlands in 1940 and got a positive reception. The novel in translation only reached the Indonesian audience in 1975. By then, it had already lost its contextual reverberation. The history of this novel illustrates the options as well as problems faced by Indonesian intellectuals in negotiating between languages and modes of writing, which is a struggle with plurality as well as with modernity. The novel's insecure position in Indonesian literary history also speaks of the precarious position of literatures written in languages other than Indonesian, which will be dealt with later.

    Manusia Bebas depicts the plight of small people in the colonial period, with a different perspective from *Hikajat Kadiroen.* The main characters, Sulastri, and her husband, Sudarmo, represent the "proletarian intellectuals" who work "for the sake of national education" through wild schools, unsubsidized but closely monitored by the colonial government. Any time, the colonial police could search such schools and withdraw the teaching permits from its teachers. The story describes the characters' struggle not only against the colonial pressures, but also against the "bourgeoisie orientation" of their society, the shortsightedness of political parties, and intrigues from competing political parties.

    The novel makes implicit reference to the existing political parties in the 1930s, and has strong political messages, expressed in Sudarmo's speech in front of the pupils' parents: "What is a good Indonesian, according to our ideal? We completely agree on this: a good Indonesian is the one that will always develop his or her potentials and use them for the sake of national movement." Yet it is not a historical novel on political movements, nor propaganda of one political ideology. This novel appears more as a diary that records the day-to-day struggle of two high-school teachers in the colonial period.[7] This novel is written in a realistic "slice of life" mode, filled with a modernist sense of alienation, doubts and ambivalence. It starts with the motivation of Sulastri to write a story based on her life, and ends in an open question: "I don't know what else to write... We have experienced a time of suffering. Is our life better now?" There is no answer, as the characters have come to where they started. The novel's last words show weariness and insecurity, accompanied at the same time by a dry sense of humour and stoic persistence: "Don't joke around... Soon they (the Dutch Indies Police) will cut you up, and what would you do then?" (p. 284).

With such explicit political criticism, it is hard to imagine that Balai Pustaka would publish this novel in the 1930s. At the same time, the self-mocking tone would not fit any political party's agenda. In the novel one character speaks — a meta-narrative or self-referring comment — that "your story is useless, having no traditional form. It is not appealing as it does not give answer to the childhood dreams of a village teacher" (p. 4). Here is the criticism against Balai Pustaka's preference for simple stories with strong didactic ends. As Ayip Rosidi points out, "the literary aspirations" of this novel, which A. Teeuw claimed to be the best among those produced by pre-Independence writers, might be considered "too advanced for her people".

There is, however, a different assessment. According to Achdiat K. Miharja, Suwarsih's novel in Sundanese was rejected by the publisher "because its Sundanese language is considered unsatisfactory". In the novel, the character has difficulty in translating her thoughts from Dutch into Sundanese, "Sulastri is not happy with her translation, because she thought that her sentences sound Dutch." (p. 250). We see similar problems in the very translation of *Manusia Bebas*. The author herself in her late years translated this novel, after spending most of her mature life in the Netherlands. As if fulfilling the prophecy of her character, Suwarsih's Indonesian translation of her novel sounds foreign to the contemporary readers of the 1970s.

With this language problem, *Manusia Bebas* comes to the precarious position of Indonesian intellectuals before and after Independence. For writers whose mother language is one of the vernacular languages, Indonesian becomes their second language. For those who were schooled in the Dutch education system during the pre-Independence era, and those brought up in a Western environment in today's gobal era, Indonesian language might be a second or even third language. Like Suwarsih's works, their writing in Bahasa Indonesia would then be a process of translating thoughts wrapped in vernacular, Dutch or English.

Sulastri's position in the border of three languages, Sundanese, Dutch and Indonesian, speaks of the multicultural dimension in the processes of nation-building in Indonesia. For Sulastri — the alter ego of the writer — language functions like home. When she was traveling to Yogyakarta, she felt alienated because "they spoke in a language foreign to me," a feeling that would not come if she were in the Netherlands. Only when she returned to the Sundanese-speaking area in Bandung, did she feel at ease: "the deadness of her feeling was broken when she could see clearly the familiar faces, the voices in the language that she knew." Sulastri admonished herself for this "sentimental" feeling, which was not congruent with nationalism: "It is so strange that I should be tied up with one region, while this vast country is called my homeland." (p. 281).[8]

Confusion in languages in this case is also a reflection of a deeper confusion in adjusting conflicting values. Sulastri who fights for women's emancipation, does not know how to deal with her father who practises polygamy without any qualms. Sudarmo who worships rationality is attracted to magic talismans. This novel depicts the continuous tugs that Indonesian intellectuals are implicated between — tradition and modernity, regionalism and nationalism.

Drama dari Krakatau

Drama dari Krakatau was one of more than fifty literary works written by the prolific and leading figure of Kwee Tek Hoay. It is not as prominent as *Drama Di Boven Digul* (1938) that has been discussed in relation to nationalism.[9] Two of his other best known novels, *Bunga Roos dari Tjikembang* (1927), and *Ruma Sekola yang Saya Impiken* (1925), lend themselves well to our discussion here. *Drama dari Krakatau* is not less pertinent. According to Claudine Salmon (in Suryadinata 1996), Chinese Malay novels that depict indigenous populations were a new phenomenon in the early 1920s. Initially talking to and about their own people, the novels broadened their horizon to include the wider population. The settings went beyond the confines of cities, where most of the Chinese Malay population lived, to remote islands and mountains that spread in the archipelago. Salmon discovered thirty-seven novels written by sixteen authors between 1923 and 1941, who wrote about the native population.

Yet, as Sumarjo (in Suryadinata 1996) explains, the Chinese Malay literature grew out of the need of the Peranakan Chinese, who was more at home in Malay language, for reading and expressing themselves in that language. The words *masjarakat* (society) and *bangsa* (people) in their writing refer to the Chinese communities.[10] Indonesian nationalism, if mentioned by the characters of these novels, usually serves as a good example, something that they respect.[11] In many, the word *tanah-air,* unlike Yamin's poems, refers to mainland China. However, novels like *Drama dari Krakatau*, through its vivid and closely researched display of geographical and cultural riches of Indonesia, play their own role: in an accessible language, they put the country within the imagination of the readers.

In his introduction to the novel, Kwee said that this story came about upon a friend's request for "a sensational story, which later could be turned into a fascinating film" (p. 428). This artistic genesis speaks the general thrust of Chinese Malay literature as a popular entertainment. The fact that it is popular underlines the wider dissemination of their imagination. The Krakatau story was so appealing, that it was staged three times in one month before Kwee could finish the book.[12]

Kwee opens his novel by locating the local setting (the district of Bantam Kidul, West Java, now called Banten) in a global perspective. Starting from 9564 BC with the sinking of Poseidonis that created a new formation of islands, the narration moves towards those spreading islands in Southeast Asia, the lesser Sunda islands, Java and Sumatra, and stops above the Krakatau volcano in Sunday Bay. After giving a history of Krakatau's eruptions (including the colonial government's oversight of its danger), the story goes into the house of the Tjakra Amidjaja, the Regent of that area, that is disturbed by the Regent's wife's ominous dreams about the mountain.

Laying out geographical panorama is a narrative technique used throughout this novel. Later in the story, the protagonist hero Raden Moelia, an Assistant Regent, climbed Ciwalirang Mountain to meet with a Baduy leader. At the peak of the mountain, he could view not only the Krakatau volcano, but also other islands as far as the tip of Sumatra, with smoke coming from steamboats entering its rich harbour. Raden Moelia's observation went as far as the southern tip of Sumatra and then zoomed back to the local village at the foot of the mountain. There the Assistant

Regents would engage with the culture and lifestyle of the Baduy society, and fall in love with their crown princess.

The interest towards isolated tribes and cultures in Chinese Malay literature can well be understood as the lure of the exotic, as some scholars believe (Salmon in Suryadinata 1996). What is more important is how novels like *Drama dari Krakatau* help the readers to imagine the geography of a nation yet to be united. By switching from a long shot of global panorama to a close-up of local details, Kwee's narrative does many things: first, it introduces to his urban readers how to appreciate the culture of an isolated ethnic group; second, it lays out the geographical and cultural map of the country that will later become Indonesia, and third, it places that location in a global perspective.

In his introduction, that serves also as a lecture of how to write a good novel, Kwee mentions Lord Lytton's *The Last Day of Pompei* as his inspiration, and advises writers to read widely to enrich their novels: "Writers who do not know language other than Malay, must learn to study Dutch or English ... By knowing one of those Western languages, a novelist holds the key to knowledge and high literature, with unbounded limit." Jedamski (in Foulcher 2002) has indicated how this fluid translation and creative adaptation from the global to the local contexts in low Malay literatures allows for the formation of new sensibilities for the "evolving postcolonial culture" (p. 45).

One of the new sensibilities that is being formed in the writing of *Drama dari Krakatau* is the will (or one might say, suspension of disbelief) and effort in "impersonating" and understanding cultures other than one's own. The Muslim characters in such stories recite prayers in Arabic, its translation given between brackets, and speak in local dialects. As the narration enters this or other characters in different cultures, it portrays their customs and beliefs from an insider's perspective.[13] Salmon (in Suryadinata 1996) notes that depiction of cultures remote from one's own is not a tendency in Balai Pustaka literature. Similarly, Sumardjo (1999) notes such an absence in Javanese literature. A rare exception in Balai Pustaka's novels is Aman Datuk Madjoindo's *Si Doel Anak Betawi* (1940), a successful rendition of the Betawi culture by a Sumatran writer.[14]

Sympathetic representation of others in this novel, like in many literatures of that period, has its limit. Here and there ethnic stereotyping occurs, depicting sentiments that abounded in the diverse population of the Dutch Indies. "Be careful of those Sundanese women! I have lost much money, ripped off by the girls in Bandung." The speaker, however, happens to be one of the two deceitful villains from Palembang, who had the lack of heart to kidnap the daughter and wife of the Baduy priest who had cured their illness.

The novel also touches on the subject of religious power struggle, i.e. the religious persecutions of the Hindu followers of Pajajaran subjects by the Islamic forces. Salmon notes that by representing isolated tribes, Chinese Malay writers speak of their own marginalization.[15] Here Kwee differentiates between religion as a faith, which he appreciates, and religion as a political force, embroiled in power struggle.

In ideological terrain, this novel also positions itself against that of *Hikajat Kadiroen*, betraying Kwee's anti-communist stance.[16] The narrator justifies Dutch colonial policy to quell the "bad influences of Red leaders, who provoke the people" (p. 459) by discharging "inept officials" who could not handle the 1926 communist rebellion. He labels the communists as "bad people". It is ironic that later in the story, the colonial fear of red scare was manipulated by the Palembang villains to support their kidnapping. In fact, it was the effort in policing and security surveillance that brought the hero — the Assistant Regent — to meet his future Baduy father-in-law. In this way, the novel shows its ideological contradictions, enacting the very forces of marginalization that it criticizes.

In terms of literary mode, this novel shares the same characteristics of *Hikajat Kadiroen*, employing mysticism, chance and romance, and all the narrative techniques of a popular novel. If *Kadiroen* envisions the future in a communist Indonesia wrapped in a religious garment, *Drama dari Krakatau* speaks of a region of theosophy where religious difference is unified in the belief of goodness. Echoing Jayabaya's famous oracle, the novel envisions the Independence of Indonesia through national movements, with a pre-Islam "return of throne" and noncommunist orientation. Compared to these two novels, *Manusia Bebas* shows a more individualized version of freedom, combined with the vision of Social Marhaenism.

The three novels intensely search for ways to educate the nation. *Hikajat Kadiroen* invents recipes for curing corrupt morality; *Manusia Bebas* depicts the struggle of intellectuals in building an alternative system of education; *Drama dari Krakatau* dramatizises a romantic journey towards an ideal society. Both Semaoen and Suwarsih's novels make strong commitments to small people against the forces of the capital or the bourgeoisie. Compared with these two, *Drama dari Krakataua* is more conservative, especially in its narrative alignment with the aristocratic saviour-heroes, although it has a strong sympathy with the marginalized. In their different cultural locations, these three novels illustrate the diverse voices and conflicting forces involved in the processes of nation-building.

Borrowing Henk Maier's words below, these novels — regardless of being written in low or high Malay — help create or envision a reading community in an emerging nation:

> Readers shaped new communities that transcended the borders of locality. They were forced to reflect on authority and power, on love, life and death in novel and confusing ways. Some of them decided they should try and play a role in these new communities in order to steer the energies they generated, either by way of dissent of by compromise, by way of centrifugality and centripetality, the interaction of which moves every discursive formation along. Forces of order and deviations, desire for control and freedom: they can be found in every field of everyday life, and in every description of it.
> (cited in Foulcher 2002, p. 67)

CONCLUSION

We have to acknowledge, however, that imagining the nation in the 1920s and 1930s is different from imagining the nation in 2003. The context that binds the three novels above is the Dutch Indies. Within that colonial structure, the three texts position themselves. First, they have to position themselves amongst competing languages (Malay, low or high, vernacular languages, Dutch and English). Second, they situate their cultural, ideological, and political orientation. The three texts show how openness towards external cultural resources (ideology, modernism, western literary style) enrich their imagination of the nation. What emerges is dynamic, creative cross-cultural translation with its own contradiction and ambivalence.

Those processes of nation-building have not stopped. Contemporary literature is still playing similar roles in constructing people's visions about their country. After the Reformasi movement that marked the fall of the thirty-two-year era of the New Order regime in May 1998, the publishing industries have been booming with escalating speed. Books on leftist ideologies, highly censored before, now can be seen on the street stalls and kiosks. Novelists and victims of repressive policies against "leftist" — as shown in *Drama dari Krakatau* — have started to rewrite the past. Their versions will compete with others in the construction of new collective memory.

Unappreciated by previous literary scholars, Chinese Malay literatures are now being reprinted by established publishers, amounting to seven volumes. In universities, courses and theses on Chinese Malay literature have become popular. Research is now being conducted to study Chinese stories written in Javanese scripts by Chinese writers (Mastuti 2003).

An interesting phenomenon is the public emergence of Inhoa (Yinhua) literature. This literature was originally written in Mandarin script in the one and only newspaper using Chinese language, the *Harian Indonesia* (Yindunixiya Ribao) which was founded during the New Order period, owned and controlled by the Government. This newspaper was a means for the New Order Government to localize and put into surveillance Chinese culture that was suppressed after the 1965 upheaval. The newspaper has a literature column that carries poems and short stories. During the Reformasi years of 1998–1999, the authors of *Harian Indonesia* joined the literary activities of the Indonesian Literary Community (KSI), reciting their poems in Chinese. Poets from KSI, most of whom are from worker poets association (*penyair buruh*), later had their works translated into Indonesian and published. Besides the translation of poetry and short-story collections, there was also a bilingual collection of Indonesian and Inhoa poems. Looking at our discussion of national literature in the previous section, the question is, what is the position of this Inhoa literature?

This question leads to another one, i.e., what is the origin of this Inhoa literature? Suryadinata (1996) mentions that "in Indonesia, besides literatures written in Chinese language, there is literature written in Chinese Malay" (p. 6). Unlike the Chinese literature in Malaysia (Mahoa) and Singapore, Chinese literature in Indonesia before *Harian Indonesia* was not as prominent as those written in Chinese Malay. Existence of other immigrant literatures, such as Arabic and Portuguese, has not been documented either. The population make-up of Indonesia, with 300 indigenous ethnic groups, and a small percentage of immigrant groups, has not been conducive for the flowering of immigrant literatures. The prominence of Peranakan Chinese culture that used Malay is another factor. The banning of Chinese schools in the 1960s, and the concentration of the culturally educated group in the *Harian Indonesia* circles, could be a place for the rebirth of Inhoa literature. Most of the Inhoa writers are over forty, supporting the evidence that they belong to the generation who had been schooled in Chinese language before 1960.

Although written in Mandarin, the contents of the poems and literature in translation show a strong orientation towards Indonesian culture. Some are strongly marked with the terms and symbols of official national ideology (Batik uniform, the dual roles of the military or *ABRI masuk desa*).[17] Like the three texts discussed above, their vision of the nation speaks of a certain ideological location, which is as valid as others. Indonesian literature by definition is literature written in Bahasa Indonesia, however, like Selasih's *Manusia Bebas*, Inhoa texts become Indonesian literature via translation.

With the crumbling of the New Order ideological paradigm, demands are raised to redefine the concepts of national literature. The decentralization movements and the regional awakenings in literature have strongly voiced the need to acknowledge literatures written in other languages as equal to that written in Bahasa Indonesia. Among literary community groups, a movement to celebrate locality and regional cultures has been growing prior to Reformasi years in line with criticism of the Java-centric and centralistic culture of the New Order Government. The inception of "Sastra Kepulauan" (Island Literature), "Sastra Pesantren" (*Pesantren* Literature), "Sastra Pedalaman" (Inland Literature), "Riau Literature" speak of this de-centering move.

The Indonesian Language Congress in 2003 puts into the agenda efforts in reversing the subordination policy towards vernacular language and literatures, which is seen to have hampered its existence. It is indeed high time to replace the concept of national literature with the equal acknowledgement of all literatures written in other languages by Indonesians — including those written in Bahasa Indonesia — as Indonesian literatures or Literatures in Indonesia

Cultural policy, however, is not the only factor in a survival of a language or literature. The competition of media and capital, as well as competition between languages, will also determine whether Inhoa literature, like Javanese, Sundanese or Bugis literature, continues to exist. Chinese language courses in Indonesia are now flourishing as people realize the reconfiguration of economic powers from the West to China. Yet, whether the popularity of Chinese language is accompanied with a heightened cultural sensibility for the production of strong Inhoa literature, like in Malaysia and Singapore, is yet to be seen. Younger generations of Indonesians — be they from Chinese or other cultural background — have been brought up in the Indonesian language, and now, in English. One or two works of Indonesian literature in English have been published, but its prevalence is insignificant, compared to those published in Malaysia and Singapore. At least within the years to come, Bahasa Indonesia will remain the most popular site for Indonesian writers to express their visions and creativity. The flourishing of Indonesian language newspapers and magazines is a strong basis for that direction. The genre of "Sastra Koran" (newspaper literature) is a result of the marriage between literature and journalism, a tendency that goes back to the Malay Chinese literature.[18]

Like Sulastri/Suwarsih, however, Indonesian intellectuals are never fully at home, nor satisfied with Bahasa Indonesia. Maier (in Foulcher, 2002) names this anxiety and quirkiness "stammer", which he believes characterizes not only Malay literature but also works by Pramoedya Ananta Toer and other contemporary writers. This is not a linguistic weakness, but a cultural anxiety of negotiating between the diverse cultures and languages in the global-national-local traffic. This anxiety is precisely what keeps Indonesian language and literature dynamically moving and obstinately diverse. Young women writers shock the reading public with their new idioms of sexuality. They have a different reading public from those with a more religious or conservative cultural idioms.[19] Others experiment with hybridity of forms, languages and cultures. In this diversified market, and in this openness for cross-cultural traffic and plurality lies the future of the multicultural Indonesian literature, where the future of Indonesia as nation-state will be continuously imagined.

Notes

1. Wong Sook Koon "Rethinking the Nation" in *Aliran Monthly* 22.
2. Initially named Comissie voor de Volkslectuur (1908), later Kantoor voor de Volkslectuur (1917) or Balai Pustaka. For the history of this institution, read Doris Jedamski (1992).
3. Damono (2003) quotes Sutan Takdir Alisjahbana's appreciation of Chinese or Market Malay, which has vast influence in the mass media of the 1930s. According to Takdir, as quoted by Damono, "the deepest and grandest feeing could be expressed in the Chinese Malay" (p. 8, English translation is mine) — which to him differs only slightly in spelling with "Bahasa Indonesia".
4. Zaidan, Abdul Rozak and Dendy Sugondo (2003). *Adakah Bangsa dalam Sastra?* (Jakarta: Pusat Bahasa and Department Pendidikan Nasional). The translation of the quotes are mine.
5. Personal communication with Harry Tjan Silalahi (2000).
6. The growth of political organizations was truncated during the Japanese occupation in 1942–45.
7. What emerges are candid descriptions of ordinary matters, which at times surpass historical or biographical works. Take as an example the description of Sukarno's first wife, Inggit, here called Zus Karno:

> After leaving Sulastri with his wife, Karno pats Sudarmo's back in a friendly's manner and invited him to his office. Karno's wife sat on wide and low bench. She is holding a cigarette, which she drew towards her mouth in a sensual and attractive way. Zus Karno talked from one thing to another, from domestic work to women's movement and her husband's involvement in political parties; from meetings to political problems, with the same gaiety, as if all of those matters are of equal importance, while inhaling the cigarette smokes from her mouth and nose and with daydreaming look in her eyes.

8. It is ironic if we contrast this closeness to the spirit of the vernacular language and culture voiced by the book, and the critics' assessment of the writer's language and cultural competence. According to Ayip Rosidi, the editors of Balai Pustaka refused Suwarsih's Sundanese manuscript because "the writer failed to depict the lives and characters of Sundanese people."

9. See Thomas Rieger's discussion in Suryadinata (1989).

10. Liem Khing Hoo's *Berjuang* (1934), for example, depicts a group of Chinese people, who were concerned that if they did not do something to improve their community, their life and culture will be erased from Indonesia's history. So they decided to transmigrate to Borneo and experimented a utopian society.

11. In Liem Khing Hoo's *Bergerak* (1935), for example, a character named Liong Seng was trying to explain to a friend what he meant by "the backbone of a movement":

> "Buat sebut satu conto, umpamanya tulang blakang Indonesia Merdika dari pergerakan bangsa Indonesiers!"

> "Tapi it toch tida bisa jadi tulang blakang dari pergerakan kita?" tanya lagi Ing Ho. "Boleh jadi tida, tapi saia melainkan hendak unjuk satu conto," saut Liong Seng (233).

12. When the Moon Opera performance was shown in Pasar Senen, Weltevreden on 28 March 1928, he was only up to Chapter 11. The second show was on 31 March, and the third on 5 April at Schouwburg Thalia, in Mangga Besar, Batavia. Kwee finished the fifteen chapters on 28 May 1928, exactly two months after the first show. The story's genealogy also shows the fluidity of genre-switching in Chinese Malay literature. What started as a novel — or even a poem — could end up being a play, and the performance of a play might modify the novel.

13. Unlike some novels of this kind (*Drama di Boven Digoel* by Kwee Tek Hoay), there are no Chinese characters in *Drama dari Krakatau*. There is only one sentence, mentioning Chinese shopowners in the districts, who were asked by the Regent to provide food supplies during emergency

14. Discussed in detail in my article "In the Margin of the capital; from "Tjerita Boedjang Bingoeng" to "Si Doel Anak Sekolahan" in Foulcher (2002).

15. Liem Khing Ho in *Berjuang* (1934), for example, puts this complaint in the mouth of one of his character: "Peranakan Chinese in Indonesia are not treated as they should be. They are considered as Dutch subjects without the rights of Dutch subjects; in law they were treated like the Indonesians (*Indonesier*), without the rights of the Indonesians; if they want to be foreign citizens of China, the Dutch government raises their eye!" (in *Kesastraan Melayu Tionghoa dan Kebangsaan Indonesia*, vol 6: 123).
16. See Leo Suryadinata's discussion of Kwee Tek Hoay's political thoughts in Sidharta (1989).
17. See my introduction to "Sastra Peranakan Tionghoa dalam Bahasa Mandarin: Kesusasteraan Diaspora atau Kesusasteraan Indonesia" (The Literature of Indonesian Chinese in Mandarin: A Diaspora Literature or an Indonesian Literature?) with co-writer Edwina Satmoko, an Introduction to the Poetry Anthology of forty Indonesian Chinese Poets, *"Menyangga Dunia di atas Bulu Mata"*, translated by Wilson Tjandinegara (Jakarta: Gitakara, 1998), pp. vii–xiii. Also "Nasi Beracun" (A Review of an Anthology of Indonesian-Chinese Mini Stories), Mitra, March 2000.
18. Sumardjo (1996) notes that a big percentage of Chinese Malay writers are journalists. Earliest stories in popular magazines also have close affinity with news reportage.
19. See Apsanti Djoko Suyatno, " Tiga Novelis Wanita Meramu Seks" in *Media Indonesia*, 2 November 2003.

References

Anderson, Benedict. *Imagined Communities: Reflections on the Origin and Spread of Nationalism*. London: Verso, 1983.
Bhabha, Homi K., ed. "Introduction: Narrating the Nation". *Nation and Narration*. London: Routledge, 1990.
Budianta, Melani and Edwina Satmoko. "Sastra Peranakan Tionghoa dalam Bahasa Mandarin: Kesusasteraan Diaspora atau Kesusasteraan Indonesia?" in Tjandinegara (1998), pp. vii–xiii.
Budianta, Melani. "Sastra dan Interaksi Lintas Bangsa". In *Adakah Bangsa dalam Sastra?*, edited by Abdul Rozak and Dendy Senggono. Jakarta: Penerbit Progress and Pusat Bahasa, 2003.
Damono, Sapardi Djoko. *Novel Sastra Indonesia Sebelum Perang*. Jakarta: Pusat Pembinaan dan Pengembangan Bahasa, 1979.
———. *Puisi Indonesia Sebelum Kemerdekaan, Sebuah Catatan Awal*. Jakarta: Pusat Bahasa, 2003.
Djojopuspito, Suwarsih. *Manusia Bebas*. Jakarta: Djambatan, 1975.
Elias, Norbert. "Processes of State Formation and Nation Building". *Transactions of the 7th World Congress of Sociology 1970* 3 (1972): 274–84. Sofia: ISA. <http://www.usyd.edu.au/su/social/elias/elias.html>.

Foulcher, Keith and Tony Day. *Clearing A Space: Postcolonial Readings of Modern Indonesian Literature*. Leiden: KITLV, 2002.

Hagen, Karen. "State Formation, Nation-Building and Mass Politics in Europe: The Theory of Stein Rokkan". *European Political Science* 1, no. 2 (Spring 2002).

Jedamski, Doris. "A Colonial Wolf in Sheep Clothes". *Archipel* 44 (1992).

Kwee Tek Hoay. "Drama dari Krakatau", originally published in 1929, republished in Marcus A.S. & Pax Benedanto, eds (2001), Vol. 2, pp. 428–589.

Liem Khing Hoo. "Berjuang: Masyarakat Antara Masyarakat", originally published by Drukkerij Hahn & Co., Surabaya, republished in Marcus A.S. & Pax Benedanto (2002), Vol. 6, pp. 109–97.

Lombard, Denys. *Nusa Jawa: Silang Budaya*, vol 1. Jakarta: Gramedia, 1996.

Marcus A.S. and Pax Benedanto, eds. *Kesasteraan Melayu Tionghoa dan Kebangsaan Indonesia*, Vol. 2 (2001), Vol. 6 (2002), Jakarta: Kepustakaan Populer Gramedia, 2001.

Semaoen. *Hikajat Kadiroen*. Semarang: Kantoor PKI, 1920.

Sidharta, Myra. *100 Tahun Kwee Tek Hoay: Dari Penjaja Tekstil sampai ke Pendekar Pena*. Jakarta: Sinar Harapan Press, 1989.

Sumardjo, Jakob. "Latar Sosiologis Pengarang Sastra Melayu-Tionghoa", in Suryadinata (1996), pp. 52–68.

———. *Konteks Sosial Novel Indonesia, 1920–1970*. Bandung: Penerbit Alumni, 1999.

Suryadinata, Leo. *Sastra Peranakan Tionghoa Indonesia*. Jakarta: Grasindo, 1996.

Suyatno, Apsanti Djoko. "Tiga Novelis Wanita Meramu Seks" in *Media Indonesia*, 2 November 2003.

Sydharta, Myra. *100 Tahun Kwee Tek Hoay: Dari Penjaja Tekstil Sampai ke Pendekar Pena*. Jakarta: Sinar Harapan Press, 1989.

Tan Boen Soan. "Bergerak?", originally published by Tan's Drukkerij, Surabaya, 1935, republished in Marcus A.S. & Pax Benedanto eds. (2002), Vol. 6, pp. 199–280.

Tjandinegara, Wilson, trans. *Menyangga Dunia di atas Bulu Mata: Antoloji Puisi 40 Penyair Keturunan Tionghoa*, Jakarta: Gitakara, c. 1998.

Wahyudi, Ibnu. "Mempertimbangkan Kembali Awal Keberadaan Sastra Indonesia Modern". *Proceedings of 11th ECIMS*. Moscow: The Institute of Asian and African Studies, 2000.

Wong Sook Koon. "Rethinking the Nation". In *Aliran Monthly* 22 (2002). Online issue 3, <http://www.malaysia.net/aliran/monthly/>.

Woro, Adiastuti. "Keindahan yang Tersembunyi dalam Sastra Cina Jawa", presented at the National Symposium on Philology. Bali, MANASA, 2003.

Zaidan, Abdul Rozak and Dendy Sugondo, eds. *Adakah Bangsa dalam Sastra?* Jakarta: Penerbit Progress dan Pusat Bahasa, 2003.

5

The Multilingual State in Search of the Nation: The Language Policy and Discourse in Singapore's Nation-Building

Eugene K.B. Tan

Around the world, especially in Asia, languages are dying out from assimilation policies as well as from oppression of minorities.[1] Even languages which hitherto had not been under threat now have to grapple with the realities of the dynamic and variable nature of language shifts.[2] Language issues have also featured prominently in manifestations of ethnic conflict in Asia.[3] In Singapore, there is no real fear of the languages of the three racial groups, viz Chinese (Mandarin), Malay, and Tamil, becoming extinct or obsolete.[4] Rather, the feeling of the intellectual and cultural elites from the Chinese, Malay and Indian communities is that more could be done to promote their respective languages and cultures. What is clear is the pivotal role of language in Singapore's socio-economic development and nation-building. Arising from the language policies, there are ramifications for politics, economics, culture and education. Thus, national language policy will retain its saliency in many societies and language planning an integral part of maintaining ethnic stability in many multilingual societies.[5]

The link between language and identity has not had much analysis in scholarly discussion.[6] Similarly, the role of language in nation-building in Singapore has not been examined in any significant way.[7] This is not surprising as race has been the dominant prism in the study of ethnic relations in Singapore. Yet language is a proxy by which issues of race and culture are often discussed in Singapore.[8] Indeed, language is construed as a less contentious context with which to deal with the tricky issues of ethnicity, broadly conceived. Language discourse is also less susceptible towards a class-based explanation of difference.

This chapter examines the role of language in nation-building in multilingual Singapore. The first part discusses Singapore's language regime and an overview of language development in Singapore since its independence in 1965. The emphasis revolves around the development of government policy towards Chinese language (and culture). The second part explores the key attributes of Singapore's language ideology and how they relate to issues of governance, political economy, and cultural policy. The third part briefly examines the state of the languages of English (and Singlish), Malay, Tamil and other Indian languages, and the Chinese dialects to demonstrate the complexities and intricacies of language planning in a postcolonial society.

THE LANGUAGE REGIME IN SINGAPORE

In recognition of Singapore's multiracial, multireligious, and multilingual society, Article 153A of the Singapore Constitution proclaims that:

(1) Malay, Mandarin, Tamil and English shall be the four official languages in Singapore.

(2) The national language shall be the Malay language and shall be in the Roman script:

Provided that —

(a) no person shall be prohibited or prevented from using or from teaching or learning any other language; and

(b) nothing in this section shall prejudice the right of the Government to preserve and sustain the use and study of the language of any other community in Singapore.[9]

Although it was and is used by only a minority of the population, the Malay language has the unique position of being the sole national language.[10] Singapore's Malay origins are reflected in the symbols of Singapore's sovereignty such as the national anthem and motto, both titled *Majulah Singapura* (Onward Singapore) in Malay.[11] Military parade commands are in Malay. Besides English, the assigned mother tongue languages of the three main races, viz Mandarin, Malay and Tamil, are adopted as official languages.

The key attributes of Singapore's language regime are evident from Singapore's Independence. First, there is a prima facie parity among the four official languages. Second, Malay, as the national language, is a symbolic political gesture recognizing the geopolitical realities in Singapore's locale. Third, since Independence, English has been dominant as the language of commerce and government. Fourth, English is the surrogate lingua franca of Singaporeans as it did not ostensibly provide any racial group, especially the ethnic Chinese majority, with any linguistic advantage. Fifth, economic concerns have played a major role in the Government's efforts in boosting the proficiency levels of the English and Chinese languages in recent years.

Recognizing that the educational system offered the best platform for socialization and social engineering, the Government swiftly established a national school system to replace the many vernacular schools established by the various communities during the colonial era. The evolution of the language ideology and language regime is poignantly manifested in Singapore's education system, a critical resource in social engineering.[12] In national schools, both English and the mother tongues are required subjects; the former is taught as the first language (and the language of instruction in all national educational institutions) while the latter were taught initially as second languages. Increasingly, the approach has been to encourage as many students to offer their mother tongues at the first language levels while also recognizing that not everyone can be effectively bilingual.

For almost forty years, success in Singapore's education system was predicated on academic ability and doing reasonably well in the languages. The bilingual education policy was originally premised on the expectation that nearly everyone could be effectively bilingual. Starting in 1979 with the implementation of the Goh Report on Education, students were first streamed at nine years of age (Primary Three) into the Normal, Extended and Monolingual streams according to their academic results. Under this streaming exercise, Monolingual stream students (academically the weakest students) were not required to study their mother tongues. Between 1991 and 2004, streaming was conducted at ten years of age (Primary Four) and the various "EM" academic streams are distinguished by the standard of the mother tongues at which students take them.[13] The brightest were chanelled into the EM1 stream where they studied English and higher mother tongues at the first language level. The majority were in the EM2 stream where they offered their mother tongue languages as a second language.

THE SALIENCY OF CHINESE LANGUAGE WRIT LARGE

In the first decade of nationhood, the Government focused on moulding an overarching Singaporean-Singapore identity in overriding preference over the formation of the spectrum of ethnic identities. Ethnic identities were regarded warily and seen as a threat to the nation-building process. Then Foreign Minister and the ruling party's ideologue, S. Rajaratnam warned that "the price for a more impressive genealogical table would be to turn Singapore into a bloody battleground for endless racial and communal conflicts and interventionist politics by the more powerful and bigger nations from which Singaporeans had emigrated."[14] It was this abiding fear of unwittingly setting off centrifugal tendencies that motivated the Government to staunchly subscribe to the nascent Singaporean-Singapore identity.

The history of language planning in Singapore had been dominated by the battle for political ascendancy between the English-educated Chinese and the Chinese-educated Chinese within the ruling People's Action Party. This subsequently manifested itself as a political struggle between the non-communist and pro-communist elements for the hearts and minds in a new society. The politically tumultuous late 1950s and early 1960s saw the Chinese-educated political activists, with links to the pro-communist elements in the labour movement in pre-independent Singapore,[15] earnestly canvassing for support from the ethnic Chinese community.

This juxtaposition of ethnic and ideological identities, of which Chinese identity, culture and education were key dimensions, was firmly imprinted in the psyche of the English-educated political elites. They went on to dominate political life and remain sensitized to the resourcefulness, passion and bravado of their Chinese-educated counterparts.[16] In the wake of their victory, the English-educated elites deliberately downplayed the ethnic Chinese accent of Singapore. The Government aggressively sidelined the key mobilisers of the Chinese community such as the Chinese chamber of commerce, clan associations, and powerful Chinese businessmen, all of which had considerable resources, commitment and charisma to exert influence on local politics, especially on Chinese education, culture and language issues.[17]

This bruising fight for political ascendancy, where language and culture figured prominently, reinforced the differences between the Chinese-educated and English-educated Chinese in subsequent years. The Chinese-educated felt deeply the significant movement towards English language within Singapore society and the perceived discrimination and prejudice against them. They also felt that their intentions and commitment to the Chinese language, education and culture were severely misunderstood.[18]

Although the conflict was ostensibly over the relative importance of Chinese language, culture and education in the new state, it masked the reality of vast differences over political ideology, values and life chances between these two broad groups. The cultural gulf and theme of alienation in various spheres of Singapore life has a residual effect today, even though the Chinese language and value system are now deemed as being of increasing importance in Singapore's political economy and cultural agenda.[19] The gradual "rehabilitation" of Chinese language and culture in the last two decades has resulted in the Government's recognition of the leadership, contributions and support provided in the 1950s and 1960s by pro-Chinese language and culture advocates such as Tan Kah Kee and Tan Lark Sye.[20] This reversal of fortunes might at first blush seem surprising. However, these developments may not be all too surprising considering the influence of Singapore's language ideology and its shaping the discourse on languages in Singapore society.

LANGUAGE IDEOLOGY:
IDEATIONAL PRAGMATISM AND CULTURAL REVIVALISM[21]

Singapore's language ideology, with its intimate linkages to the political, economic and socio-cultural fundamentals, constrains and intimately influences the direction of language planning and the development of the various languages. "Language ideology", refers to the substantive content and ideational principles that undergird the state discourse, policies and action on language in Singapore. The key organizing principles in Singapore's language ideology can be summarized as follows: (1) the cornerstone of bilingualism and the race-based, state-ascribed mother tongue policy; (2) language as a cultural transmission vehicle providing each race with the critical cultural ballast; (3) the creation of a core of cultural elites for each race with urgency being accorded to the Chinese language; and (4) a pragmatic approach to the learning of mother tongue languages and the fundamental of economic relevancy in language planning.

The Bilingual Imperative

Bilingualism is a cornerstone of Singapore's language ideology and policy. However, prior to the advent of a national school system, the education system was fragmented into English and the three vernacular streams of Chinese, Malay, and Indian.[22] It was only with self-government in 1959 and independence from Malaysia in 1965 that the political imperative to create an indigenous and integrated national school system united by a common language policy acquired added urgency.[23]

Rather than the common understanding of literacy in two languages, bilingualism in Singapore is configured on the study of the English language plus a mother tongue. Between 1959 and 1965, bilingualism often included the learning of Malay, with either English or Mandarin or Tamil depending on the student's language stream. This was changed in 1966. Since then, "mother tongue" has a particularistic definition: "the symbolic language of the group of one's paternal ancestry, rather than the language of one's primary socialization, or one's 'native speech'."[24] This formulaic definition, founded on the state's rigid Chinese-Malay-Indian-Others (CMIO) racial classification, has caused problems for children of mixed marriages where the state-ascribed mother tongue has no correlation to the language spoken at home.[25]

Indeed, the Government's efforts to bond the heterogeneous Chinese community necessitated a radical remaking of the meaning of mother tongue. To enforce the invented pan-ethnic mother tongue for the Chinese community, the linguistic homogenization of the ethnic Chinese was necessary.[26] This change required the invention of a linguistic and cultural norm, viz Mandarin, as the mother tongue of Chinese Singaporeans and the marginalization of Chinese "dialects". This mandated the official consignment of the natural mother tongues of the various ethnic Chinese sub-groups such as Hokkien, Cantonese, Teochew, Hakka, etc., as "dialects", and thus excluded from Government support.[27]

Bilingualism in Singapore seeks to enable students to "keep in touch with their cultural links whilst being equipped with skills to function in a modern economy".[28] The economic dimension looms large and is manifested in English being the first language in national schools. The political imperatives of social engineering ensure that meticulous and centralized language planning remains a focus of the Government's efforts in the governance of a multiracial, multilingual society. Over time, the aspirations of the bilingual policy have grown. For instance, the cultural fortification element was grafted onto the bilingualism framework in the late 1970s. With China's dramatic rise, the Chinese language is now seen as having economic relevance nearly on par with its English counterpart. Increasingly, Singapore's bilingual framework emphasizes the economic pragmatism in its language discourse and ideology.

The bilingual policy in national schools, while successful on most fronts, appears to have induced primary school children to mix with fellow students of the same race. A study conducted by academics from Singapore's National Institute of Education noted that as school children got older, the preference to mix with students of the same race became more pronounced even though they were fluent in English. Students studying English and the mother tongue at the first language level (EM1) were also found to be least likely to mix.[29] These findings are a cause of concern. It suggests that the emphasis on the mother tongues under the energized bilingual policy may have heightened ethnic consciousness and reduced the incentive to communicate and interact using the English language. That EM1 students, who are likely to be the cultural elites of their communities, were least likely to mix does not augur well, especially when this tendency towards separateness is learned or acquired at a formative age.

Mother Tongues: Transmission and Fortification of Cultural Ballast

Language is the alter ego of race in Singapore's political discourse. Language and race are intimately linked and ethnic policies are increasingly being enunciated through the matrix of the language ideology. The Government's official stance is that cultural values are encoded and transmitted through the mother tongue. The caution exercised in the State's downplaying the expression of genealogical roots began to relax towards the end of the 1970s.

The rapid and impressive rise of the East Asian economies of Japan, Hong Kong, Singapore, South Korea and Taiwan provided the celebratory hubris and much vaunted empirical support for "culture as destiny" in economic development. Culture, as a derivative of race and encoded in the "cultural DNA" of a nation-state, was seen as the driving force behind much of East Asia's impressive economic achievements. The Confucian core of these economies was regarded as the explanatory variable in the remarkable achievement of socio-political stability and sustainable economic prosperity.

The waxing and waning of the importance of the Chinese language was not an arbitrary development. Instead, the evolving primacy of the Chinese language over the last twenty-five years is also the result of a confluence of mutually reinforcing factors such as the belief in cultural revivalism as an engine of economic growth and political stability, the positive, if exuberant, prognosis of the political economy of China, and the particularistic nuances of political governance in Singapore, where the dictates of race, language, and culture are strong.[30] The heightened concern that the Chinese Singaporeans were becoming deculturalized gave further impetus to the return to one's genealogical roots. Further, the loss of the cultural ballast was perceived as being detrimental to Singapore's long-term economic sustainability, and a fundamental correction was urgently needed. To stem the tide of Westernization and the loss of cultural heritage, the mother tongues are envisaged to play a facilitative role in this cultural revitalization effort.[31] Thus, to further the cultural endeavour and to promote the Chinese language and culture within the national education system, nine established Chinese schools were designated as "Special Assistance Plan (SAP) schools" in 1979, catering to the top ten per cent of each graduating primary school cohort.[32]

The Speak Mandarin Campaign graduated from one of reducing the usage of "dialects" by the Chinese community to the present elevation of Mandarin as the high language of Chinese Singaporeans. A prominent spokesman for the "language as culture" belief, BG (NS) George Yeo, then the Information and the Arts Minister declared that:

> If the majority of Chinese Singaporeans use Chinese, not as the mother tongue but as a second language, not used at home and taught only in school, the nature of our society will change, and it will be for the worse... It is worth recapitulating why promoting Mandarin as a high language for Chinese Singaporeans is necessary. The reasons are both cultural and economic. The use of Mandarin will help us preserve and develop our cultural roots. Chinese Singaporeans are the proud inheritors of 5,000 years of Chinese civilization, the longest continuous civilization in human history. Chinese culture and the Chinese language give us a sense of who we are, where we came from and what we can be... The culture of a people gives its members their internal strength. Without that internal strength, we will not be able to survive disasters, political turmoil and war. If we use only English, and allow our mother tongue to degenerate into a second language, with Chinese not used at home and taught only in school, we will lose much of our internal strength and become a weak people with shallow roots. There is also a powerful economic reason to promote Mandarin. The re-emergence of China will have a growing impact on world economics and world politics in the coming decades. Those who speak and write Mandarin, and understand

Chinese culture, will enjoy a considerable advantage in the next
century. Those who are able to master both Chinese and English
at a high level will be much sought after.[33]

Larger movements within the cultural revivalism era were also launched
in the late 1970s. Two landmark documents, the Goh Keng Swee education
report and the Ong Teng Cheong moral education report, provided the
impetus for the fundamental movement towards a nuanced cultural
essentialist approach in political governance and the development of core
societal values.[34] These two reports laid the groundwork for the
introduction of an ersatz neo-Confucian ethos in Singapore's political
governance[35] and the introduction of Confucian Studies as an approved
subject under the compulsory religious knowledge programme in the
mid-1980s.[36] By 1990, English and Chinese as first languages were offered
to selected primary schools.

Impressive economic success and increased security encouraged a more
confident and extensive assertion of "Chineseness" in Singapore. The
theme of cultural revitalization, with the younger generation Chinese as
the target beneficiaries, continues to resonate, ensuring the visibility of
mother tongue languages, especially Chinese.[37] In the process, the
"legitimization of the primordial — or the traditional — that had been
vilified"[38] requires the motif of language as a carrier of high culture.

Nurturing the New Generation of Cultural Vanguards[39]

With the closure of Nanyang University (Nantah) — through its merger
with the University of Singapore to form the National University of
Singapore in 1980 — the fate of Chinese education appeared uncertain.
In a shrewd move, however, the fanfare that accompanied the formation
of SAP schools enabled the Government to avoid some criticism that it
was unsupportive and suspicious of Chinese education.[40] The implicit
mission of the SAP schools is to regenerate a new core of cultural elites
without the political, cultural and emotional baggage of their Nantah
predecessors.

By 1997, although Mandarin was gaining popularity at the expense of
Chinese dialects, the Government expressed concern over the lack of a
sufficient pool of cultural elites who have "deep knowledge of Chinese
language, culture, history, literature and traditions".[41] The promotion of
Chinese language, culture and political values requires a core of Chinese
cultural elites to provide the intellectual and cultural capital to drive the

civilizational discourse in Singapore's nation-building efforts. The graduates of the now defunct Nantah, who form a large part of the present ageing Chinese cultural elites, are declining in numbers. The determined push for the catchment pool to be both significantly and rapidly enlarged has now taken centre-stage in Singapore's language planning framework.

Although the Speak Mandarin campaign succeeded in greatly reducing the usage of Chinese dialects, Chinese Singaporeans are still not reading or writing sufficiently in Chinese. This translates to declining readership of Chinese newspapers among the younger generation.[42] Thus, the campaign's objective in recent years has also promoted "Mandarin as the social language of the Chinese".[43]

That language and culture are inseparable is inherent in Singapore's language ideology: language unlocks the wisdom, legacy and virtues of a 5,000 year-old civilizational culture. The mother tongue policy, a critical component of the bilingual education framework, is deemed critical in maintaining social discipline and facilitating economic relevancy.[44] Then Deputy Prime Minister (DPM) Lee Hsien Loong put it succinctly:

> English is and will remain our common working language... But the mother tongue gives us a crucial part of our values, roots and identity. It gives us direct access to our cultural heritage, and a world-view that complements the perspective of the English-speaking world. It provides us the ballast to face adversity and challenges with fortitude, and a sense of quiet confidence about our place in the world. Maintaining our distinctiveness and identity as an Asian society will help us to endure as a nation. This applies to all ethnic groups.

In 1999, the Government announced changes to the teaching of Chinese language in schools with the twin aims of "reproducing a core group of Singaporeans who are steeped in the Chinese cultural heritage, history, literature and the arts. We need them to be Chinese language teachers, writers, journalists, community leaders, MPs and Ministers; and to set realistic standards in CL [Chinese language] for all pupils, including those from English-speaking homes."[45] DPM Lee elaborated on the need for the sustained production of the Chinese cultural elite:

> The Chinese cultural elite are an important source of strength for our multi-racial, multi-religious society. Their group instincts, political and social values, and social cohesion complement the

> different spirit and outlook of English educated Singaporeans....
> So the Chinese elite in Singapore must develop, and help Chinese
> culture to play its rightful role in shaping our cosmopolitan society
> and knowledge economy of the 21st century.

At the same time, there is also the policy imperative of ensuring the general appreciation for the Chinese language among Chinese Singaporeans. As then DPM Lee Hsien Loong put it:

> Our desired outcome is the emergence of a core group of Chinese
> educated elite who go beyond mastering the Chinese language, to
> be at home with Chinese culture, history, literature, art and
> contemporary developments. Outside this core, there should be
> widespread appreciation of the Chinese language by Chinese
> students. Levels of language proficiency will vary, but hopefully
> the students will all find learning Chinese a worthwhile and
> enriching experience, and acquire the foundation to deepen their
> knowledge later in life if they choose to.[46]

Closer attention to the health of the Chinese language in Singapore, not least by Singapore's founding Prime Minister Lee Kuan Yew, has somewhat assuaged the concern of the Chinese-educated over the health of the Chinese language, culture and heritage in Singapore.[47] The White Paper on the Report of the Chinese Language Curriculum and Pedagogy Review Committee was tabled in November 2004. The Report details the fundamental rethink and recommended significant and wide-ranging changes to the teaching of the Chinese language in order to promote conducive learning of the language.[48] In a fundamental shift in language planning and ideology, it also recognized the difficulties and limitations of learning two languages at an equally high level of proficiency.

The concerted efforts to establish a larger pool of Chinese cultural elites has attracted muted criticisms and concerns of the perceived differential treatment and urgency towards cultural preservation among the ethnic groups.[49] Being the main provider of Chinese cultural elites, the SAP schools have been criticized for being effectively racially exclusive, while there are no SAP-type schools for the minorities.

The Constancy and Language of Pragmatism in Language Planning

Given Singapore's heavy reliance on trade and investment, the theme of economic relevancy within the national language ideology is evident. As

English is the de facto international language for trade, science and politics, the decision to emphasize English language in national schools has been proven to be far-sighted. On the other hand, with China becoming an increasingly important economic and political partner, the Chinese language has become more important.[50]

The Singapore Government presciently saw the potential economic opportunities if Singapore were to participate substantively in China's economic revolution. Since its launch in 1979, the Speak Mandarin campaign has been unequivocal in emphasizing this development. To optimally harness the offerings of the Chinese market, the Government has reiterated that Singaporeans must not only communicate effectively in Mandarin, but also need to possess intimate knowledge of Chinese culture, society, and psyche. This cultural intimacy and affinity is believed to provide a significant advantage to Singapore businesses and would reduce the transaction costs in business activities. In this regard, the Government has overhauled the Chinese language curriculum on no fewer than three occasions in the last decade.[51] The current strategy is to encourage Chinese students to learn as much of the Chinese language as possible, without a one-size-fits-all approach. With an eye on the Indian economy as well as the potentially lucrative Sino-Indian trade, it is likely that the Indian languages will become more important in the years ahead.[52] Thus, the economic imperative for this emphasis on Mandarin and the Chinese culture conveniently dovetails with the imperative for cultural fortification.[53]

Given the recent recognition that not all students can be effectively bilingual, the Government has been more cognizant and accommodative of the difficulties that some students face in learning the mother tongue languages.[54] For the Singapore Government, pragmatism does not mean expediency. Rather the goal is to do what is necessary to attain the objective, without being overly encumbered by tradition, ideology or convention. As a consequence of Chinese not being the "natural" mother tongue for an increasing number of ethnic Chinese, the learning of the language has posed varying levels of difficulties for these students. Students (and many teachers) see it as an examination subject that they need to pass in order to progress in the academic ladder; few see it as the mother tongue from which they can learn about their civilizational culture.[55] The challenge for Chinese language educationists is to make the learning of the language fun, without compromising standards, and to engage the students such that they would not treat it as an examination subject.[56]

Two widely publicized approaches in the Chinese language pedagogy approach can be cited. The first is the implementation of the "bilingual approach" in the teaching of Chinese. Under this pedagogic device, there is selective use of English in the instruction of Chinese language beginners, in order to achieve "the best possible results with the widest group of students" given the "diverse home language backgrounds".[57] Another move was the introduction of the Chinese Language 'B' syllabus ("CLB") in 2001, to help students struggling to meet the minimum mother tongue requirements for admission to junior colleges and the local universities without compromising their ability to learn other subjects.[58] On the need for CLB, Deputy Prime Minister Lee Hsien Loong reasoned:

> But we must look at this issue practically. The language environment at home is changing rapidly. When I did the report four years ago, which was in 1999, the statistics were — 40 per cent of primary one students lived in families with English-speaking environment, 20 per cent of Pre U two students came from English-speaking families. So within 12 years, the number of English-speaking families doubled. This year, statistics showed that the number of primary one students who speak English at home has grown to 44 per cent. So this is a problem, and it will become worse in the long run. We would be unrealistic to ignore the problems faced by our English-speaking students in learning Chinese. This will inflict much pain to the students and the parents. I think we will not be able to sustain our mother tongue education policy that way. Therefore, to continue to uphold the ideals of mother tongue education, we must set realistic goals. The disparity in language environment among students is very great. So some students will take Higher Chinese while others take CL. Some will try their best but still can only study CL 'B'. In this case, we should let them take CL 'B'.[59]

However, the initial take-up rate was low.[60] As the *Straits Times* editorialized, "the CLB has morphed into a badge of dishonour that strikes fear in many parents' hearts. Why did a scheme meant to teach Chinese without tears end up shunned?"[61]

The foregoing discussion has attempted to weave trends, recent developments in Singapore's language ideology and its policies with the focus being on the "language of primacy", the Chinese language. It is to an overview of the various languages in Singapore that we now turn to for a better grasp of the complex language environment in Singapore.

ENGLISH AND SINGLISH — STILL DOMINANT

The English language has a secure status within Singapore's language regime. Its status as a global language in education, commerce, technology, and the access and transmission of new knowledge ensures its dominance and importance.[62] Yet the English language poses two key concerns for the Government. The widespread use of the English language in Singapore is argued to have an enervating effect on the traditional cultures and languages of Singaporeans. The other, the Government argues, is that the widespread use of English in many homes is now threatening the valuable home environment needed for the mother tongues to flourish. Nonetheless, the English language (its proficiency and its widespread use) is too valuable to Singapore's economic prosperity to be downgraded in importance.[63]

For many years, Singapore's bilingual policy was described as "English-based bilingualism", wherein English was taught as the first language and the mother tongues were taught at the second language level. The choice of English as the declared household language has increased with each census, particularly among the younger generation.[64] This language shift raises the popularity of English at the expense of the mother tongues. Chua Beng Huat points to the "ideological illusion" surrounding English language in Singapore — English is not a neutral language as it has been made out to be.[65] The choice of the English language was not only pragmatic but shrewd. "[I]t enables the state to articulate, in English, its own interests distinctly apart from the interests of all racial groups. It also effects a separation of state/national interests from those of the racial majority, and prevents state/national interests from being captured by the majority."[66]

Since the implementation of the single national stream under the New Education System (NES) in 1987, all Singapore school students learn English as a first language.[67] At the primary and at upper secondary levels, more classroom time is allocated to English than the mother tongues.[68] However, and much to the Government's chagrin, the English language standard did not benefit from such a concentration of resources and classroom time on the teaching of the language. In recent years, the political leadership has been extremely concerned with the English proficiency level of Singaporeans and the popularity of Singlish. Again, the economic implications flowing from lacking a good command of the dominant international language galvanized the Government to act resolutely. In April 2000, the Speak Good English Movement (SGEM) was launched with the twin objectives of promoting among Singaporeans the use of Standard English and discouraging the use of Singlish.[69]

Singlish — A Threat or a Unique Singaporean Attribute?

Although English is taught as a first language in schools, the prevalence of Singlish, the local variant of colloquial English, is blamed for the declining standards in standard English proficiency. Lee Kuan Yew has pithily described Singlish as "a handicap we must not wish on Singaporeans".[70] The Government regards Singlish as pidgin English and is working concertedly towards eradicating it in order not to undermine Singapore's competitive strength.[71] Singlish, while serving the younger generation well informally, is "often troubling their elders".[72] On the other hand, Singlish is also viewed as a uniquely Singaporean identity marker, and a "symbolic expression of the country's novel, bicultural identity".[73] However, such views have not persuaded the Government to grant Singlish a reprieve. Then Prime Minister Goh first declared the untenable status of Singlish in his 1999 National Day rally speech:

> Most of our pupils still come from non-English speaking homes. For them, English is really a second language, to be learnt almost like a foreign language, and not their mother tongue. For them to master just one version of English is already quite a challenge. If they get into the habit of speaking Singlish, then later they will either have to unlearn these habits, or learn proper English on top of Singlish. Many pupils will find this too difficult. They may end up unable to speak any language properly, which would be a tragedy. ... We learn English in order to communicate with the world. The fact that we use English gives us a big advantage over our competitors. Parents send children to English language schools rather than Chinese, Malay, or Tamil schools, because they hope the children will get jobs and opportunities when they grow up... We cannot be a first-world economy or go global with Singlish... if we carry on using Singlish, the logical final outcome is that we too will develop our own type of pidgin English, spoken only by three million Singaporeans, which the rest of the world will find quaint but incomprehensible. We are already half-way there. Do we want to go all the way? We would be better off sticking to Chinese, Malay or Tamil; then at least some other people in the world can understand us.[74]

Clearly, economic concerns take precedence and no concession is given to Singlish being a putative marker of Singaporean identity (and to be tolerated).[75]

MALAY LANGUAGE — STILL THE NOMINAL NATIONAL LANGUAGE

Although Singapore is at the heart of the Malay world, little effort since Independence had been made to encourage the study of Malay in schools to non-Malay students or to promote it to the policy-makers and bureaucrats. Contrast that with the constitutional exhortation for the promotion of Malay as the national language.[76] Furthermore, Singapore's future and well-being is intimately connected with Indonesia's and Malaysia's.[77] However, things are changing gradually and the promotion of the Malay language is slowly extended beyond the Malay community.

From 2007, the Ministry of Education (MOE) has allowed Secondary One students to offer another mother tongue language in addition to their native mother tongue language "as long as they have the interest and inclination". The MOE noted that, "the ability to speak a third language is useful, and will help young Singaporeans of all races operate effectively in the region and beyond. Proficiency in non-native mother tongue languages (MTLs) would also help increase interaction among the ethnic communities and facilitate inter-racial understanding."[78] Prior to this, Malay can be studied as a third language under the Malay (Special Programme) scheme only by the more academically inclined, non-Malay secondary school students.[79]

The ambivalent state of affairs and treatment of the Malay language is not surprising as Malay is the symbolic national language merely observed in the trappings of state symbols, such as the national anthem and state motto. As a national language, the recognition accorded is minimal, more form than substance. Such a situation only reinforces the belief that its selection as the national language was an instrumental political act during the throes of Singapore's turbulent separation from Malaysia.[80] Many students merely utter the lyrics of the national anthem, which is sung daily at the start of each school day, without appreciating its meaning and significance since they do not understand Malay.

Although the last Malay-medium vernacular school closed in 1979, the establishment of enrichment programmes in Malay culture and language is relatively recent. The secondary-level Enrichment Programme in Malay Language (EMAS) and the pre-university level Malay Language Elective Programme (MLEP) were introduced only in

2001.[81] While the Government has no objections to a SAP-type school for top Malay students, it believes that "the best way" to produce top Malay students is to "integrate them into the national schools and stretch their ability".[82]

INDIAN LANGUAGES — A MULTIPLICITY OF TONGUES

Constituting approximately eight per cent of Singapore's population, the generic Indian community comprises eleven main sub-groups, with the Tamils being the largest group (63.9 per cent) followed by the Malayalees (8.6 per cent).[83] Not all the sub-groups' mother tongues are offered at the national schools from primary to pre-university levels. Bengali, Gujarati, Hindi, Punjabi and Urdu are offered as mother tongue language options for non-Tamil Indian students. However, this expanded range of Indian languages came about only in 1989 at the secondary school level. It was expanded to pre-university students in 1991 and primary school students in 1993.[84] Apart from Tamil, none of the other Indian languages are offered for study at the university level.

There are additional constraints for students learning these mother tongues as compared with their peers who learn Chinese and Malay in their schools. Given the small numbers of Tamil students in many schools, it is not cost-effective for schools to have Tamil mother tongue language teachers on their staff. As a consequence, there are nine Tamil language centres to cater to students from schools without a Tamil language programme. These students, however, have to travel to these centres and attend the lessons outside normal school hours. For the non-Tamil Indian languages (abbreviated by the Education Ministry as "NTILs"), the self-help exercised by the various non-Tamil Indian communities becomes critical. The task falls on them to establish and maintain the language centres for the study of their respective mother tongues.[85] Such mother tongue language centres have the onus of supplying the teachers, producing teaching materials, as well as setting examination policies and standards.[86]

As is the case for ethnic Chinese students, Indian Singaporeans are increasingly coming from homes where English is the dominant language. This is especially the case for Tamil students where a substantial number of them do not have adequate home exposure to the language.[87] Like the Chinese language, concerns persist over the quality of Indian mother-tongue language instruction in schools.[88]

CHINESE DIALECTS: THEIR AMBIVALENT
RELEVANCE AND POTENTIAL RESILIENCE

Despite the Government's efforts to discourage the use of Chinese dialects and to linguistically homogenize the Chinese population, Chinese dialects demonstrate a streak of resilience, entrenching their subtle relevance and political saliency.[89] While the Government is encouraging the various clan associations to attract younger members, the homogenization of the various sub-identities (dialect groups) under the generic Chinese/Mandarin label has meant that a powerful and intimate organizing and motivating force is removed. On the home front, the transmission mechanism of mother tongues has not worked as well. Younger generation Chinese and their elders could not intimately understand and communicate with each other since there is no common language between the younger and older generations. For the former, English or Mandarin is the standard fare; for the latter, Chinese dialects remain their mother tongue.[90]

Despite the Government's reluctance to acknowledge the role of Chinese dialects in Singapore society, Chinese dialects continue to demonstrate their utility. For instance, dialects are commonly used during the general elections when electoral candidates, from both the ruling and opposition parties, would campaign in door-to-door visits and election rallies using Chinese dialects to reach out to older Chinese Singaporeans. Another instance of dialects demonstrating their "usefulness" was during the Severe Acute Respiratory Syndrome (SARS) outbreak in Singapore in mid-2003. In order to reach out to every Singaporean "in a language that he or she understands", the Government permitted the use of dialect on television and radio. The Media Development Authority (MDA) explained such an adjustment of programming guidelines was necessary "in these exceptional circumstances... so that everyone will be aware of the SARS problem". In particular, the target audience was the elderly who spoke only dialects and did not read the newspapers.[91]

Beyond the pragmatic response during the SARS crisis, there appears to be pockets of latent appreciation for the intrinsic worth of dialects. Oddly enough, the Censorship Review Committee in its 2003 report recommended the continuation of allowing films with limited use of dialects.[92] It also recommended allowing "full dialect use" on cable television, the Arts Central television channel, some radio news programmes, and allowing limited screening of full Chinese dialect films at cinemas on a single film print per title basis.[93] In 2003, the Advisory Committee for Chinese Programmes (ACCESS), which assists the MDA in monitoring Chinese programme standards and public service programmes broadcast, recommended a relaxation of the restrictions on the use of dialects in TV programmes "without causing a setback to the Speak Mandarin Campaign". The Committee noted that "ideally more research needs to be done to better understand the relationship between exposure to dialects in the media and how it affects the learning of the Chinese language and skill in the speaking of Mandarin." It added that "dialects form a rich part of the Chinese culture."[94] However, the Government responded quickly and cautioned that any exercise of flexibility over Chinese dialect programming on television must not undermine the efforts to promote Mandarin as well as the hard-won progress made "to get the Chinese community in Singapore to speak and communicate in Mandarin, and to bond as one community". It added that:

> Many children today still have difficulty coping with two languages in school and the use of dialects will only worsen the problem. Furthermore, we run the risk that dialects would be mixed into Mandarin, resulting in a pidgin Mandarin which will be worse than what we started with.[95]

The notion that the monolithic Mandarinization in Singapore can undermine the unique attributes and essence of the (heterogeneous) Chinese culture in Singapore was underscored by the Remaking Singapore Committee. The Committee's July 2003 report highlighted "the origins and development of the various communities in Singapore (including the multi-layered cultural links of the micro-communities within each of the major races with the rest of the region) have not been adequately captured in our social history."[96] It proposed the establishment of a Community Museum to showcase and "celebrate the rich heritage of the diverse communities in Singapore". It also proposed the setting up of a Community Radio to broadcast in the "languages, dialects and even patois of the various ethnic communities" in which the use of local dialects will give the radio station "a distinctively Singaporean flavour". Both recommendations, however, were not accepted on the basis that community history and life are already incorporated into the existing heritage framework.[97]

The Government has also urged Chinese clan associations, often organized along dialect lines, to reconceptualize their role in today's rapidly changing world in order to remain relevant. Besides playing a role in preserving cultural traditions, clan associations have been encouraged to use their innate resources in "forging business networks to exploit global opportunities".[98] On the role of clan associations in facilitating cultural renewal, then Deputy Prime Minister Lee Hsien Loong remarked:

> But it is more difficult for the younger generation to do that ["anchor our unique identities"]. They are the second, third even fourth generation of overseas Chinese. Many no longer speak their parent's dialect, or perhaps even Chinese. Their sense of heritage and tradition is less strong. And without strong roots, it is harder for them to face the challenges of globalization with confidence and security.[99]

Ironically, both these challenges require proficiency in the Chinese dialects if kinship ties are to be successfully harnessed for cultural continuity and to capitalize on kinship economic networks. The marginalization of Chinese dialects, as a consequence of the Speak Mandarin Campaign, seems to have been ignored in this development in which the younger generation is no longer proficient in the original mother tongue of their forefathers.

CONCLUSION

In Singapore, language is clearly a socio-economic and political resource. If mismanaged, the implications are grave for Singapore's social cohesion and political stability. Language planning is taken seriously for a variety of reasons, not least economic, political and cultural ones; it also requires a delicate balance of competing objectives, interests, and emotions, as well as pragmatic and effective approaches. As a result of its competing objectives, governmental interventions in the language and cultural realm do not always produce the convergence of goals much sought after. Furthermore, public demands by one group for more state resources and recognition for their language could trigger off competing demands by other groups.

In constructing the language regime, the prevailing language ideology has played a critical function in the state-building and nation-building discourse. Language is a dominant ethnic and cultural marker in Singapore society. Language policy and planning is instrumental and premised on particularistic ideas of culture vis-à-vis political governance and the economic imperative of achieving high economic growth rates.

The economic dimension of language competency is a significant motivator in the promotion of Chinese (and, to a lesser extent, Indian languages) given the putative rise of China and India as economic powers, as well as the immense potential of Sino-Indian trade. As part of Singapore's economic agenda, Singapore is seeking to establish a brand state niche as a "cipher for other Asian civilizations" where Singaporeans have "a knowledge and intuitive understanding" of Asian economic networks.[100] This cultural bandwidth requires not just bilingual competency (English and mother tongue), but also bicultural (East and West) knowledge and sensitivity. The bilingual policy is now enhanced with the policy objective of producing bicultural elites starting with the Chinese biculturalists.

With increasing attention being placed on the Chinese language, Singapore must be mindful of the potential for the minorities' perception of the Chinese language's apparent hegemony. In the political economy of governance in Singapore, the salience and high profile accorded to the Chinese language are evident. This dominance is not by virtue of the enrolment numbers of ethnic Chinese in the national schools. Rather, it is dominance by virtue of the singular importance of the Chinese language in the minds of the political elite.[101] As a carrier of culture and heritage, the Chinese language acts as the cornerstone and a legitimizing force in the moulding of the Chinese Singaporean cultural identity. It is also a useful resource for expanding political and economic relations between Singapore and China. Both these developments could potentially shape the political and socio-economic discourse and significantly influence Singapore's cultural and linguistic footprint.

Given the likely longevity of the high-profile Chinese language policy, what needs to be borne in mind is that an excessive focus on the Chinese language can lead to the minority groups' self-perceived insecurity, and their reactive response of canvassing for more recognition and resources as a means of cultural redemption. In the nation-building process, language has the "capacity for generating imagined communities, building in effect *particular solidarities*".[102] Conversely, the relentless search for one's ethnic identity — whether through the prism of race, language, religion, and culture — could transmogrify into a worrying centrifugal force. In searching for the Singapore nation, Singapore's multiethnic society and the political elite must remain alive to, in Toynbee's words, the "shibboleth of language".

Appendix 1

The tables below tabulate the figures on the language spoken most frequently at home for the Chinese, Malays, and Indians.

TABLE A.1
Ethnic Chinese — Language Most Frequently Spoken At Home

	1990	2000
English	19.3	23.9
Mandarin	30.1	45.1*
Chinese dialects	50.3	30.7
Others	0.3	0.4

Notes
* Although literate in both English and Chinese, younger Chinese families are more likely to be English-speaking. In 1988, 20 per cent of Primary 1 cohort came from English-speaking homes; by 1998, the figure has doubled to 40 per cent. See "Ministerial Statement on Chinese Language in Schools", *Singapore Parliamentary Debates, Official Record*, 20 January 1999, cols 1809-1854 and the ensuing debate at cols 1855-1903.
Source: *Singapore Population*, Singapore Department of Statistics, May 2001, p. 11.

TABLE A.2
Ethnic Malays — Language Most Frequently Spoken At Home

	1990	2000
English	6.1	7.9
Malay	93.7	91.6
Others	0.1	0.5

Source: *Singapore Population*, Singapore Department of Statistics, May 2001, p. 11.

TABLE A.3
Ethnic Indians — Language Most Frequently Spoken At Home

	1990	2000
English	32.3	35.6
Tamil	43.2	42.9
Malay	14.5	11.6
Others	10.0	9.9

Source: *Singapore Population*, Singapore Department of Statistics, May 2001, p. 11.

Notes

1. On threatened languages generally, see Mark Abley, *Spoken Here: Travels among Threatened Languages* (New York: Houghton Mifflin, 2003).

2. Even the Arabic language, which is not faced with a threatened existence, has to rise to the challenges of remaining relevant and of its ability to assimilate the knowledge society. See further the United Nations Development Programme's *The Arab Human Development Report 2003: Building a Knowledge Society* (New York: United Nations Development Programme, 2003), especially at pp. 121–26. In response to political and economic realities, even the Hong Kong SAR is contemplating the need to move away from Cantonese to Mandarin: see "Hong Kong Schools May Teach in Mandarin", *Straits Times*, 22 October 2003, p. A5.

3. See, for instance, the multi-country case studies in Michael E. Brown and Sumit Ganguly (eds.), *Fighting Words: Language Policy and Ethnic Relations in Asia* (Cambridge, MA: MIT Press, 2003).

4. Singapore is an island-state of about 3.3 million citizens comprising 76.8 per cent Chinese, 13.8 per cent Malay (the indigenous people), 7.9 per cent Indian, and 1.4 per cent "Others". These are the latest figures from the 2000 population census. For an overview of census data on literacy and language, see <http://www.singstat.gov.sg/keystats/c2000/literacy.pdf> (last accessed on 20 October 2004). Literacy rate as at 2003 is 94.2 per cent: see <http://www.singstat.gov.sg/keystats/annual/yos/yos112.pdf> (last accessed on 20 October 2004).

5. For a sampling of recent work on language and nation-building affecting countries across the globe, see Jennifer Lindsay and Tan Ying Ying (eds.), *Babel or Behemoth: Language Trends in Asia* (Singapore: Asia Research Institute, National University of Singapore, 2003); T. K. Oommen, "Language and Nation: For a Cultural Renewal of India", *Asian Journal of Social Science* 31, no. 2 (2003): 286–303; William F. S. Miles, "The Politics of Language Equilibrium in a Multilingual Society", *Comparative Politics* 32, no. 2 (January 2000): 215–30; Norrel A. London, "Entrenching the English Language in a British Colony: Curriculum Policy and Practice in Trinidad and Tobago", *International Journal of Educational Development* 23 (2003): 97–112; Grigory Ioffe, "Understanding Belarus: Questions of Language", *Europe-Asia Studies* 55, no. 7 (2003): 1009–47; Zane Goebel, "When do Indonesians Speak Indonesian? Some Evidence from Inter-ethnic and Foreigner-Indonesian Interactions and its Pedagogic Implications", *Journal of Multilingual and Multicultural Development* 23, no. 6 (2002): 479–89; Webb Keane, "Public Speaking: On Indonesian as the Language of the Nation", *Public Culture* 15, no. 3 (2003): 503–30.

6. But see useful overview in Stephen May, *Language and Minority Rights:*

Ethnicity, Nationalism and the Politics of Language (Harlow: Longman, 2001), pp. 5–9.

7. But see Nirmala Srirekam PuroShotam, *Negotiating Language, Constructing Race: Disciplining Race in Singapore* (Berlin: Mouton de Gruyter, 1998) for her ethnomethodological study on how the Indian Singaporean community dealt with the Government's language policy.

8. See the seminal piece by Geoffrey Benjamin, "The Cultural Logic of Singapore's 'Multiracialism' ", in *Singapore: Society in Transition*, edited by Riaz Hassan (Kuala Lumpur: Oxford University Press, 1976).

9. This provision is also found in section 7 of the Republic of Singapore Independence Act (Act 9 of 1965), passed on 22 December 1965, but having retrospective effect to 9 August 1965 ('Singapore Day').

10. Malay is, of course, the lingua franca of Singapore's immediate neighbours. Indonesia, had on its Independence, opted for Bahasa Indonesia as the national language although the Javanese were by far the dominant ethnic group.

11. Written between 1956 and 1957 as a patriotic song, 'Majulah Singapura' was launched on 3 December 1959 and was adopted as the national anthem upon Independence. The national motto is also incorporated into Singapore's national coat of arms (state crest).

12. On education and its social engineering effects, see further H.E. Wilson, *Social Engineering in Singapore: Educational Policies and Social Change 1819–1972* (Singapore: Singapore University Press, 1978).

13. 'EM1' is the abbreviation for English and mother tongue languages taken at the first language level. On average, between 1991 and 2004, the top 20 per cent of pupils in each cohort qualified for EM1, about 75 per cent for EM2 (English taken as the first language with the mother tongue taken at the second language level) and the rest, EM3. Students could move from one stream to another if their academic performance required it. EM1 and EM2 streams were merged in 2004: see the Education Ministry's media statement of 18 March 2004 at <http://www.moe.gov.sg/press/2004/pr20040318.htm> (accessed on 31 October 2004). Those in EM3 offer three subjects only — foundation English, mother tongue at basic proficiency level and mathematics. There is also a ME3 stream for the weakest students if "there is a sufficient demand". In this stream, pupils will learn Mother Tongue at the higher level (Higher Malay, Higher Chinese or Higher Tamil) and Basic English Language. Teaching of English Language will emphasize oral/aural skills, reading and listening comprehension, as well as conversation. The language of instruction for all subjects will be in Mother Tongue: see <http://www.moe.gov.sg/corporate/primary4.htm; http://schools.moe.edu.sg/gps/P4Streaming.pdf> (last accessed on 31 October 2004).

14. Chan Heng Chee and Obaid ul Haq (eds.), *The Prophetic & The Political:*

Selected Speeches & Writings of S. Rajaratnam (Singapore: Graham Brash, 1987), p. 149. On the long-standing phenomenon of diasporas and their consequence for ethnic politics, see Gabriel Sheffer, *Diaspora Politics: At Home Abroad* (Cambridge: Cambridge University Press, 2003).

15. Two recent analyses are Carl A. Trocki, "Development of Labour Organisation in Singapore, 1800–1960". *Australian Journal of Politics and History* 47, no. 1 (2001): 115–29; and Michael Barr, "Trade Unions in an Elitist Society: The Singapore Story". *Australian Journal of Politics and History* 46, no. 4 (2000): 480–96.

16. Although the non-communist, English-educated elites won the political and ideological battle, the political landscape was scarred. See further Tim Harper, "Lim Chin Siong and the 'Singapore Story' ", in *Comet in Our Sky: Lim Chin Siong in History*, edited by Tan Jing Quee and K.S. Jomo (Kuala Lumpur: INSAN, 2001), p. 15:

> However, recent writing has challenged the stereotypical notion – perpetuated in many accounts since – that the politics of the 'Chinese-educated' was driven by an innate ethnocentrism and a natural susceptibility to a 'secret society complex' and to Communism.... Student politics was fuelled by a wider sense of exclusion for the Chinese-educated with a colonial society in which fluency in English was the route to employment and advancement. It was underpinned by resentment of the privileges of the Anglophone Chinese. Yet within the Chinese community, graduates of Chinese middle schools were themselves something of an elite.

17. The stalwart role played by the Chinese vanguards from the ruling People's Action Party's (PAP) is captured in Sai Siew Min and Huang Jianli, "The 'Chinese-educated' Political Vanguards: Ong Pang Boon, Lee Khoon Choy & Jek Yeun Thong", in *Lee's Lieutenants: Singapore's Old Guard*, edited by Lam Peng Er and Kevin Y.L. Tan (St Leonards, NSW: Allen & Unwin, 1999), pp. 132–68.

18. See also Wong Ting-Hong's detailed study of Chinese education during the post-war and independence period in his *Hegemonies Compared: State Formation and Chinese School Politics in Postwar Singapore and Hong Kong* (New York: Routledge Falmer, 2002); "Rethinking the Education/ State Formation Connection: Pedagogic Reform in Singapore, 1945–1965". *Comparative Education Review* 46, no. 2 (May 2002): 182–210; "Education and State Formation Reconsidered: Chinese School Identity in Postwar Singapore". *Journal of Historical Sociology* 16, no. 2 (June 2003): 237–65.

19. For instance, Lee Kuan Yew recently noted in his *From Third World to First: The Singapore Story 1965–2000, Memoirs of Lee Kuan Yew* (Singapore: Singapore Press Holdings & Times Editions, 2000), pp. 546–47 that:

A people steeped in Chinese values had more discipline, were more courteous, and respectful to elders. The result was a more orderly society. When these values were diluted by an English education, the result was less vigour and discipline and more casual behaviour. Worse, the English-educated generally lacked self-confidence because they were not speaking their own native language. The dramatic confrontations between the communist-led Chinese middle school students and my own government brought home these substantial differences in culture and ideals, represented in two different value systems.

However, for Lee Kuan Yew and his Old Guard generation, the Chinese-educated robust stance on Chinese culture and the need to preserve Chinese traditions through Chinese schools in the 1960s, was portrayed as "a proletarian issue; it was plain, simple chauvinism": see Lee, *The Singapore Story*, pp. 185–86.

20. They were previously characterized as being pro-communist China in the 1950s and 1960s. See the persuasive analysis of Hong Lysa and Huang Jianli, "The Scripting of Singapore's Heroes: Toying with Pandora's Box," in *New Terrains in Southeast Asian History*, edited by Abu Talib Ahmad and Tan Liok Ee (Athens, OH and Singapore: Ohio University Press and Singapore University Press, 2003).

21. My conception of the organizing framework of language ideology has benefited from the insights of Paul V. Kroskrity, "Regimenting Languages: Language Ideological Perspectives", in *Regimes of Language: Ideologies, Polities, and Identities*, edited by Paul V. Kroskrity (Oxford: James Currey, 2000).

22. The British colonial authorities left each community to structure their own education system. Colonial education policy in British Malaya resulted in "different perceptions of these different groups towards each other". See Keith Watson, "Rulers and Ruled: Racial Perceptions, Curriculum and Schooling in Colonial Malaysia and Singapore", in *The Imperial Curriculum: Racial Images and Education in the British Colonial Experience*, edited by J.A. Mangan (London: Routledge, 1993).

23. This process started tentatively with the 1956 All-Party Committee on Chinese Education. In its report, it noted that "Malay is important because of its regional importance…" The committee went so far as to recommend bilingual education in the primary stage followed by trilingualism in the secondary stage: see the *Report of the All-Party Committee of the Singapore Legislative Assembly on Chinese Education* (Singapore: Government Printing Office, 1956).

24. Nirmala Srirekam PuroShotam, *Negotiating Language, Constructing Race: Disciplining Race in Singapore* (Berlin: Mouton de Gruyter, 1998), pp. 49–50.

25. Thus it was no surprise that the Eurasian and Peranankan communities found difficulties coping with the mother tongue language requirements since they were trying to learn a language that had little connection with the home environment. For instance, 43 per cent of Eurasian students passed the mother tongue language at the 'O' Level 2000 but this figure jumped to 65 per cent in 2002. Then Acting Education Minister Tharman Shanmugaratnam provided these figures in his speech at the Eurasian Association Education Awards Ceremony, 30 August 2003.

26. On the linguistic ideology as part of the political ideology of nation-building, see Wendy Bokhorst-Heng, "Singapore's Speak Mandarin Campaign: Language Ideological Debates and the Imagining of the Nation", in *Language Ideological Debates*, edited by Jan Blommaert (Berlin: Mouton de Gruyter, 1999).

27. Linguistically, these "dialects" are in reality "languages" like Mandarin. See <http://www.ethnologue.com/show_language.asp?code=CHN>. What is also little known, at least in Singapore, is that Mandarin is itself based on a Beijing dialect with heavy influence from other varieties of northern Beijing dialects. Benedict Anderson has termed such endeavours as "linguistic nationalism" where "each true nation was marked off by its own peculiar language and literary culture, which together expressed the people's historical genius": see his "Western Nationalism and Eastern Nationalism: Is there a Difference that Matters?" *New Left Review* 9 (May–June 2001): 31–42 at 40.

28. *Education Statistics Digest 2002* (Singapore: Ministry of Education, 2002), p. v.

29. See "Pupils aren't Mixing, Study Finds", *Straits Times*, 26 July 2003, p. 1. See also related stories at pp. H2 and H3. The Education Ministry has acknowledged the study's findings: see "Yes, There's Little Racial Mixing, but Schools are Trying: MOE", *Straits Times*, 31 July 2003, p. 4. See also the editorial, "Why Pupils Should Mix", *Straits Times*, 31 July 2003, p. 14. The study is published as Christine Lee et al., "Children's Experiences of Multiracial Relationships in Informal Primary School Settings", in *Beyond Rituals and Riots: Ethnic Pluralism and Social Cohesion in Singapore*, edited by Lai Ah Eng (Singapore: Eastern Universities Press, 2004).

30. Until the onset of the Asian financial crisis in 1997, Singapore's cultural motivations in governance and economic development enjoyed limelight as one exemplar of the World Bank-popularized "East Asian Miracle" phenomenon. This provided boisterous incentive for Singapore to be the self-declared "Asian Values" spokesman. The essence of "Asian values" postulates a particularistic style of political governance premised on state-defined community interests having precedence over the individual. The

literature on the Asian Values and human rights debate is voluminous. A succinct discussion of the 'Singapore School' can be found in Chua Beng Huat, *Communitarian Ideology and Democracy in Singapore* (London: Routledge, 1995); Daniel A. Bell, *East Meets West: Human Rights and Democracy in East Asia* (Princeton, NJ: Princeton University Press, 2000) and Eva Brems, *Human Rights: Universality and Diversity* (The Hague: Martinus Nijhoff, 2001), pp. 36–49. See also Donald K. Emmerson, "Singapore and the 'Asian Values' Debate", *Journal of Democracy* 6, no. 4 (October 1995): 95–105.

31. On the "Asianisation" policy and its emphasis on the return to one's cultural roots and heritage in the modernization drive, see Raj Vasil's *Asianizing Singapore: The PAP's Management of Ethnicity* (Singapore: Heinemann Asia, 1995).

32. The SAP schools' prestige was enhanced by their being exclusively designated "Special Stream" schools, the top-tier education rank within the secondary school system (the other two educational streams at the secondary school level are the Express and Normal streams). SAP students study English and Chinese as first languages. The SAP school scheme has now enlarged to cover an additional fifteen primary schools. At the pre-university level, the Language Elective Programme (LEP) in Chinese is offered to encourage academically able and linguistically talented students to study Chinese at GCE 'A' Level in three selected junior colleges. Students in the LEP (Chinese) programme will take the GCE 'A' Level Higher Chinese papers, and will be given the option to offer the Higher Chinese Special Paper.

33. Speech (delivered in Mandarin) by George Yeo, Minister for Information and the Arts and Second Minister for Trade and Industry at the 1998 Speak Mandarin Campaign Launch, 12 September 1998.

34. Education Study Team, *Report on the Ministry of Education 1978* (Singapore: Singapore National Printers, 1979); and Moral Education Committee, *Report on Moral Education 1979* (Singapore: Singapore National Printers, 1979).

35. The 1991 White Paper on Singapore's Shared Values gave the imprimatur for the idealized honourable gentlemen or *junzi* (a Confucian gentleman) as a key component of Singapore's conception of good government.'

36. Confucianism is generally not regarded as a religion. See Eddie C.Y. Kuo, "Confucianism as Political Discourse in Singapore: The Case of an Incomplete Revitalization Movement," in *Confucian Traditions in East Asian Modernity: Moral Education and Economic Culture in Japan and the Four Mini-Dragons*, edited by Tu Wei-ming (Cambridge, MA: Harvard University Press, 1996), pp. 294–309. See also Joseph B. Tamney, *The Struggle over Singapore's Soul: Western Modernization and Asian Culture* (Berlin: Walter de Gruyter, 1996).

37. As Wee questions, "why does a triumphant modernity [Singapore] breed a longing for 'tradition'?": see C.J. W.-L. Wee, *Culture, Empire, and the Question of Being Modern* (Lanham, MD: Lexington Books, 2003), p. 198. On the phenomenon of diasporic re-Sinification, see Michael Pinches, "Cultural Relations, Class and the New Rich of Asia", in *Culture and Privilege in Capitalist Asia*, edited by Michael Pinches (London: Routledge, 1999), pp. 1–55.

38. C.J. W.-L. Wee, *Culture, Empire, and the Question of Being Modern* (Lanham, MD: Lexington Books, 2003), p. 209.

39. Unless otherwise stated, quotes in this section are from Deputy Prime Minister Lee Hsien Loong's Ministerial Statement on Chinese Language in Schools in Parliament, 20 January 1999.

40. The concerns the Government had with Chinese education (epitomized by Nantah) date back to the 1950s. See also Justus M. Van Der Kroef, "Nanyang University and the Dilemma of Overseas Chinese Education", *The China Quarterly* 20 (Oct–Dec 1964): 96–127.

41. Prime Minister Goh's National Day Rally speech in Mandarin, 24 August 1997.

42. See Prime Minister Goh's speech at the *Lianhe Zaobao* 75th Anniversary Gala Dinner, 6 September 1998; "Fewer Here Reading and Writing Chinese", *Straits Times*, 7 March 2001, p. H5. However, the future of the main Chinese language newspaper, Zaobao, is secure as the Government has indicated that it is a 'national project' to maintain it as a high quality Chinese language newspaper: see Senior Minister Lee Kuan Yew's speech at the *Lianhe Zaobao* 80th Anniversary Gala Dinner on 6 September 2003. On *Zaobao*'s reach to mainland China's readers and other stories in conjunction with its 80th anniversary celebrations, see Presslines, July 2003, pp. 3–7, 18–19 (*Presslines* is the monthly journal of the Singapore Press Holdings, the publisher of *Zaobao*, as well as the other Chinese newspapers: *Shin Min Daily News* and *Lianhe Wanbao*).

43. Prime Minister Goh's 1997 National Day Rally speech in Mandarin, 27 August 1997. On the evolution of the Speak Mandarin campaign, see Promote Mandarin Council, *Mandarin: The Chinese Connection* (Singapore: Ministry of Information and the Arts, 2000). The campaign's website is at <http://mandarin.org.sg/>. Complementing the Speak Mandarin campaign is the biennial Chinese Cultural Festival, which serves to highlight the "self-renewal and splendid spirit of Chinese culture ... and to promote the understanding of Chinese culture." See speech by then Environment Minister Lim Swee Say at the 2002 festival opening, 1 March 2002.

44. *Cf.* "There does not seem to be a realization of the fact that moral concepts or values can best be transmitted in the language the child is most proficient in." This little known throw-away line is in the 1979 *Report on Moral Education* prepared by Ong Teng Cheong and the Moral Education Committee, p. 5 at para 3.4.1.

45. See also "Learn Chinese for Cultural Value, Say Some", *Straits Times*, 31 August 2001, p. 46. The Chinese community leaders were reported to be planning to start a school that will place emphasis on the learning of Chinese, see "Plans for New School with Emphasis on Chinese", *Straits Times*, 12 October 2002, p. 8.

46. Speech by Deputy Prime Minister Lee Hsien Loong at the opening of the Chinese High Boarding School, 10 January 2003.

47. The earlier Chinese language reviews did not go far enough in arresting the decline in standards. Although Mandarin is the most popular language among the Chinese, the proficiency level leaves much to be desired. Chinese Singaporeans, in speaking Chinese, are said to speak "something like Chinese", suggesting mediocre standards. See further "Will Chinese become a Dumpling House Language?", *Straits Times*, 31 March 2001, p. H16; "Arresting the Chinese Language Decline", *Straits Times*, 5 May 2002, p. 22. For an elucidation of some of the concerns of the Chinese-educated and Chinese-speakers, see Lee Guan Kin, "Singapore Chinese Society in Transition: Reflections on the Cultural Implications of Modern Education", in *Chinese Migrants Abroad: Cultural, Educational, and Social Dimensions of the Chinese Diaspora*, edited by Michael W. Charney, Brenda S.A. Yeoh and Tong Chee Kiong (Singapore: Singapore University Press and World Scientific, 2003).

48. A White Paper is needed as the proposed changes are a "sea change in the way Chinese is taught... [and] expected to attract intense scrutiny": see "Chinese Teaching to Go Flexible", *Straits Times*, 12 October 2004. For more details, see the various local newspaper reports on 12 October 2004.

49. On the difficulties of creating a Tamil elite, see Vanithami Saravanan, "Indians in Multilingual and Multicultural Settings: Tamil Education in Singapore", in *Challenges Facing the Singapore Education System Today*, edited by Jason Tan, S. Gopinathan and Ho Wah Kam (Singapore: Prentice Hall, 2001), pp. 252–53. For the Indians, heterogeneity is more complex given the non-existence of a common Indian language as well as the divisive caste system. Further, the notion of a pan-Indian culture "is alien even in India".

50. China is Singapore's fourth largest trading partner (after Malaysia, the United States and Japan) with bilateral trade expanding rapidly at thirty per cent annually. China is also Singapore's largest foreign investment destination. Singapore's trade with Greater China — the People's Republic of China, Hong Kong SAR, and Taiwan — surpassed that with the United States in 2002. On the close ties between China and Singapore and how it impacts on Singapore, see Eugene K.B. Tan, "Re-engaging Chineseness: Political, Economic and Cultural Imperatives of Nation-Building in Singapore". *The China Quarterly* 175 (September 2003): 751–74.

51. The reviews took place in 1992, 1999 and 2004. In 1992, the Chinese

Language Review Committee recommended the use of "Higher Chinese" in place of CL1 [Chinese as a first language] and Chinese Language in place of CL2 [Chinese as second language]. This arose from concerns that the CL2 label, "the de facto standard of Chinese language in all schools", is "not conducive to the teaching and learning of CL as the mother tongue" and has caused some parents and pupils to regards CL2 as being of lesser importance. See *Chinese Language Teaching and Learning in Singapore* (Singapore: Chinese Language Review Committee, 1992), paras 2.3.2-2.3.3.

52. Conversely, until the Malay world demonstrates its economic potential, the promotion of the Malay language as a language of commerce is unlikely to happen. In the words of political commentator Lee Han Shih, "Does Singapore think it can compete in the region when its people are armed with English alone?" See his "Singapore, Love thy Neighbours", *Today*, 28 October 2003.

53. The emphasis on economic motivation is, of course, not popular with the champions of Chinese language and culture, see "Learn Chinese for Culture or for Economics", *Straits Times*, 28 August 2003, p. H6; "Learn Chinese for Cultural Value, Say Some", *Straits Times*, 31 August 2003, p. H6; "Profit from Chinese, But Where's the Passion?", *Straits Times Interactive*, 29 October 2004.

54. Minister Mentor Lee Kuan Yew remarked that for the majority of Chinese Singaporeans, an 80 per cent mastery of English and 60–70 per cent mastery of Chinese would be adequate. See "Chinese Teaching to Go Flexible", *Straits Times Interactive*, 12 October 2004.

55. As Minister Mentor Lee Kuan Yew observed, "By forcing them to achieve the standard [being equally good in English and Chinese], we have turned off one generation, which is a great pity. They are fed up. They are forced by their parents, forced by their school. They have bad results, they hate it, they want nothing more to do with it, which I think is a tragedy." See "Change Needed as More Speak English at Home", *Straits Times Interactive*, 12 October 2004.

56. In recent years, new forms of learning the language and culture, such as Chinese calligraphy and letter writing to students of the opposite sex, have been introduced. See speech by Mr Tharman Shanmugaratnam, then Acting Minister for Education, at the 12th Singapore Young Calligraphers' Exhibition, 18 October 2003. The effusive praise for this art form is evident in the Acting Education Minister's remarks:

> I am also told that for learners of the Chinese language, calligraphy allows discovery of the poetic beauty of the language, and stimulates a desire to gain greater proficiency in the Chinese language. ... Our schools have been promoting this fine art, as a way of

developing the skills and character of our young, as well as nurturing an appreciation of the Chinese language and culture. Besides being taught in formal art lessons, from the Primary school levels upward, some schools have also incorporated the learning of calligraphy into Chinese language lessons so as to make learning the language more engaging.

57. Speech by then Deputy Prime Minister Lee Hsien Loong at the opening of the Chinese High Boarding School, 10 January 2003. Echoing the Deputy Prime Minister, then Senior Minister of State for Education, Tharman Shanmugaratnam, in endorsing the bilingual approach urged teachers to bear in mind that "whatever we do in education, we should remain pragmatic, not doctrinaire, in our approach": see "Effective Teaching and Learning of the Mother Tongue: Innovating and Adapting to New Circumstances", a speech delivered at "The Significance Of Speaking Skills For Language Development" seminar on 15 February 2003. See also "Teaching Chinese: English Serves as 'Float' ", *Straits Times*, 6 March 2003, p. H4; "Bilingual Way to Learn Chinese 'Gives Support' ", *Straits Times*, 21 March 2003, p. H10. *Cf.* "Only for the Weakest Kids, Please", *Straits Times*, 13 January 2003, p. H5.

58. Under this arrangement, only students with a C grade or lower at the Primary School Leaving Examinations (PSLE) can offer CLB in Secondary 3. To offer it at 'O' level, a student has had to fail Chinese Language in Secondary 3 and a E8 grade or worse in the Secondary 4 mid-year exams.

59. "Official translation of excerpts of DPM Lee Hsien Loong's interview with *Lianhe Zaobao* published on 16 November 2003", available at <http://www.gov.sg/singov/interviews/161103lhl.htm> (last accessed on 20 November 2003). See also "More Chinese Language Students Opting for Plan B", *Straits Times*, 9 October 2003; "Ministry to Review Criteria for Chinese 'B' Option", *Straits Times*, 17 October 2003, p. H1; "More Help for Kids Struggling with Chinese", *Straits Times*, 17 November 2003, p. 3.

60. Only 2.4 per cent offered it as a subject at 'O' level in 2002. Over time, this figure is expected to be between ten and twenty per cent.

61. "Clear the CLB Cloud", *Straits Times*, 13 October 2003, p. 14.

62. On an early observation of the linguistic balance of power in Singapore, and that English was here to stay, see the sardonic comments by D.J. Enright, *Memoirs of a Mendicant Professor* (London: Chatto and Windus, 1969), pp. 120–21.

63. On the global sprawl of the English language, see Mark Abley's *Spoken Here: Travels among Threatened Languages* (New York: Houghton Mifflin, 2003), pp. 83–94 (chapter entitled, *Don't Vori, Bi Khepi*). On the global

dominance of English, see works by David Crystal, especially his *English as a Global Language* (Cambridge: Cambridge University Press, 1997) and *Language Death* (Cambridge: Cambridge University Press, 2000).

64. See Appendix 1. This is not surprising as the parents of the current school students are themselves products of the bilingual education system in which English was the first language and the mother tongue as the second language.

65. English was, of course, introduced by the British and, during the colonial regime, was a language for the colonial administrators and the small privileged population who had the opportunity of learning the language.

66. Chua Beng Huat, "Multiculturalism in Singapore: An Instrument of Social Control", *Race & Class* 44, no. 3 (Jan–Mar 2003): 58–77 at 71–72.

67. Within a decade of Singapore's independence, it was widely accepted that social and professional advancement prospects are highest for the English-educated. This reinforced the enhanced status of English language and made the closure of non-English stream schools inevitable. See John A. MacDougall and Chew Sock Foon, "English Language Competence and Occupational Mobility in Singapore", *Pacific Affairs* 49, no. 2 (Summer 1976): 294–312.

68. Moral Education is also taught in the mother tongue. Even more time was allocated for English for the EM2 and EM3 students in the primary schools and in the less academically demanding programmes. Information extracted from *Report of the Committee on Compulsory Education in Singapore* (Singapore: Committee on Compulsory Education, 2000), Annex 7, pp. 40–42.

69. The SGEM's website is at <http://www.goodenglish.org.sg/SGEM/home.php>. See further Rani Ruby, "Creative Destruction: Singapore's Speak Good English Movement", *World Englishes* 20, no. 3 (2001): 341–55.

70. See speech by Senior Minister Lee Kuan Yew at the Tanjong Pagar 34th National Day Celebration, 14 August 1999. See also Chng Huang Hoon, " 'You see me no up': Is Singlish a Problem?" *Language Problems and Language Planning* 27, no. 1 (2003): 45–62.

71. The Government immediately launched a three-pronged campaign to urgently raise English standards in Singapore schools. First, the Education Ministry revised the English Language syllabuses to make them more rigorous and to strengthen the teaching of grammar. Second, the Education Ministry conducted a 60-hour course, leading to the Singapore-Cambridge Certificate in the Teaching of English Grammar, for 8,000 English language teachers to strengthen and update their skills. Third, a handbook on common errors in English usage in Singapore was published.

72. Tom McArthur, "English as an Asian Language", *English Today* 19, no. 2 (April 2003): 19–22 at 21.

73. Edgar W. Schneider, "The Dynamics of New Englishes: From Identity

Construction to Dialect Birth", *Language* 79, no. 2 (June 2003): 233–81 at 265.

74. National Day Rally Speech, "First-World Economy, World-Class Home", 22 August 1999.

75. Vivienne Fong, Lisa Lim and Lionel Wee suggest that the concern over Singlish may be exaggerated: "Official policies and general attitudes that are linguistically naïve can only have negative effects on attempts to cultivate linguistic confidence and, ultimately, national pride in the local standard variety." See their " 'Singlish': Used and Abused", *Asian Englishes* 5, no. 1 (Summer 2002): 18–39 at 33.

76. Article 152 of the Singapore Constitution reads (emphasis mine):

> (1) It shall be the responsibility of the Government constantly to care for the interests of the racial and religious minorities in Singapore.
> (2) The Government shall exercise its functions in such manner as to recognise the special position of the Malays, who are the indigenous people of Singapore, and accordingly *it shall be the responsibility of the Government to protect, safeguard, support, foster and promote* their political, educational, religious, economic, social and cultural interests and the Malay language.

77. As the 1956 All-Party Committee on Chinese Education noted in its report, "Malay is important because of its regional importance...": see the *Report of the All-Party Committee of the Singapore Legislative Assembly on Chinese Education* (Singapore: Government Printing Office, 1956). A nuanced understanding of Singapore's closest neighours can be facilitated through the Malay language and ameliorate the possibility of bilateral tensions. One could proffer the argument that the substantive disputes with Malaysia, and to a lesser extent Indonesia, are a reflection of a mutual lack of understanding between Singapore and its neighbours. Before English became commonly spoken, bazaar Malay was the de facto lingua franca for Singaporeans. Indeed, we can still observe the older generation of non-Malay Singaporeans communicating with the Malays in bazaar Malay.

78. See the Ministry of Education press release, "Non-Native Mother Tongue Language as a Third Language", 29 September 2004, available at <http://www.moe.gov.sg/press/2004/pr20040929c.htm> (last accessed 30 September 2004).

79. Non-Malay students are reminded that their offering Malay as a third language is to their benefit as they will be in "an advantageous position for scholarship awards". See the Education Ministry's Language Centre's website at <http://www.moe.gov.sg/moelc/benefits.htm> (last accessed on 30 October 2004).

80. In his *Memoirs of a Mendicant Professor* (London: Chatto and Windus,

1969), pp. 120–21, D.J. Enright described Malay as the "nominal" national language used as a "linguistic red herring to distract attention from the real problem, or the real problem as reflected in the rivalry between the English and Chinese languages."

81. EMAS is conducted at the Bukit Panjang Government High School although students from other secondary schools can participate in the programme. The intake averages 120 students a year. The MLEP is based at the Tampines Junior College and had about 20 students in 2001 and 2002 and 11 in 2003. Information obtained from then Deputy Prime Minister Lee Hsien Loong's interview with *Berita Harian* published on 23 and 24 October 2003.

82. Ibid.

83. Figures obtained from Vanithami Saravanan, "Indians in Multilingual and Multicultural Settings: Tamil Education in Singapore", in *Challenges Facing the Singapore Education System Today*, edited by Jason Tan, S. Gopinathan and Ho Wah Kam (Singapore: Prentice Hall, 2001), p. 249.

84. See speech by then Acting Education Minister Tharman Shanmugaratnam at the Hindi Centres' Day 2003, 2 August 2003.

85. For instance, the Hindi Society caters to 2500 students enrolled at its three Hindi Centres. It also has a Parallel Hindi Programme with nine schools where Hindi Centre teachers teach Hindi during the mother tongue lesson periods, obviating the need for the students in these schools to travel to a Hindi Centre after school hours for Hindi classes. For Punjabi, the Singapore Sikh Education Foundation oversees the delivery of Punjabi language education in Singapore to about 2,000 students each year. (Information obtained from speech by Acting Education Minister Tharman Shanmugaratnam at the Hindi Centres' Day 2003, 2 August 2003.)

86. The non-Tamil Indian Languages ("NTILs") jointly established a Board for the Teaching and Testing of South Asian Languages in 2002 to "maintain common policies and standards through combined examinations in the NTILs."

87. Speech by Acting Education Minister Tharman Shanmugaratnam at Tamil Murasu's Most Inspiring Tamil Language Teacher Award Presentation Ceremony, 4 October 2003.

88. In 1998, a review committee was formed to look into the Tamil language curricula. On the review committee's work and recommendations, see Vanithami Saravanan, "Indians in Multilingual and Multicultural Settings: Tamil Education in Singapore", in *Challenges Facing the Singapore Education System Today*, edited by Jason Tan, S. Gopinathan and Ho Wah Kam (Singapore: Prentice Hall, 2001), pp. 250–52.

89. For a vivid portrayal of the marginalization of the non-English speakers, dialects, and Singlish in Singapore cinema, see Chua Beng Huat and Wei-Wei Yeo, "Singapore Cinema: Eric Khoo and Jack Neo — Critique from the

Margins and the Mainstream", *Inter-Asia Cultural Studies* 4, no. 1 (2003): 117–25.

90. This mismatch is less observed for the Malay-speaking and Tamil-speaking despite the linguistic switch to English. See also Anne Pakir, "English-Knowing Bilingualism in Singapore", in *Imagining Singapore*, edited by Ban Kah Choon, Anne Pakir and Tong Chee Kiong (Singapore: Times Academic Press, 1992).

91. See MDA news release, "Allowing the use of dialect on television and radio", 30 April 2003.

92. Censorship Review Committee, *Censorship Review Committee Report: Towards Greater Diversity* (Singapore: Ministry of Information, Communications and the Arts, July 2003), pp. 54–55, para 5.9 (also available on-line at <http://www.mica.gov.sg/pressroom/press_030904.html>; last accessed on 31 October 2004). The committee was mindful that its recommendations should not undermine the Speak Mandarin Campaign and also noted that "… there has not been any recent research study on the possible impact of the use of dialect in films and TV programmes on the level of Mandarin proficiency."

93. The Government had agreed in principle to the recommendations, see "Working Together Towards a Responsible and Vibrant Society", MITA's response to the CRC Recommendations, 8 September 2003; available at <http://www.mita.gov.sg/pressroom/press_030908.pdf> (last accessed on 31 October 2004).

94. All quotes in this paragraph are taken from the ACCESS Annual Report 2002/2003. See also "Let's Hear it for Dialect", *Straits Times*, 5 March 2003, p. L4; "More Dialect Shows on TV?", *Streats*, 27 February 2003, p. 3; "Dialects on TV? Needs more Study", *Straits Times*, 18 April 2003, p. L24; "Back to *gong hokkien* on TV", *Today*, 27 February 2003, p. 2.

95. "More Dialect Shows will Hit Mandarin Use", *Straits Times*, 10 March 2003, p. 15.

96. All quotes in this paragraph are taken from the Remaking Singapore Committee report, *Changing Mindsets, Deepening Relations* (Singapore: Remaking Singapore Committee, 2003), pp. 68–70.

97. See the Government's response at <http://www.remakingsingapore.gov.sg/Dialogue%20session%20-%20govt%20response%20_full__final_.pdf>, para 59 (p. 26). *Cf.* Can-Seng Ooi, "Identities, Museums, and Tourism in Singapore: Think Regionally, Act Locally", *Indonesia and the Malay World* 31, no. 89 (March 2003): 80–90. Ooi argues that museums are geared towards the Government's social engineering and economic goals and that heritage is politically irrelevant in Singapore today. See also the discussion on the survival prospects of Peranankan (Straits Chinese) culture and the government agencies' tendency to exoticise it in J. Henderson, "Ethnic Heritage as a

Tourist Attraction: The Peranakans of Singapore", *International Journal of Heritage Studies* 9, no. 1 (March 2003): 27–44.
98. Speech by then Deputy Prime Minister Lee Hsien Loong at the opening ceremony of the Char Yong building, 3 December 2002. Another similar message can be discerned from then Prime Minister Goh Chok Tong's speech at the celebration dinner for the 5th World Anxi Convention and the 80th Anniversary of the Singapore Ann Kway Association, 9 November 2002.
99. Speech by then Deputy Prime Minister Lee Hsien Loong at the opening ceremony of the 12th Teochew International Conference, 22 November 2003.
100. Quotes are taken from Acting Education Minister Tharman Shanmugaratnam's speech at the opening ceremony of the "Conference on the cultures of Southeast Asia", 22 August 2003.
101. The Government has mooted the idea of requiring future government scholars studying in the US to also enroll in Chinese universities under a dual scholarship scheme. The goal is to nurture a large pool of Singaporeans who understand China. See "Scholarship May Mean China Stint", *Straits Times Interactive*, 21 November 2003.
102. Benedict Anderson, *Imagined Communities Reflections on the Origin and Spread of Nationalism*, revised and extended edition (London: Verso, 1991), p. 133. Anderson's emphasis.

References

Books and Articles
Abley, Mark. *Spoken Here: Travels among Threatened Languages*. New York: Houghton Mifflin, 2003.
Anderson, Benedict. *Imagined Communities: Reflections on the Origin and Spread of Nationalism* (revised and extended edition). London: Verso, 1991.
Anderson, Benedict. "Western Nationalism and Eastern Nationalism: Is there a Difference that Matters?" *New Left Review* 9 (May–June 2001): 31–42.
Barr, Michael. "Trade Unions in an Elitist Society: The Singapore Story". *Australian Journal of Politics and History* 46, no. 4 (2000): 480–96.
Bell, Daniel A. *East Meets West: Human Rights and Democracy in East Asia*. Princeton, NJ: Princeton University Press, 2000.
Benjamin, Geoffrey. "The Cultural Logic of Singapore's 'Multiracialism' ". In *Singapore: Society in Transition*, edited by Riaz Hassan. Kuala Lumpur: Oxford University Press, 1976.
Bokhorst-Heng, Wendy. "Singapore's Speak Mandarin Campaign: Language Ideological Debates and the Imagining of the Nation". In *Language Ideological Debates*, edited by Jan Blommaert. Berlin: Mouton de Gruyter, 1999.

Brems, Eva. *Human Rights: Universality and Diversity*. The Hague: Martinus Nijhoff, 2001.

Brown, Michael E. and Sumit Ganguly, eds. *Fighting Words: Language Policy and Ethnic Relations in Asia*. Cambridge, MA: MIT Press, 2003.

Chan, Heng Chee and Obaid ul Haq, eds. *The Prophetic & The Political: Selected Speeches & Writings of S. Rajaratnam*. Singapore: Graham Brash, 1987.

Chua, Beng Huat. *Communitarian Ideology and Democracy in Singapore*. London: Routledge, 1995.

————. "Multiculturalism in Singapore: An Instrument of Social Control". *Race & Class* 44, no. 3 (Jan–Mar 2003): 58–77.

Chua, Beng Huat and Wei-Wei Yeo. "Singapore Cinema: Eric Khoo and Jack Neo — Critique from the Margins and the Mainstream". *Inter-Asia Cultural Studies* 4, no. 1 (2003): 117–25.

Chng, Huang Hoon. " 'You see me no up': Is Singlish a Problem?" *Language Problems and Language Planning* 27, no. 1 (2003): 45–62.

Crystal, David. *English as a Global Language*. Cambridge: Cambridge University Press, 1997.

————. *Language Death*. Cambridge: Cambridge University Press, 2000.

Emmerson, Donald K. "Singapore and the 'Asian Values' Debate". *Journal of Democracy* 6, no. 4 (October 1995): 95–105.

Enright, D.J. *Memoirs of a Mendicant Professor*. London: Chatto and Windus, 1969.

Fong, Vivienne, Lisa Lim and Lionel Wee. " 'Singlish': Used and Abused". *Asian Englishes* 5, no. 1 (Summer 2002): 18–39.

Goebel, Zane. "When do Indonesians Speak Indonesian? Some Evidence from Inter-ethnic and Foreigner-Indonesian Interactions and its Pedagogic Implications". *Journal of Multilingual and Multicultural Development* 23, no. 6 (2002): 479–89.

Harper, Tim. "Lim Chin Siong and the 'Singapore Story' ". In *Comet in Our Sky: Lim Chin Siong in History*, edited by Tan Jing Quee and Jomo K.S. Kuala Lumpur: INSAN, 2001.

Henderson, J. "Ethnic Heritage as a Tourist Attraction: The Peranakans of Singapore". *International Journal of Heritage Studies* 9, no. 1 (March 2003): 27–44.

Hong, Lysa and Huang Jianli. "The Scripting of Singapore's Heroes: Toying with Pandora's Box". In *New Terrains in Southeast Asian History*, edited by Abu Talib Ahmad and Tan Liok Ee. Ohio, Athens and Singapore: Ohio University Press and Singapore University Press, 2003.

Ioffe, Grigory. "Understanding Belarus: Questions of Language". *Europe-Asia Studies* 55, no. 7 (2003): 1009–47.

Keane, Webb. "Public Speaking: On Indonesian as the Language of the Nation". *Public Culture* 15, no. 3 (2003): 503–30.

Kroskrity, Paul V. "Regimenting Languages: Language Ideological Perspectives". In *Regimes of Language: Ideologies, Polities, and Identities*, edited by Paul V. Kroskrity. Oxford: James Currey, 2000.

Kuo, Eddie C.Y. "Confucianism as Political Discourse in Singapore: The Case of an Incomplete Revitalization Movement". In *Confucian Traditions in East Asian Modernity: Moral Education and Economic Culture in Japan and the Four Mini-Dragons*, edited by Tu Wei-ming. Cambridge, MA: Harvard University Press, 1996.

Lee, Christine et al. "Children's Experiences of Multiracial Relationships in Informal Primary School Settings". In *Beyond Rituals and Riots: Ethnic Pluralism and Social Cohesion in Singapore*, edited by Lai Ah Eng. Singapore: Eastern Universities Press, 2004.

Lee, Guan Kin. "Singapore Chinese Society in Transition: Reflections on the Cultural Implications of Modern Education." In *Chinese Migrants Abroad: Cultural, Educational, and Social Dimensions of the Chinese Diaspora*, edited by Michael W. Charney, Brenda S.A. Yeoh and Tong Chee Kiong. Singapore: Singapore University Press and World Scientific, 2003.

Lee, Kuan Yew. *From Third World to First: The Singapore Story 1965–2000, Memoirs of Lee Kuan Yew*. Singapore: Singapore Press Holdings & Times Editions, 2000.

Lindsay, Jennifer and Tan Ying Ying, eds. *Babel or Behemoth: Language Trends in Asia*. Singapore: Asia Research Institute, National University of Singapore, 2003.

London, Norrel A. "Entrenching the English Language in a British Colony: Curriculum Policy and Practice in Trinidad and Tobago". *International Journal of Educational Development* 23 (2003): 97–112.

MacDougall, John A. and Chew Sock Foon. "English Language Competence and Occupational Mobility in Singapore". *Pacific Affairs* 49, no. 2 (Summer 1976): 294–312.

May, Stephen. *Language and Minority Rights: Ethnicity, Nationalism and the Politics of Language*. Harlow: Longman, 2001.

McArthur, Tom. "English as an Asian Language". *English Today* 19, no. 2 (April 2003): 19–22.

Miles, William F.S. "The Politics of Language Equilibrium in a Multilingual Society". *Comparative Politics* 32, no. 2 (January 2000): 215–30.

Ommmen, T.K. "Language and Nation: For a Cultural Renewal of India", *Asian Journal of Social Science* 31, no. 2 (2003): 286–303.

Ooi, Can-Seng. "Identities, Museums, and Tourism in Singapore: Think Regionally, Act Locally". *Indonesia and the Malay World* 31, no. 89 (March 2003): 80–90.

Pakir, Anne. "English-Knowing Bilingualism in Singapore". In *Imagining Singapore*, edited by Ban Kah Choon, Anne Pakir and Tong Chee Kiong. Singapore: Times Academic Press, 1992.

Pinches, Michael. "Cultural Relations, Class and the New Rich of Asia". In *Culture and Privilege in Capitalist Asia*, edited by Michael Pinches. London: Routledge, 1999.

PuroShotam, Nirmala Srirekam. *Negotiating Language, Constructing Race: Disciplining Race in Singapore*. Berlin: Mouton de Gruyter, 1998.

Ruby, Rani. "Creative Destruction: Singapore's Speak Good English Movement". *World Englishes* 20, no. 3 (2001): 341–55.

Sai, Siew Min and Huang Jianli. "The 'Chinese-educated' Political Vanguards: Ong Pang Boon, Lee Khoon Choy & Jek Yeun Thong". In *Lee's Lieutenants: Singapore's Old Guard*, edited by Lam Peng Er and Kevin Y.L. Tan. St Leonards, NSW: Allen & Unwin, 1999.

Saravana, Vanithami. "Indians in Multilingual and Multicultural Settings: Tamil Education in Singapore". In *Challenges Facing the Singapore Education System Today*, edited by Jason Tan, S. Gopinathan and Ho Wah Kam. Singapore: Prentice Hall, 2001.

Schneider, Edgar W. "The Dynamics of New Englishes: From Identity Construction to Dialect Birth". *Language* 79, no. 2 (June 2003): 233–81.

Sheffer, Gabriel. *Diaspora Politics: At Home Abroad*. Cambridge: Cambridge University Press, 2003.

Tamney, Joseph B. *The Struggle over Singapore's Soul: Western Modernization and Asian Culture*. Berlin: Walter de Gruyter, 1996.

Tan, Eugene K.B. "Re-engaging Chineseness: Political, Economic & Cultural Imperatives of Nation-Building in Singapore". *The China Quarterly* 175 (September 2003): 751–74.

Trocki, Carl A. "Development of Labour Organisation in Singapore, 1800–1960". *Australian Journal of Politics and History* 47, no. 1 (2001): 115–29.

United Nations Development Program. *The Arab Human Development Report 2003: Building a Knowledge Society*. New York: United Nations Development Program, 2003.

Van Der Kroef, Justus M. "Nanyang University and the Dilemma of Overseas Chinese Education". *The China Quarterly* 20 (Oct–Dec 1964): 96–127.

Vasil, Raj. *Asianizing Singapore: The PAP's Management of Ethnicity*. Singapore: Heinemann Asia, 1995.

Watson, Keith. "Rulers and Ruled: Racial Perceptions, Curriculum and Schooling in Colonial Malaysia and Singapore". In *The Imperial Curriculum: Racial Images and Education in the British Colonial Experience*, edited by J.A. Mangan. London: Routledge, 1993.

Wee, C.J. W.-L. *Culture, Empire, and the Question of Being Modern*. Lanham, MD: Lexington Books, 2003.

Wilson, H.E. *Social Engineering in Singapore: Educational Policies and Social Change 1819–1972*. Singapore: Singapore University Press, 1978.

Wong, Ting-Hong. *Hegemonies Compared: State Formation and Chinese School Politics in Postwar Singapore and Hong Kong*. New York: Routledge Falmer, 2002.

———. "Rethinking the Education/State Formation Connection: Pedagogic Reform in Singapore, 1945–1965". *Comparative Education Review* 46, no. 2 (May 2002): 182–210.

———. "Education and State Formation Reconsidered: Chinese School Identity in Postwar Singapore". *Journal of Historical Sociology* 16, no. 2 (June 2003): 237–65.

Government Sources

Government of Singapore. *White Paper on Singapore's Shared Values*. Cmd. 1 of 1991.

Media Development Authority. *Annual Report 2002/2003* (English version), available at <www.mda.gov.sg/MDA/documents/ACCESS_Annual_Report_English.pdf> (last accessed on 3 November 2004).

Media Development Authority. News release, "Allowing the use of dialect on television and radio", 30 April 2003.

Ministry of Education, Singapore. Education Study Team, *Report on Education*, 1978.

———. Moral Education Committee, *Report on Moral Education*, 1979.

———. Chinese Language Review Committee, *Chinese Language Teaching & Learning in Singapore: Report of the Chinese Language Review Committee*, 1992.

———. Committee on Compulsory Education in Singapore, *Report of the Committee on Compulsory Education in Singapore*, 2000.

———. *Education Statistics Digest* 2002.

———. "Non-Native Mother Tongue Language as a Third Language", <http://www.moe.gov.sg/press/2004/pr20040929c.htm> (last accessed 30 September 2004).

———. "Benefits of Studying a Third Language", <www.moe.gov.sg/moelc/benefits.htm> (last accessed on 30 October 2004).

———. "Refinements to Primary School Streaming", <http://www.moe.gov.sg/press/2004/pr20040318.htm> (last accessed on 31 October 2004).

———. White Paper on the Report of the Chinese Language Curriculum and Pedagogy Review Committee (Paper Cmd 9 of 2004).

Ministry of Information and the Arts. Promote Mandarin Council, "Mandarin: The Chinese Connection 2000", <http://mandarin.org.sg/>.

———. Censorship Review Committee Report, "Towards Greater Diversity". Singapore: Ministry of Information, Communications and the Arts, July 2003, <www.mica.gov.sg/pressroom/press_030904.html> (last accessed on 31 October 2004).

———. "Working Together Towards a Responsible and Vibrant Society", MICA's Response to the CRC Recommendations, 8 September 2003, <http://www.mica.gov.sg/pressroom/press_030908.pdf> (last accessed on 31 October 2004).
Remaking Singapore Committee. *Changing Mindsets, Deepening Relations*, 2003.
Singapore Legislative Assembly. *Report of the All-Party Committee of the Singapore Legislative Assembly on Chinese Education*. Singapore: Government Printing Office, 1956.

Newspapers
"More Dialect Shows on TV?". *Streats*, 27 February 2003.
"Fewer Here Reading and Writing Chinese". *Straits Times*, 7 March 2001.
"Will Chinese Become a Dumpling House Language?". *Straits Times*, 31 March 2001.
"Learn Chinese for Cultural Value, Say Some". *Straits Times*, 31 August 2002.
"Arresting the Chinese Language Decline". *Straits Times*, 5 May 2002.
"Plans for New School with Emphasis on Chinese". *Straits Times*, 12 October 2002.
"Only for the Weakest Kids, Please". *Straits Times*, 13 January 2003.
"Let's Hear it for Dialect". *Straits Times*, 5 March 2003.
"Teaching Chinese: English Serves as 'Float'". *Straits Times*, 6 March 2003.
"More Dialect Shows will Hit Mandarin Use". *Straits Times*, 10 March 2003.
"Bilingual Way to Learn Chinese 'Gives Support' ". *Straits Times*, 21 March 2003.
"Dialects on TV? Needs More Study". *Straits Times*, 18 April 2003.
"Pupils Aren't Mixing, Study Finds". *Straits Times*, 26 July 2003.
"Yes, there's Little Racial Mixing, but Schools are Trying: MOE". *Straits Times*, 31 July 2003.
"Why Pupils Should Mix". *Straits Times*, 31 July 2003.
"Learn Chinese for Culture or for Economics". *Straits Times*, 28 August 2002.
"More Chinese Language Students Opting for Plan B". *Straits Times*, 9 October 2003.
"Clear the CLB Cloud". *Straits Times*, 13 October 2003.
"Ministry to Review Criteria for Chinese 'B' Option". *Straits Times*, 17 October 2003.
"Hong Kong Schools May Teach in Mandarin". *Straits Times*, 22 October 2003.
"More Help for Kids Struggling with Chinese". *Straits Times*, 17 November 2003.
"Scholarship May Mean China Stint". *Straits Times Interactive*, 21 November 2003.
"Chinese Teaching to Go Flexible". *Straits Times*, 12 October 2004.

"Change needed as more speak English at home". *Straits Times Interactive*, 12 October 2004.
"Profit from Chinese, but Where's the Passion?". *Straits Times Interactive*, 29 October 2004.
"Back to Gong Hokkien on TV". *Today*, 27 February 2003.
"Singapore, Love Thy Neighbours". *Today*, 28 October 2003.
Deputy Prime Minister Lee Hsien Loong's interview with *Berita Harian*, published on 23 and 24 October 2003.

Ministerial Speeches

Goh Chok Tong. National Day Rally Speech in Mandarin, 24 August 1997.
———. *Lianhe Zaobao* 75th Anniversary Gala Dinner, 6 September 1998.
———. National Day Rally Speech, 22 August 1999.
———. National Day Rally Speech, 18 August 2002.
———. 5th World Anxi Convention and the 80th Anniversary of the Singapore Ann Kway Association, 9 November 2002.
Lee Hsien Loong. Ministerial Statement on Chinese Language in Schools in Parliament, 20 January 1999.
———. Opening ceremony of the Char Yong building, 3 December 2002.
———. Opening of the Chinese High Boarding School, 10 January 2003.
———. Opening ceremony of the 12th Teochew International Conference, 22 November 2003.
Lee Kuan Yew. (Tanjong Pagar Constituency's) 34th National Day Celebration, 14 August 1999.
———. *Lianhe Zaobao* 80th Anniversary Gala Dinner, 6 September 2003.
Lim Swee Say. Chinese Cultural Festival Opening, 1 March 2002.
Tharman Shanmugaratnam. "Effective Teaching and Learning of the Mother Tongue: Innovating and Adapting to New Circumstances", speech delivered at "The Significance of Speaking Skills For Language Development" Seminar, 15 February 2003.
———. Hindi Centres' Day 2003, 2 August 2003.
———. Opening ceremony of the 'Conference on the Cultures of Southeast Asia', 22 August 2003.
———. Eurasian Association Education Awards Ceremony, 30 August 2003.
———. Tamil Murasu's Most Inspiring Tamil Language Teacher Award Presentation Ceremony, 4 October 2003.
———. 12th Singapore Young Calligraphers' Exhibition, 18 October 2003.
George Yeo. Speak Mandarin Campaign Launch, 12 September 1998.

Others

Presslines, July 2003, pp. 3–7, 18–19 (*Presslines* is the monthly journal of the Singapore Press Holdings, the publisher of *Zaobao*).
Speak Good English Movement. <www.goodenglish.org.sg/SGEM/>.

Legislation
Republic of Singapore Independence Act (Act 9 of 1965), 1985 Revised Edition
Constitution of the Republic of Singapore, 1999 Revised Edition.

6

Ethnic Politics, National Development and Language Policy in Malaysia

Lee Hock Guan

INTRODUCTION

One could argue that Malay nationalism, after the Japanese Occupation, was largely one that imagined the nation in terms of a people sharing a common culture and language; that is, the nation as a culturally and linguistically homogenous entity. While this led the Malay nationalists to take for granted that the future Malay(si)an national culture and identity should be fashioned out of their own, nevertheless, various factors and circumstances prevented them from pursuing an unambiguously assimilationist policy. This paper indeed will trace how language and education policy in post-Independence Malay(si)a became circumscribed and shaped by the politics of inter-ethnic bargaining, or "consociational politics", that arose in the post-World War Two period and became, subsequently, the dominant political form in the country.

In a nutshell, conflicts over the language and education issues had oscillated between the Malays' aims to consolidate the status of their mother tongue as the sole official language and main medium of instruction on the one hand, and the Chinese's insistence on their language rights as Malaysian citizens, including a state-funded Chinese-medium primary and secondary education system, on the other hand. In a sense, Tunku Abdul Rahman, the first Prime Minister, accurately observed that the language controversies have never been over Malay language as the sole national language, as everyone accepts this, but rather about Malay as the sole official language and main medium of instruction.[1]

The first two sections of this paper examine the language and education issues prior to the achievement of political independence; the formation of a multilingual society and multilingual education system prior to World War Two, and then how the emerging politics of consociation shaped the language and education discourses and policies. The third section focuses on the immediate post-Independence period's escalating passionate language and education controversies. The fourth section examines the rise of Malay dominance and the institutionalization of Malay language as the sole official language and main medium of instruction. The final section shows how globalization has led to the re-emergence of a limited multilingual education system in Malaysia.

BILINGUAL STATE AND MULTILINGUAL EDUCATION BEFORE THE SECOND WORLD WAR (WWII)

Prior to WWII, even though colonial rule had transformed Malaya into a multilingual society, language and education policies were not formulated to facilitate the construction of a common national community and identity. Rather, the colonial state adopted a laissez faire approach that was influenced by three key factors, which at times were at odds with one another. One factor, the British State's designation of Malays as the indigenous group and Chinese as "alien residents" led to the adoption of differential language and educational policies towards the different ethnic groups. Secondly, the formation of colonial language and education policies was also dictated by economic considerations, such as the costs of financing education and the demand of "educated manpower for government service and the commercial economy". Thirdly, the success of an Orientalist view that favoured education in the vernacular language, over an Anglicist approach that supported English-medium education, decisively shaped the development of colonial education policy (Loh 1975, pp. 2–4; Pennycock 2001, pp. 51–53, 56–57).[2]

British Malaya was administered in the form of two distinct colonial entities: the Crown Colony of the Straits Settlements (SS) and the Protected Malay States (PMS) of the Federated and Unfederated Malay States.[3] While the SS came under the direct rule of the British Crown, the PMS came under British indirect rule,[4] formally introduced into the PMS through treaty agreements with the various Malay Rulers. Since the Malay States were classified as Protected States, it meant that they were recognized as sovereign governments, which were established by Malays, the indigenous group, and presided over by Malay Rulers.

British indirect rule endeavoured to tweak the indigenous political systems so as to facilitate economic development, while preserving as much as possible their Malay character and social structure. A feature found in all the PMS was a shared common language of governance, the Malay, or Melayu, language. Although spoken Melayu varied from place to place, the official script throughout the peninsula was Jawi.[5] The British kept Melayu as an official language of the PMS,[6] but began, starting in the last decade of the nineteenth century, to romanize its written form. Importantly, in later negotiations with the British, a few of the Malay elites demanded that Melayu be formally designated as an official language; for example, the Kedah Treaty of 1 November 1923 stipulated that Melayu should be the official language "in all departments of the Government of Kedah except where it is provided in the law of the State or by special authority of Government that any other language may be used".

However, although Melayu was retained as an official language, in practice, the colonial State largely used English as the working language of governance. The official usage of English in fact became more and more prevalent over time with the expansion of the size and function of the colonial administrative apparatus and the recruitment of increasing numbers of non-Malays[7] and non-Melayu-speaking British into the colonial service. English also became the foremost language of communication in the local and federal legislative councils, among the colonial elites and professional class, as well as, with the growing presence of British businesses,[8] gained wider usage in the business world. Thus, although Melayu and English were both official languages, by and large official communications and documents were in English only; indeed, in practice, the colonial State's treatment of Melayu was only slightly better than that of the Chinese and Indian languages. Moreover, in the urban areas, one would find more public signboards displayed in Chinese and English, than the official language Melayu.

In colonial Malaya, the British felt obliged to look after first, the Malay ruling elites, their "partners" in the business of governance, and second, the Malay subjects. Acting as the Malays' trustees, the British claimed to administer the PMS on behalf of and for the benefit of the Malays. Hugh Clifford, one of the earliest and important Malayan pioneers, insisted that "the public servants to whom is entrusted the task of administering and developing" the Malay States should be aware "that the welfare and well-being of the indigenous inhabitants [i.e. Malays] must always be the first care of the Federal and State Governments".[9] In contrast, British policy towards the Chinese continued to regard them as foreigners who did not "belong" to Malaya; a policy that was only revised after WWII. The colonial State hence felt morally obliged to, among other things, educate the Malays, but not the Chinese.

A dual track strategy was constructed by the colonial State in the provision of education for the Malays; one for the ruling elites and the other for the commoners. While selected members of the ruling elites were given an English education to prepare them for service in the colonial State, for the commoner, a Melayu education was thought sufficient. Government-funded Melayu vernacular schools were built to provide free education for Malay boys and girls throughout Malaya (Loh 1975, pp. 13–15; Stevenson 1975; Rosnani 2004 (1996), pp. 44–61). The primary objective of colonial education for the Malay commoners was:

> not to turn out a few well-educated youths nor a number of less well-educated boys: rather it [was] to improve the bulk of the people and to make the son of a fisherman or the peasant a more intelligent fisherman or peasant than his father had been, and one whose education will enable him to understand how his life fits in with the scheme of life around him (Maxwell in Kratoska 1983, p. 406).[10]

Colonial education policy for the Malays hence was designed not to upset the existing Malay social structure. It tried to keep " a balance between an elite English education for the minority destined to be "administrators" and an elementary but practical education for the great bulk of the people required to remain as "cultivators" (Stevenson 1975).

After their British India experience, the British became wary of furnishing an English-medium education to their colonial subjects — in Malaya, the Malays in particular. Swettenham warned that "it is not advisable to teach English indiscriminately" because a "mere smattering of English and English ideas … is harmful, and which in India causes the country to "swarm with half-starved, discontented men, who consider manual labour beneath them, because they know a little English" (Barlow 1995, p. 337). Thus, in spite of of their stated objective to "educate a small number of young noblemen in English so that they might enter the service of the Government" (Stevenson 1975, p. 194), it was only after the departure of Swettenham that the Malay College Kuala Kangsar (MCKK) was established in 1905.[11]

In contrast to the colonial State's reticence about providing English education, Christian missionaries, motivated by the "civilizing mission" and desire to convert the "heathens" to Christianity, became important purveyors of English education in the colony (Loh 1975, Chapter III). Since missionary schools were only allowed in non-Muslim areas, and were largely located in towns, they enrolled primarily Chinese and Indian students, who saw an English education as a means to employment in the colonial service or British companies. Initially, Malays were suspicious of the missionary schools, but, by the 1910s, an "increasing Malay demand for English had arisen" (ibid, p. 52). After the First World War, expansion of the administrative machinery and British business in the colony forced the colonial State to grudgingly expand the English education system, though this should not be interpreted as a radical departure from the Orientalist view.

As early as 1872, the colonial State-supported schools were classified into two categories: "government schools" which were managed and financed by government, and "aided schools" which were controlled by civil society groups and received government grants-in-aid. Melayu vernacular schools, which were managed and financed by the colonial State, were of course government schools. English schools fell into both categories, some funded and managed by the colonial State, while the missionary schools who received grants-in-aid became "aided schools". Hence, the official languages-medium schools were either government or aided schools.

The colonial State, however, did not feel obliged to provide the Chinese community with education because it regarded them as transient aliens. Conversely, the majority of Chinese also saw themselves as sojourners and did not expect, or press, the colonial State to take care of their educational needs. The Chinese thus established, financed and managed the development of Chinese schools by and for themselves. Besides providing their children with the " three Rs", Chinese schools were also viewed as transmissions of Chinese culture and identity.[12] Also, the British colonial State did not compel students in the Chinese schools to learn either of the official languages as subjects.

The founding of the Republic of China in 1919 led, in Malaya, to a rise in demand for Chinese education, proliferation of new schools and, above all, politicization of the schools.[13] While previously the colonial State left the Chinese to manage, administer and fund their schools, the increasing politicization of the schools led the British to introduce steps to regulate and control them.[14] One of the methods adopted by the colonial State to curtail nationalist and leftist politics in Chinese schools was that of government financial assistance (Loh 1975, pp. 92–100). On the one side, Chinese schools were torn between needing state funds to address perennial financial shortfalls and the strong desire to protect their autonomy. On the other side, although the colonial State wanted to exert control over the Chinese schools, it was reluctant to incur the additional financial burden that funding the Chinese schools would result in. Consequently, by 1938, federal grants to Chinese schools made up only 1.5 per cent of the total federation education expenditure, which meant that the majority of Chinese schools continued to be completely self-funded and autonomous.

In summary, Melayu, the language of governance of the indigenous State, and English, the language of the British imperial State, assumed the status of official languages in British Malaya. But, as the British were not concerned with formulating and implementing language and educational policies to build a nation-state, the Chinese were not forced to learn or be taught in any of the official languages; instead, they were permitted to build schools that taught in their own mother tongue. The colonial State financially supported the Melayu and English schools, including providing grants-in-aid to missionary schools, but left the Chinese schools to source their own funds; except from the 1920s, when a few Chinese schools were provided with some public funds as a means to control them. Although the British felt obliged to educate the Malays, that obligation was circumscribed by the prevalence of the Orientalist view, which feared the dangers of furnishing English education to and over-education of the natives. Prior to WWII then, the language and education landscape in colonial Malaya was rather multifaceted: a bilingual official language, Melayu was the lingual franca, a multilingual society and education system, and the majority of Malays educated in Melayu schools, Chinese in Chinese schools, Indians in Indian schools, and a minority of each ethnic group in English schools.

BETWIXT BILINGUALISM AND MULTILINGUALISM

After WWII, the de-colonization of British Malaya divided colonial officials into one group "in favour of making the old system work better" and another "advocating a break with the past" (Stockwell 1979, p. 164). While the former advocated a return to the pre-WWII, pro-Malay policy,[15] the latter proposed the creation of a Malayan Union with a common national citizenship, where every fully recognized citizen would have equality of rights, regardless of ethnicity or place of birth.[16] The Malayan Union Plan was rejected and defeated by the Malays, led by the United

Malay National Organization (UMNO), who successfully re-negotiated a return to a pro-Malay policy, albeit modified. The 1948 Federation of Malaya (*Persekutuan Tanah Melayu*) Agreement[17] signified a major victory for UMNO-led Malay nationalists.

Convinced by the then predominant concept of nation as a culturally homogenous community, Malay nationalists[18] envisioned making Melayu the sole national and official language. The 1948 Federation Agreement indeed officially sanctioned Melayu as the sole national and official language. Aware that the Melayu language had fallen in use in spite of its official language status in colonial Malaya, in post-WWII, Malay nationalists insisted that it be given equal usage and application as English.[19] To foster the development of a common national community and identity, they were determined to re-make the pre-WWII multilingual education system into a Melayu-medium national education system, open to children of all ethnic groups, provided they qualified as citizens.

In 1951, the colonial State established the Barnes Committee to look into the state of education of the Malays. Largely influenced by the Malay nationalists,[20] the Barnes Report asserted: "We have given prolonged thought to the language question. It has been clear throughout that two languages, and only two languages should be taught in the National Schools, and that those two must be official languages of the country, namely, Melayu and English." (Barnes Report 1951, Article 7) If a bilingual education system were established, then the Chinese would have to give up their vernacular schools and send their children to Melayu or English schools. In other words, this would mean the elimination of the pre-WWII multilingual education system.

The Barnes Committee rationale was that the establishment of a bilingual national education system would facilitate the development of a common national identity and community. Hence, the Barnes Report stated:

> We have set up bilingualism in Malay and English as its objective because we believe that all parents who regard Malaya as their permanent home and the object of their undivided loyalty will be happy to have their children educated in those languages. If any parents were not happy about this, their unhappiness would properly be taken as an indication that they did not so regard Malaya. On the other hand, all non-Malay parents who avail themselves of the new facilities, and who set aside their vernacular attachments in the interests of a new social unity, have a right to

be welcomed without reserve by the Malay people as fellow-builders and fellow-citizens." (Barnes Report 1951, Article 18)

While the Chinese accepted Melayu as the sole national language, they strongly objected to the Barnes Report anointment of Melayu and English as the only official languages and establishment of a bilingual national education system. Given the precarious political conditions then, with the communist insurrection in full force, the colonial State, afraid of pushing the Chinese into the arms of the communists, agreed to the Chinese demands to look into their educational needs. In 1951, the colonial State established the Fenn-Wu Committee[21] to review the Chinese education and schools in the colony.

In contrast to the Malay nationalists' aim to establish a culturally homogeneous national community, the Fenn-Wu Report clearly supported the idea of constructing a national community that would preserve the existing multiculturalism found in the peninsula:

> By virtue of its composite population it should be a land where the developing culture draws its validity from acceptance of the high values of other cultures. The people of Malaya will have to learn to understand and appreciate their cultural differences. They should be proud of their spirit of mutual tolerance. (ibid, p. 4)

The Fenn-Wu Report thus argued against the Barnes Report's proposal to create a Malay rather than a 'Malayan' society because it would result in "the elimination of Chinese schools" and relegate "the Chinese language to an inferior status, with the ultimate result, if not the present purpose, of the extinction of Chinese culture in Malaya" (ibid, p. 5).

Consequently, the Fenn-Wu Report would have accepted the establishment of a multilingual national education system where the media of instruction would be Melayu, because it is the national and official language, English, because it is a world language and the language of business, science, and so on, and Chinese and Tamil, because they are "great language[s] of the world and key[s] to [two] of the world's great culture[s]" (ibid, p. 6). The Report asserted that most Chinese would be trilingual because for practical reasons they would see the advantages of learning Melayu and English and "would probably accept" them as "required subjects in … Chinese primary school".

The Barnes and Fenn-Wu Reports hence proposed diametrically opposing educational systems; while the former proposed the construction of a bilingual Melayu and English educational system, the latter "advocated a pluralistic and open approach which would allow schools teaching in different languages to be part of the Malayan system of education" (Tan 1997, p. 59). Towards the end of 1951, the colonial State established another committee, the Central Advisory Committee (CAC), to review the Barnes and Fenn-Wu Reports. But because the CAC was unduly influenced by UMNO and Malay nationalists, as well as by pro-Malay British officials, its proposals, which were incorporated in the 1952 Education Ordinance, largely reflected the Barnes Report's suggestions with only a "token gesture to the Fenn-Wu Report" (Kua 1999, p. 43).

The 1952 Education Ordinance proposed the establishment of a bilingual national school system, where schools would be in either Melayu or English medium, with the longer view of establishing a Melayu-medium only national school system. It also suggested that the English and Chinese schools should gradually be converted to "become multi-racial National Schools ... and in return for full government aid, these schools should be expected to conform to conditions in Government National Schools" (Education Ordinance 1952, p. 21). In other words, since National Schools would be in Melayu medium only, it meant that Chinese schools that received full government assistance would eventually have to convert to Melayu medium. As a compromise, the Ordinance proposed a Pupils Own Language (POL) concession where Mandarin and Tamil would be provided "to those children whose parents so desire where there are at least fifteen pupils in any standard" (Tan 1997, p. 62).

The Chinese educationist movement or Dongjiaozong[22] was critical of the 1952 Education Ordinance and argued vociferously for the building of a multiethnic and multicultural nation "in which there would be equal treatment and respect for the languages and cultures of all races" (ibid, p. 284). For the Dongjiaozong, as citizens, the Chinese have the right to be instructed in their mother tongue, their language be granted official language status, and Chinese schools be included in the national education system.

At that time, the Dongjiaozong had the support of and worked closely with the Malayan Chinese Association (MCA) to protect and advance Chinese language and education. Subsequently, when the MCA and UMNO formed a coalition to contest the 1955 general election, the two parties had to iron out, among other things, the Chinese language and education issues.[23] The UMNO-MCA negotiations led to the inclusion of a number of issues raised by the Dongjiaozong into the Alliance Agreement (Tan 1997, pp. 155–60). In return, the Dongjiaozong promised "not to raise the issue of Chinese as an official language until after the 1955 elections" (ibid, p. 285).

Selected elements of the Alliance Agreement were subsequently incorporated in the Razak Committee's 1956 Report — which became the blueprint of the national education system in post-independent Malaysia. The Razak Committee's task was to set an educational policy that would be "acceptable to the people of the Federation as a whole" with the "guiding principle ... to make Malay the national language of the country whilst preserving and sustaining the growth of the languages and cultures of non-Malay peoples living in the country" (Razak Report 1956, Articles 8 and 9). This guiding principle, however, juxtaposed ambiguously with Article 12:

> the ultimate objective of educational policy in this country must be to bring together the children of all races under a national development system in which the national language is the major medium of instruction, though we recognize that progress towards this goal cannot be rushed and must be gradual.

At the primary school level, the Razak Report proposed the establishment of two type of schools: a National Primary School in Melayu medium, and a National-type Primary School in which the language of instruction may be English, Tamil or Mandarin (Article 13a). At the secondary school level, although it recommended a single type of National Secondary School, the Razak Report also asserted that there must be "some flexibility", and specifically mentioned there was no reason to alter "the practice in Chinese secondary schools of using Kuo Yu as a general medium provided that these Chinese schools" accept teaching Melayu, because it was the national language and everybody was expected to know it, and English, for pragmatic reasons, as compulsory subjects. The Chinese secondary schools were, however, expected to follow a common syllabus and work towards common examinations set by the State.

Importantly, although many in the Malay community were critical of the Razak Report — accusing it of letting down Melayu as the sole national and official language and making too many concessions to the Chinese — the UMNO leaders strongly defended the terms of the Report. Conversely, despite strong objections from the Dongjiaozong, the Government insisted that the two common secondary school public examinations would only be offered in the two official languages, English and Melayu. For the Chinese schools that received state financial assistance, the Government dictated that to continue receiving funding they would have to prepare their students for the two common secondary school public examinations by 1957, later negotiations extended it to 1961, which meant that the Chinese schools would have to convert to English medium.

Although the Dongjiaozong endorsed Chinese as an official language, it refrained from pushing this issue because of the overriding "common objective of wanting an end to British rule" (Tan 1997, p. 285). Recognizing the existing multilingual conditions, the Reid Commission[24] proposed that Chinese and Tamil be accepted along with English and Melayu as official languages of the country for a period of ten years or more after Independence. UMNO, Malay nationalist groups, and former Malayan British officials were adamantly against the idea of a multilingual official languages policy and rejected this proposal. In the end, a compromise reached between UMNO, MCA and the British was integrated into the Constitution in Article 152 where Melayu was granted the status of sole national and official language. The role of English as an official language was to be continued for, and evaluated, ten years after Independence, and the non-Malays would not be "prohibited or prevented from using (otherwise than for official purposes), or from teaching or learning" their mother tongues.

POST-INDEPENDENCE LANGUAGE AND EDUCATION CONTROVERSIES AND STRUGGLES

Immediately after Independence, the ambiguities of the Alliance compromise on language and education issues, which were incorporated into the Razak Report and 1957 Education Ordinance, quickly generated heated controversies and mounting opposition. On the one side, Malay language nationalists intensified their pressure on the Government to entrench Melayu as the sole national and official language and establish a Melayu monolingual education system. Moreover, they objected vociferously to the idea of extending English as an official language beyond the stipulated ten years after Independence. On the other side, the Dongjiaozong intensified their campaign to have Chinese granted official language status, Chinese primary schools be granted equal status as Melayu and English schools, and the inclusion of Chinese secondary schools in the national secondary school system.

Disappointed with the MCA over the failure of the party to protect Chinese language and education in the run-up to Independence, the Dongjiaozong began to turn to the non-Malay opposition political parties for support. Also, an emerging group of MCA leaders, led by Lim Chong Eu, tried to win back the Dongjiaozong by pressuring UMNO to reconsider the Chinese language and education issues. UMNO, when it was clear that their Malay electoral base would not accept any changes to the language and education compromises, and that the Islamic Party of Malaysia (PAS) was fishing for Malay votes by manipulating the language and education issues, refused to revise the terms of the compromises.[25]

Needless to say, the 1960 Talib Report proposals further heightened the Dongjiaozong's concern over the future of the Chinese language and schools. While the Talib Report reiterated its support for the provision of primary education in each of the four main languages with full state funding and promised "to preserve and sustain the four main languages and cultures of Malaysia" (p. 13), the Report's Article 18 also states:

It would, however, be incompatible with an educational policy designed to create national consciousness and having the intention of making the Malay language the national language of the country to extend and to perpetuate a language and racial differential throughout the publicly-financed educational system.

For the Dongjiaozong, Article 18 could be interpreted to mean that in the long term, the national education system must be Melayu medium only, which would spell the gradual elimination of the state-supported primary Chinese schools.

Furthermore, the Report also suggested that public-funded secondary schools "shall be conducted mainly in the medium of one of the two official languages with the intention of ultimately using the national language as the main medium of instruction, except that other languages and literatures may be taught and learnt in their own media" (Article 19). In other words, the Talib Report proposed the elimination of Chinese secondary schools from the national system and thus students of all races would have no choice but to attend Melayu or English secondary schools. To further facilitate this policy, the Talib Report suggested that all public examinations at secondary level be "conducted only in the country's official languages" (Article 175) and, in fact, Article 187 recommended outright the gradual discontinuation of Chinese secondary schools and their respective examinations.

An ultimatum was thus given to the Chinese secondary schools by the Talib Report; to receive state funding and remain in the national education system, they must conform fully to the requirements of a national-type secondary school, in other words, convert to English medium. The UMNO-dominated Government was uncompromising in not extending the deadline beyond 1961 and hence Chinese secondary schools had to make their decision before 1 January 1962. Consequently, "given that government financial assistance was vital to the survival of many of the Chinese secondary schools, more than half the forty-one Chinese secondary schools had little choice but to comply with the ultimatum and ... converted to English-medium 'National-Type' " (Kua 1999, p. 83). Chinese secondary schools that refused to comply, and thus deprived themselves of any government recognition and financial support, became the Independent Chinese Secondary Schools (ICSS). For the ICSS, while they used Chinese as the medium of instruction, they also had to teach Malay and English as compulsory subjects as well as follow the same syllabus as the public secondary schools. However, the ICSS set and conducted their own examinations, which were not accredited by the Government and thus could not be use for admission into local public tertiary institutions.

Spurned by the Talib Report and the 1961 Education Ordinance, the Dongjiaozong ratcheted up its campaign to get Chinese recognized as an official language and for Chinese secondary schools to be included in the national secondary school system. Non-Malay opposition parties became the Chinese education movement's strongest supporters in advancing their language and education objectives.

The Dongjiaozong's rigorous challenge alarmed the Malays and prodded some of them, especially Malay intellectuals and teachers, to form the National Language Action Front (NLAF) in 1964.[26] Besides stridently voicing their support for Melayu to be the sole national and official language, the NLAF also insisted that the State take steps to entrench the Melayu language after 1967. Consequently, the NLAF made several demands (Funston 1980, pp. 63–67) such as: multilingual news broadcasts by radio and televisions be abolished by 1967 and after which, be broadcasted in Melayu only; college and university students be promoted to second year only if they pass a Melayu course; Form Five students would be eligible for college and university admissions only if they pass a compulsory Melayu subject; and university and college lecturers would be given two years to learn Melayu language and if they failed to master it by that time, they would be sternly dealt with.

The language and education controversies heightened as the deadline 1967 approached; that is, the 1957 Constitution suggestion that "after a period of ten years … and thereafter until Parliament otherwise provides, the English Language may be used in both Houses of Parliament, in the Legislative Assembly of every state, and for all other official purpose" (Article 11). The Alliance Government decided to use the occasion to formulate a national language policy and as such, tabled the National Language Bill in Parliament in 1967. Opposing sides of the language and education spectrum rigorously canvassed for their respective positions before and as the National Language Bill was debated in Parliament.[27] Predictably, while UMNO and PAS came down on the side of the NLAF, the non-Malay opposition parties supported the Dongjiaozong's position; the MCA leadership, however, was divided.

The 1967 National Language Bill rejected the Dongjiaozong's demands to grant Chinese official language status and include Chinese secondary schools in the national secondary schools. Although UMNO concurred with the NLAF to make Melayu the sole national and official language, its top leadership, however, sought to extend the official usage of English beyond 1967. Hence the 1967 National Language Bill stipulates that:

> (a) Federal and state governments could use translations of official documents or communications in other languages where this was considered necessary; (b) the Yang Di-Pertuan Agung could permit the continued use of English for such official purposes as are deemed fit; (c) English could continue to be used in the federal parliament or state legislatures with the sanction of the speaker or president; (d) bills and ordinances would continue to be published in English; and (e) proceedings in federal court could be conducted in English" (Funston 1980, p. 73).

Led by the NLAF, a broad spectrum of Malay groups, including factions from within UMNO, raised a number of objections over the National Language Bill. Besides their disapproving the preservation of Chinese and Indian primary schools, the NLAF were also very critical of the decision to extend the usage of English in official capacity beyond 1967. Indeed, the NLAF "considered the concessions a betrayal of the Malay cause and accused the Tunku [Abdul Rahman] of having sold the Malays down the drain" (Kua 1999, p. 90). On the other side, the

Dongjiaozong became disillusioned with their failure to get the Government to recognize Chinese as an official language and reinstate the status of Chinese secondary schools. The Chinese educationists were particularly frustrated with the MCA's refusal to support their language and educational objectives.

Invariably, the language and education policies and issues featured prominently in the 1969 General Election campaign. On the one side, the Dongjiaozong mobilized the Chinese community to support the non-Malay opposition parties, who proclaimed their support to make Chinese an official language,[28] the maintenance of the four language streams of primary education, the recognition of Chinese secondary schools, and, above all, the "equal treatment of all educational institutions irrespective of race" (Means 1976, p. 394). On the other side, PAS roundly condemned the Dongjiaozong's demands and extending the official usage of English beyond 1967, which garnered party support especially from the NLAF and their supporters. Undoubtedly, the language and education issues contributed to the major setback suffered by the Alliance, especially the MCA, in the 1969 General Election. When a series of events culminated in ethnic rioting on 13 May 1969, the crisis was seized by UMNO as an opportunity to restructure the political, economic and cultural, including language and education, landscape of the nation.

ENTRENCHING A PARTIAL BILINGUALISM

In the aftermath of the 1969 ethnic rioting, UMNO leaders successfully "persuaded" a number of the non-Malay opposition political parties to form a new multiethnic coalition party, the National Front (Barisan Nasional or BN).[29] Unlike the Alliance, which was a democratic consociation of sorts,[30] in the BN, UMNO became the 'pre-eminent' party such that it clearly dictated the coalition's agendas and policies. For UMNO, after 1969, winning Malay electoral support became its number one priority and this has led successive UMNO-dominated governments to uphold and implement the New Economic Policy (NEP). UMNO also went about reconfiguring the electoral and political system in order to strengthen and entrench Malay dominance. In terms of language and educational policies, the Malay language nationalists', especially the NLAF's, demands gained considerable currency and influence during the NEP period.

One of the first steps taken by the UMNO-dominated Government was to put a lid on the passionate public debate on language policies. In the 1960s, the NLAF's aggressive push to entrench Melayu as the sole official language was countered by an equally forceful struggle by the Dongjiaozong to get Chinese elevated to official language status. The Malays interpreted the Chinese demand for a multilingual official languages policy as a direct challenge to Melayu as the sole official language, which they claim was stipulated in Article 152 of the Constitution. In 1971, the Government amended the Sedition Act[31] making it an offence to question the status of Melayu as the sole official language.[32] Effectively, this move made it not only an offence to question the status of Melayu as the official language, but also to advocate a multilingual official language policy.

In addition, because the meaning of "official purpose" in Article 152, which stipulated: "Bahasa Malaysia should be the National Language without preventing or prohibiting the use of other languages except for official purposes", was never properly defined, an amendment was made to clarify the term. "Official purpose" was taken to mean "the purpose of Government whether Federal or State and including the purpose of a public authority" and Article 162 defined "public authority" to mean: "the Yang di-Pertuan Agung, the Ruler or Governor of a State, the Federal Government, the Government of a State, a local authority, statutory authority exercising powers vested in it be Federal or State law, any court or tribunal, other than the Federal Court or High Courts, or any officer or authority appointed by or acting on behalf of any of those persons, courts, tribunals or authorities." Given its wide-ranging definition, "official purpose" has been interpreted to mean that Melayu would be the only language used in all public institutions and documents and communications. Indeed, the definition could even be, and had been, interpreted to sanction a public officer's refusal to serve a member of the public if the latter could or would not speak in Melayu. From the 1970s onwards then, the State forcefully pursued and implemented Melayu as the official language, which perhaps appeased the Malays, but definitely, alienated the Chinese.

The 1970s also marked the beginning of aggressive state policies to develop a common national identity in Malaysia.[33] In the realm of language, significant resources and energies were devoted to the development of the Melayu language in order to consolidate its status as the sole national and official language and the main medium of instruction for the purposes of fostering national unity and identity (Asmah 1982 and 1979). The notion of Melayu as the national language was linked to the restoration of the originally Malay character of the peninsula before

British colonization, albeit with modifications. In the state-controlled television and radio stations, steps were taken to switch most news broadcast and programmes to Melayu language at the expense of non-Malay news broadcast and programmes. National literature became equated with literature written in Melayu, and only movies and films produced in Melayu language were eligible for state funding.

The display of public signboards by private sector institutions and businesses became a hotly debated issue in the contest over language policies. The Malay language nationalists claimed that "to evolve a Malaysian identity of Malaysian cities and towns, such that they do not appear to be duplicates of Hong Kong or India, the people have to be made to realize that they have to go all the way to conform to the official language policy" (Asmah 1979, p. 47). That is, all public signboards, the State insisted, must appear in Melayu prominently. The Dongjiaozong, however, insisted that the Chinese as citizens have the right to display public signboards in their mother tongue as stipulated in Article 152: "... no person shall be prohibited or prevented from using (other than for official purposes) or for teaching or learning any other language." The State circumvented this argument by declaring that "signboards of shops and privately owned buildings is an instance of official language use", thus subjected to official language regulations. From the 1970s then, non-Malay languages experienced a shrinking presence in public spaces, which was most apparent in the urban areas where English and Chinese languages signboards historically dominated the landscape.

The gradual conversion of English schools to Melayu medium began in 1970 when the medium of instruction of Primary One in the English schools was switched to Melayu medium. At the secondary level, from 1973, all Arts subjects (History, Geography, etc.) in Form One were taught in Melayu, and from 1976, all subjects were taught in Melayu medium in Form One. Thus through a staggered approach, all primary and secondary English schools were converted to Melayu medium by 1982 such that 1983 marked the beginning of the use of Melayu for all subjects in the universities. Moreover, Melayu was made a compulsory subject in the Lower and Malaysian Certificate Examinations (LCE & MCE) such that a pass in this subject was necessary in order to obtain the two certificates.[34]

For pragmatic reasons, the State retained English as a second language that was taught as a compulsory subject from Primary One onwards in all schools at all levels. The importance attached to the English language was most evident at the university level where it was made a compulsory subject that students must pass to graduate. Although Melayu became the main medium of instruction for all subjects at university from 1983 onwards, nevertheless, in practice its implementation was, for many reasons, not consistently applied. One problem was the shortage of available reading materials in Melayu which meant that for many subjects the bulk of reading materials assigned were in English. Also, foreign university lecturers, employed because of the shortage of local expertise, were permitted to teach in English instead of Melayu. In some universities, at undergraduate level, certain courses in faculties such as Science, Engineering, Law, Dentistry and Medicine, were regularly granted permission to use English as the medium of instruction. Above all, at the graduate level, many of the faculties would conduct their courses in English, and the majority of Master and doctoral courses were indeed written in English (Asmah 2003, p. 90).[35]

A parallel trend that emerged with the staggered conversion of English primary schools to Melayu medium was the increasing enrolment of Chinese students in the Chinese primary schools. Indeed, by the 1990s, more than ninety per cent of Chinese primary school students were enrolled in the Chinese primary schools. In the urban areas, rising demand for Chinese primary education, coupled with the limited number of urban Chinese primary schools resulted in "over enrollment", especially in the Klang Valley. Yet, the State, for the most part, consistently refused to grant the Chinese permission to build more Chinese primary schools in the urban areas.[36] Moreover, although the Chinese primary schools are government-assisted schools, in practice, they were not treated equally, for example, they received far less funding than the national primary schools. Consequently, Chinese primary schools had to depend on financial contributions from their community and this has led to major discrepancies in the quality and wellbeing of the different Chinese schools.[37]

Several episodes in the 1980s led the Dongjiaozong, and the Chinese community in general, to doubt the UMNO-dominated State's sincerity in preserving the Chinese primary school. In 1980, the MOE declared its intention to implement a 'three R' (Reading, Writing and Arithmetic) system in all primary schools where the Chinese primary schools would teach Chinese as a subject and Mathematics in Chinese, and all other subjects were to be taught in Melayu. In 1984, the Kuala Lumpur Education Department issued a circular decreeing "all Chinese primary schools to use only Melayu in school assemblies and other functions" (Kua 1999, p. 131). In 1985, the MOE proposed to establish "integrated schools" where three schools of varied media of instruction were to be integrated.[38] Two years later, when Anwar Ibrahim, then the Minister of Education, announced the State's aim to appoint non-Mandarin-educated headmasters and senior assistants in Chinese primary schools, it triggered a robust response from the Chinese community.[39] Although all the above episodes were not implemented, they, nevertheless, reinforced the Dongjiaozong's, and the Chinese in general, suspicions that the UMNO-dominated State ultimately aimed to do away with Chinese primary schools.

In 1975, the Dongjiaozong announced its intention to establish a common examination, the Unified Examination Certificate (UEC), for the ICSS. The then Minister of Education, Dr Mahathir, ordered the Dongjiaozong to withdraw this move and alleged that the ICSS "were trying to set up a separate education system and that this would disrupt national unity" (Kua 1999, p. 106). However, the Dongjiaozong went ahead with the UEC simply because the ICSS students no longer could sit for the national secondary examinations which were first conducted in English and Melayu, and later only in Melayu. The Government refused to accredit the UEC and thus ICSS graduates could not apply for admission into local public universities. The Malaysian Government also refused accreditation to Taiwanese universities and Nanyang University, Singapore,[40] essentially the only places that would accept ICSS graduates in the 1970s and 1980s.

More generally, during the NEP period, conditions were such that Chinese students' tertiary educational opportunities became severely circumscribed. Chinese students, already facing a limited supply of tertiary educational opportunities in the country that then affected all students,[41] also found themselves discriminated by the implementation of an ethnic quota admission policy to increase Malay enrolment in tertiary education in 1971. Indeed, although the stipulated ethnic quota breakdown was fifty-five per cent Malays and forty-five per cent non-Malays, in practice, the in-take of Malay students into the university usually exceeded the fifty-five per cent target.

The combination of the ethnic quota admission policy, the limited supply of tertiary educational opportunities and the non-accreditation of Taiwan universities and Nanyang University propelled the Dongjiaozong to push for the establishment of the Merdeka University, a privately-funded Chinese-medium tertiary institution. This project was first conceived and promoted in the late 1960s. The Merdeka University movement received passionate support and financial support from a broad spectrum of the Chinese community, and indeed it was one of the few issues that would galvanize the majority of the Chinese population. The

UMNO-dominated State, however, would not budge on this issue and subsequently the Dongjiaozong mounted a long, losing legal battle against the Government to establish the Merdeka University in the 1980s.

GLOBALIZATION AND THE RETURN OF MULTILINGUALISM

From the 1990s onwards, two key features of globalization as well as the emerging worldwide multicultural discourses led to major shifts in the language and education policies and developments in Malaysia.[42] One key feature of globalization was the growing intensification of economic competition among nations, which forced the Malaysian State to speed up its objective to develop a knowledge economy. A second feature is related to the rise of China as an emerging economic power in the world. These two features had, however, different impacts; one led to the resurrection of English as an important medium of instruction, and the other to freeing up the space for Chinese language and education.

To transform Malaysia into a knowledge-based economy would entail, among other things, upgrading the skill and knowledge levels of the country's human resource. In the 1990s, the Malaysian State began to expand its tertiary education sector so as to increase the supply of knowledge workers; in the public education sector, the number of polytechnics increased from seven in 1990 to eleven in 2004, and the number of universities from seven to eighteen during the same period. More significantly was the State's decision to allow and encourage the private sector, in this case meaning businesses, to play a larger role in the provision of tertiary education. To facilitate and regularize the entry of businesses into the tertiary education sector, the State formulated and implemented the Private Higher Education Institutions Act in 1996.[43]

The growth of private tertiary education has been most impressive indeed; the number of private colleges increased from 280 in 1995 to 611 in 1999, local private universities and university colleges from none in 1995 to nineteen in 1999, and five foreign universities had established branch campuses in Malaysia since 1999. Consequently, in 1990 the enrolment of students in the public and private institutions was 122,340 and 35,600 respectively, but, by 2000, the enrolment in the private institutions had surpassed the public institutions; 203,391 to 167,507.

A consequence of the privatization of education was that it led to the re-emergence of English as an important medium of instruction at the tertiary education level. Private tertiary institutions have existed since Independence, and English had always been its medium of instruction simply because the certificate and diploma courses offered were franchised from primarily British-based institutions. When the private education sector expanded in the 1990s, especially with the introduction of twinning programmes[44] with American, British and Australian tertiary institutions, this also enhanced the role of English as a medium of instruction. Unsurprisingly, when the State was revising the higher education policy in order to permit private tertiary institutions to conduct and grant undergraduate, and later graduate, degrees in English medium, Malay language nationalists and their supporters protested because they felt that this would dilute Malay as the main medium of instruction. For utilitarian reasons,[45] the State stood firm and permitted the private education sector to use English as the medium of instruction, but, nevertheless, as a compromise, insisted that "the national language shall be taught as a compulsory subject" (Education Act 1996, s. 23).[46]

More importantly, the status and function of English medium in the national education system received a major boost as a result of new state policies in the 1990s. Among the Malay political and administrative elites, there was a growing sentiment that the switch to Malay as the medium of instruction has not helped, indeed it may have retarded the growth of scientific and technical knowledge and research in the country, especially among the Malays.[47] It was to redress the falling standards and dismal knowledge of science and technology that led the State to reintroduce English as the medium of instruction for subjects in these areas. English competency was judged to be necessary in order to upgrade the skills and knowledge of the country's human resource, especially in the information and communication technologies, which form the bedrock of a knowledge economy.

English is of course also the language of business, both locally, in spite of the State's aggressive promotion of Melayu as the sole official and national language, and globally (Gill 2002). In the local context, English has continued to be the main language of communication in the world of business, especially among the professional and executive classes. Indeed, since English is still the dominant language in multinational corporations and Malaysian economic growth remains dependent on foreign investments, an individual's lack of command of the English language would be a major handicap. As a matter of fact, in the 1990s it emerged that the employability of public universities graduates had become negatively affected by their poor command of the English language — and the majority of them were Malays.[48]

When the State decided to reintroduce English as the medium of instruction for science and technical subjects, there were, however, emotional objections from Malay language nationalists who argued that it would diminish Melayu as the medium of instruction and that, in turn, would weaken its status as the national language and role in the construction of a national identity. Nevertheless, the then Prime Minister, Dr Mahathir, insisted that "learning the English Language will reinforce the spirit of nationalism when it is used to bring about development and progress for the country ... True nationalism means doing everything possible for the country, even if it means learning English language" (Mahathir cited in Gill 2002, p. 41) In fact, as early as the 1990s, Dr Mahathir was already convinced that Malays needed to master English in order to upgrade their scientific and technical knowledge and skills as well as for the community to stay relevant and competitive in the increasingly globalized knowledge economy.[49]

In December 1993, Dr Mahathir announced that universities in Malaysia would be allowed to use English as a medium of instruction in courses related to science and technology. Two years later in 1995, the MOE issued an education guideline that permitted public universities and higher institutions to

> determine the percentage of their courses to be taught in English and this should be in accordance with the relevance and needs of the use of the language, as well as with the ability of these institutions to conduct academic courses in the language. Apart from this, a hundred percent use of English is allowed if the courses concerned are taught by foreign lecturers, or if the courses are post-graduate ones which are attended by foreign students as well. ... The guideline also proposes that these institutions should increase the use of English in tutorials, seminars, assignments etc. (cited in Asmah 2003, p. 91)

The Government thus "gave the legal green light to [higher educational] institutions to seek official approval" for the use of English medium in the science and technical subjects (Gill 2002). In 2003, the Government announced the more stunning policy to re-introduce English as the medium of instruction for mathematics and science at all levels; the policy was implemented in a staggered fashion.[50] Effectively then, the previously partial bilingual education national system would eventually become a multilingual system again, albeit in a different way from the pre-NEP period.

Broadly speaking, a number of factors contributed positively to the fortunes of Chinese language and education from the 1990s onwards. Unlike the 1970s and 1980s, the State in the 1990s adopted a more liberal language policy which accordingly opened up the public space for non-Malay languages. For example, the State allowed more non-Malay programmes on public television and radio, and in the privatized cable sector, far more English and Chinese than Malay channels were offered. The opening of China and its expanding ties with Malaysia also included increasing cultural exchanges, which has invariably re-invigorated the local Chinese culture. Besides cultural liberalization and globalization, the growing global influence of the multicultural discourse would have a positive impact on the status of Chinese language and education in Malaysia.

Notably, the multicultural discourse in Malaysia was also linked to an economic dimension, specifically in relation to the emergence of China as a major economic force. The Government was quick to recognize the existing Chinese language and education in the country as a valuable resource that could help to enhance the country's business relations with and investments in and from China. At the individual level, in 2000, more than 60,000 non-Chinese, the majority of them Malays, were enrolled in Chinese primary schools and the trend appears to be on the upward cycle. A reason given by non-Chinese parents for enrolling their children in Chinese schools was because they want their children to learn Mandarin in order to take advantage of the opportunities in China.

Since the 1990s, several developments have helped to expand the tertiary education opportunities of ICSS graduates. Several Chinese secondary schools had adapted by preparing their students to sit for the public examinations as well, so that their graduates could also apply to enter the local universities. Although the Malaysian Government still would not accredit the UEC, ICSS graduates have gained admission into a wide range of overseas universities that accepted the UEC, and the Malaysian Government accredits many of those universities. In recent years, the Malaysian Government have also extended recognition to qualifications obtained from Taiwanese universities, and increasingly universities in China[51] as well.

Above all, the expansion of the private tertiary education sector greatly enhanced the opportunities for Chinese students to obtain tertiary educational qualifications. For the ICSS graduates in particular, a major development was that of the State granting licences for the establishment of tertiary institutions largely funded and managed by the Chinese community; the Southern College was established in 1990, the New Era

College in 1997, and lastly the University of Tunku Abdul Rahman (UTAR) in 2001. All these institutions are tri-lingual in that the two main media of instruction are Chinese and English, while Malay is also used as the medium of instruction in the Malay Studies programme. Unlike the public tertiary institutions, the two colleges and UTAR recognized the UEC as admission exams and admission is open to all qualified students based largely on merit.

CONCLUSION

Broadly speaking, the language and education issues in Malaysia have undergone five different stages. The first stage saw how differential treatment of the different ethnic groups, economic considerations and the prevailing Orientalist view resulted in a bilingual state and multilingual education system. In the second stage, the British helped to form a consociational political system, which, in turn, led the ethnic groups to meet half way, in a manner of speaking, on language and education issues. Also, although the Chinese educationists disagreed with the compromises, they promised not to raise their objections in the larger interest of attaining independence from the British. The disagreements especially between the Malay language nationalists and Chinese educationists rapidly degenerated into heated controversies in the immediate post-Independence period such that it contributed to the breakdown of the consociational politics. The 1970s and 1980s saw the rise and assertion of a UMNO-led Malay dominance, including the institutionalization of Melayu as the sole official language and medium of instruction, and, conversely, the marginalization of Chinese language and education.

The latest twist in the story of language and education in Malaysia is twofold. On the one hand, globalization has led the Malaysian State to liberalize its cultural and education policies and re-introduce English as a medium of instruction for science and technical subjects. On the other hand, the emergence of China as an economic power and regional power has re-invigorated the status and function of Chinese language, education and culture in Malaysia.

Notes

1. The Tunku made this remark around the time when the 1967 National Language Bill was tabled in Parliament. Of course, there are debates over the meaning and role of "national language". This paper will focus on West Malaysia.

2. The Orientalist-Anglicist controversy first emerged over the issue of Indian education in British India (see Evans (2002) for a discussion of this controversy). In Malaya, the Orientalist view had a pronounced influence over key colonial officials. Importantly, as pointed by Pennycock, the Anglicist and Orientalist in actual fact "were two sides of the same coin, both designed to facilitate trade while maintaining social control of the native population" (Ricento 2001, p. 3).
3. Composed of Penang, Malacca and Singapore, the Straits Settlements became a Crown Colony in 1867. Federated Malay States were made up of Perak, Selangor, Negeri Sembilan, and Pahang, and the Unfederated Malay States of Johore, Trengganu, Kelantan, Perlis, and Kedah.
4. The principle of indirect rule meant governing through the traditional Malay leaders "operating within the traditional institutional framework", but modifying according to British "needs and preconceptions" (Emerson 1937 [1970], p. 7).
5. An adapted Arabic alphabet for writing the Melayu language.
6. In the early years of British colonialism, Frank Swettenham claimed that: "In the Malay States we have always insisted upon officers passing an examination in Malay, and the standard is a high one" (Swettenham in Kratoska 1983, p. 190).
7. This was because of the British failure to live up to its stated pro-Malay employment policy.
8. English usage was, however, unevenly distributed in the colony; it was more widely used in the Straits Settlements and the Federated Malay States and Johore than in the less developed and almost ethnically homogenous Malay states of Trengganu and Kelantan.
9. Hugh Clifford's sentiment was widely shared and often throughout the duration of colonial rule reiterated by members of the British administrative elite.
10. Melayu vernacular education thus primarily focused on providing a sound grounding in the three basic subjects of reading, writing and arithmetic, and to teach practical arts and relevant skills that would enhance the various Malay traditional agricultural and cottage handicrafts. Generally, in the Malay schools, in the morning lessons were conducted in Melayu and in the afternoon lessons were devoted to the Koran.
11. The man responsible for this was R.J. Wilkinson, then Inspector of Schools. The best book on MCKK is Khasnor Johan's *Educating the Malay Elite: the Malay College Kuala Kangsar, 1905–1941* (1996).
12. Indeed, "Chinese parental concern that their children did not become culturally alienated from 'the land of their ancestors' was a major motivating factor in the community's maintenance of a school system whose curriculum emphasized the teaching of Chinese literature and language" (Loh 1975, p. 124).

13. "Before the founding of the Republic, Overseas Chinese in SEA did not get education as we know it now. At that time there were very few schools. Although there were private schools, they too were extremely limited in scope. For example, the British colonial Government did establish English language schools, but the education they provided was only enough to prepare the students for working for the British. Not only were there no technical schools or universities, even relatively acceptable high schools were hard to find. … After the founding of the Republic, the Overseas Chinese in the various colonies began to take a renewed and active interest in their native land …, became actively involved in establishing schools in the countries in which they lived." (Tan Kah Kee 1994, p. 47)

14. British intervention in the Chinese schools began with the 1920 Registration of Schools Enactment.

15. This position was supported by a prominent group of ex-Malayan Officials who publicly voiced their rejection of the Malayan Union proposals. Among the Malays, the opposition to the Malayan Union cut across class and parochialism.

16. The Malayan Union Plan projected a generous set of criteria for the acquisition of Malayan citizenship. Categories of persons who would be conferred citizenship included: (1) any person born in the peninsula before the date when the Order comes into force, (2) any person aged 18 or above who has resided in the peninsula for a period of ten years during the fifteen years preceding 15 February 1942, and who swears allegiance, (3) any person born in the peninsula after the date when the order comes into force, and (4) any person whose father is a Malayan citizen (Malayan Union and Singapore, 1946). Through the naturalization process of acquiring Malayan citizenship, applicants must satisfy; (1) have resided in the peninsula for a period of one year immediately preceding the date of application and for a further period of four years during the last eight years before application, (2) are of good character and have an adequate knowledge of the Malay or English language, and (3) intend, if the application is granted, to reside in the Malayan Union or Singapore.

17. A document essentially negotiated and agreed to by the British and Malay political elites.

18. It appears that there was a consensus among the Malay nationalists, regardless of their political leanings, on this issue.

19. Their aim was to redress the unequal usage of the two official languages in the pre-war period in which Melayu was largely neglected as a language of governance.

20. That the Barnes Report ignored the interests and needs of the Chinese community was not surprising given that the Committee was composed of only British officials and Malay representatives, and only solicited the views of different Malay groups.

21. This was at the request of Sir Henry Gurney, who had just replaced Edward Gent as the High Commissioner.

22. The United Chinese School Teachers' Association (UCSTA), formed in 1951 as a result of the Barnes Report, and later on by the United Chinese Schools Committees' Association (UCSCA) (Tan 1992), initially led it.

23. The British were far-sighted enough to realize that stability in the plural Malaysian society was best achieved by getting the rival ethnic communities to work together. This insight led to the invention of the consociational paradigm in Malaysian politics. The Alliance Party fairly resembled the democratic consociational model in that consensus on decision-making was reached through consultations and deliberations that took into account the disparate and conflicting ethnic interests the ethnic leaders represented, and every ethnic leader had, more or less, equal vetoing power.

24. It was tasked with drafting the constitution for the future independent Malaya.

25. This UMNO and MCA confrontation eventually led to the resignation of Lim Chong Eu and his faction from MCA, and a group acceptable to the UMNO leadership replaced them.

26. The main supporters of the NLAF were Malay teachers who at that time constituted the largest — and most influential — bloc in UMNO.

27. In the debates on the National Education Bill, the Tunku Abdul Rahman made a keen observation: "The question of this national language has been the subject of much debate and negotiations between all sections of the community … However what impressed me is that there has been no one, in the course of the discussion, who is opposed to Malay being made the national language of this country. … The controversies arising from the national language issue were not spurred on by the people's rejection of Malay as the national language, but rather of Malay as the official language and as medium of instruction." (Asmah 1979, pp. 13–14).

28. The two opposition parties that strongly supported the Chinese language and education issues were the Democratic Action Party and People's Progressive Party. See DAP (1969).

29. Some of the non-Malay political leaders became convinced that it was better to have a subordinate role in a Malay-dominated government than to have no role at all. Their willingness to join in a Malay-dominated government did not mean their agreement with the permanence of Malay political dominance legacy. Rather, they saw Malay political dominance as a temporary means for the Malays to uplift themselves and not as an end in itself. Hence, they believed that when the Malays have achieved economic equality, they would be more inclined and open to the idea of equal citizenship for all Malaysians, regardless of ethnicity.

30. The consociational paradigm in Malaysia has deviated from the democratic model to one in which one ethnic party, that is UMNO-Malay, is pre-eminent and has a disproportionate share of vetoing power. (Crouch 1996, chapter 9; Mauzy 1983)

31. Three issues considered "sensitive" were removed from public debate under the revised Sedition Act. On the one side, Malay "special rights" and the official status of the Malay lanuguage and Islam were made neither debatable nor negotiable (Articles 152 and 153 of the Constitution). On the other side, the non-Malay citizenship status cannot be questioned.

32. From the 1970s onwards, to further assert the Melayu language's claim as the sole official language, the language was renamed as Bahasa Malaysia or Malaysian Language.

33. The National Culture Policy was formulated and implemented during this period.

34. In later years, for the MCE a pass will get a candidate a Grade 2 certificate and a credit a Grade 1 certificate.

35. Also, in the Chinese and Indian Studies departments, courses were largely taught in Chinese and Tamil languages.

36. For example, in the then emerging satellite township of Petaling Jaya, only one out of a total of fifteen primary schools was Chinese and this was a place where the Chinese population formed the majority; 80 per cent of 100,000.

37. In general, the urban Chinese schools are better off simply because they served a wealthier Chinese community, while those in the rural and semi-rural are rather dilapidated and faced a dwindling enrolment due to a shrinking Chinese community.

38. Later, the "integrated schools" were basically repackaged as "Vision Schools". While the rationale for "integrated schools" is to facilitate interaction of Malay, Chinese and Indian students, the Dongjiaozong feared that the Chinese primary schools would lose their autonomy and character.

39. According to Kua, "Parents objected as they feared the quality of education in the schools would be affected since some of these teachers had to teach subjects in Mandarin. Furthermore, they feared the administration of the school would be affected by the non-Mandarin educated administrators since they would not be able to communicate effectively with the rest of the staff." (1999, p. 134) Importantly, this announcement degenerated into a heated argument between Malays and Chinese, and because it was made in the midst of a power struggle within UMNO, Mahathir used the heightened ethnic situation to clamp down on his critics and opposition.

40. The Chinese medium Nanyang University was a private university funded by the Chinese of Malaysia and Singapore and started its first classes in 1956. It was, however, merged with the University of Singapore in 1980 to form the English-medium National University of Singapore.

41. The expansion of tertiary education only began in the 1990s in line with the growing demand for workers with higher educations and skills.

42. In the 1990s, multiculturalism became increasing recognized as a human rights issue and also sometimes as a desirable good. Numerous scholars and activists have advocated a notion of language rights as a tool by which

minority ethnic groups may protect their cultural integrity against the incursions of hegemonic groups. At the same time, critics have problematized language rights as a dangerous notion that may provoke inter-ethnic competition or worse.

43. Before the 1990s, although there was a huge demand, the private sector has remained relatively small because of state policy to restrict the privatization of education. By the 1990s, a number of factors compelled the State to expand the role of the private sector in the provision of tertiary education. The increasing numbers of tertiary institutions in the developed world driven to recruit more full fees-paying foreign students in order to generate more revenues assisted this privatization. Also, financially, the country was losing a huge sum of money in having tens of thousands of Malaysian students studying overseas. This problem became especially painful during the 1997 financial crisis. Also, the State came to see the business potential in education and thus proceeded with plans to turn Malaysia into an educational hub in the region. An additional factor was that the brain drain of young non-Malay Malaysians — bound for Australia, Britain, Canada, New Zealand, Singapore and the United States — was depriving the local economy of the skilled human resource the country badly needed for its objective to be a knowledge economy. (Tan 2002).

44. Twinning programs usually are degree courses where the students complete, say, the first two years of his/her courses in Malaysia and the last two years in the foreign university.

45. Perhaps the main reason was that the State regarded the private tertiary education sector as a potential business that would attract students from all over the world, and, obviously, an English medium would be more accessible as well as more marketable.

46. Initially, this was made compulsory for both Malaysian and foreign students. However, later foreign students were exempted from this requirement.

47. Scientific and technical publications and translations in and into Malay remained miniscule. It was felt that the Chinese did not suffer the same fate because they were trilingual in that they were competent in Malay, English and Chinese languages.

48. The irony is that even the Malay language nationalists now recognized the policies that had pushed the Chinese students to become trilingual, with the Malay students remaining essentially monolingual, has turned out to be an advantage to the former.

49. In 1991, Prime Minister Mahathir made a press statement highlighting his concerns regarding the poor results of the national English language examination given at the end of secondary school. He was perturbed that Malaysia might not only lose its economic competitiveness, but also find it hard to progress in the industrial and technical fields if its workforce was not competent in English.

50. Interestingly, this state decision moved the Malay language nationalists and Chinese educationists to work together to oppose this new policy — but for different reasons. While the former felt that this would dilute the status of Malay as the official and national language, the latter objected because they felt that it would dilute the use of Chinese as the medium of instruction in the Chinese schools. Nevertheless, the State went ahead with the policy and the Chinese schools reluctantly accepted the new policy; a compromise was worked out where the students studied mathematics and science subjects in both Chinese and English at different times.

51. There were 841 Malaysian students in China in 2003, covering those pursuing associate, bachelor's and master's degrees. One worry is that presently the Malaysian Government only recognize degrees from the world-class Tsinghua and Peking universities, alongside medical degrees from Peking University, Fudan University, Shanghai University of Traditional Chinese Medicine, Sun Yat-sen University, Jinan University and Tongji University.

References

Asmah Haji Omar. *Language Planning for Unity and Efficiency: A Study of the Language Status and Corpus Planning of Malaysia*. Kuala Lumpur: Penerbit Universiti Malaya, 1979.

———. *Language and Society in Malaysia*. Kuala Lumpur: Dewan Bahasa dan Pustaka, 1982.

———. *Language and Language Situation in Southeast Asia: With Focus on Malaysia*. Kuala Lumpur: Hakcipta Akademi Pengajian Melayu, 2003.

Barlow, H.S. *Swettenham*. Kuala Lumpur: Southdene, 1995.

Chai Hon-Chan. *Education and Nation-Building in Plural Societies: The West Malaysian Experience*. Australian National University, Development Studies Centre, Monograph no. 6, 1977.

Crouch, Harold. *Government and Politics in Malaysia*. Sydney: Allen & Unwin 1996.

Democratic Action Party. *Who Lives if Malaysia Dies?: The DAP's Case for a Multi-Racial Society*. Kuala Lumpur: DAP, 1969.

Emerson, Rupert. *Malaysia: A Study in Direct and Indirect Rule* (first published in 1937). Kuala Lumpur: University of Malaya Press, 1970.

Evans, Stephen. *Macaulay's Minute Revisited: Colonial Language Policy in Nineteenth-century India*. Journal of Multilingual and Multicultural Development 23, no. 4 (2002): 260–81.

Funston, John. *Malay Politics in Malaysia: A Study of UMNO and PAS*. Kuala Lumpur: Heinemann Educational Books (Asia) Ltd, 1980.

Gill Saran Kaur. *English Language Challenges for Malaysia: International Communication*. Serdang, Selangor: Universiti Putra Malaysia Press 2002.

Government of Malaya. *Report of the Committee on Malay Education, Federation of Malaya* (or Barnes Report). Kuala Lumpur: Government Publication, 1951.

———. *Chinese Schools and the Education of Chinese Malayans* (or Fenn-Wu Report). Kuala Lumpur: Government Publication, 1951.

———. *Education Ordinance 1952.* Kuala Lumpur: Government Publication, 1952.

———. *Report of the Education Committee 1956* (or Razak Report). Kuala Lumpur: Government Publication, 1956.

———. *Report of the Education Review Committee 1960* (or Talib Report). Kuala Lumpur: Government Publication, 1960.

Khasnor, Johan. *Educating the Malay Elite: the Malay College Kuala Kangsar, 1905–1941.* Kuala Lumpur: Pustaka Antara, 1996.

Kua Kia Soong. *A Protean Saga: The Chinese Schools of Malaysia.* Selangor, Malaysia: Dong Jiao Zong Higher Learning Center, 1999 (third edition).

Loh Fook Seng, Philip. *Seeds of Separatism: Educational Policy in Malaya 1874–1940.* Kuala Lumpur: Oxford University Press, 1975.

Maxwell, George. "Some Problems of Education and Public Health in Malaya". In *Honourable Intentions: Talks on the British Empire in Southeast Asia delivered at the Royal Colonial Institute 1874–1928*, edited by Paul H. Kratoska. Singapore: Oxford University Press 1983.

Mauzy, Diane. *Barisan Nasional: Coalition Government in Malaysia.* Kuala Lumpur: Maricans, 1983.

Means, Gordon. *Malaysian Politics.* London: Hodder and Stoughton Ltd, 1976.

Pennycook, Alastair. "Language, Ideology and Hindsight: Lessons from Colonial Language Policies". In *Ideology, Politics and Language Policies: Focus on English*, edited by Thomas Ricento. Amsterdam: John Benjamins Publishing Co., 2001.

Ricento, Thomas, ed. *Ideology, Politics and Language Policies: Focus on English.* Amsterdam: John Benjamins Publishing Co., 2001.

Rosnani, Hashim. *Educational Dualism in Malaysia: Implications for Theory and Practice.* Kuala Lumpur: The Other Press, 2004.

Rudner, Martin. *Malaysian Development: A Retrospective.* Ottawa, Ontario: Carleton University Press, 1994.

Stevenson, Rex. *Cultivators and Administrators: British Educational Policy towards the Malays 1875–1906.* Kuala Lumpur: Oxford University Press, 1975.

Stockwell, A.J. *British Policy and Malay Politics During the Malayan Union Experiment 1942–1948.* Kuala Lumpur: Malaysian Branch of the Royal Asiatic Society, 1979.

Swettenham, F.A. "British Rule in Malaya". In *Honourable Intentions: Talks on the British Empire in Southeast Asia delivered at the Royal Colonial Institute 1874–1928*, edited by Paul H. Kratoska. Singapore: Oxford University Press, 1983.

Tan Ai Mei. *Malaysian Private Higher Education: Globalization, Privatization, Transformation and Marketplaces*. London: ASEAN Academic Press, 2002.
Tan Kah Kee. *The Memoirs of Tan Kah-Kee*. Edited and translated with notes by A.H.C. Ward, Raymond W. Chu, Janet Salaff. Singapore: Singapore University Press, 1994.
Tan Liok Ee. "Dongjiaozong and the Challenge to Cultural Hegemony 1951–1987". In *Fragmented Vision: Culture and Politics in Contemporary Malaysia*, edited by Joel S. Kahn and Loh Kok Wah Francis. Sydney: Allen & Unwin Pty Ltd, 1992.
———. *The Politics of Chinese Education in Malaya 1945–1961*. Kuala Lumpur: Oxford University Press, 1997.
Thomas, R.M. "Malaysia: Cooperation versus Competition". In *Politics and Education: Cases from Eleven Nations*, edited by R. Murray Thomas. Oxford: Pergamon Press, 1983.

7

The Politics of Language Policy in Myanmar: Imagining Togetherness, Practising Difference?

Kyaw Yin Hlaing

Although Myanmar has been an independent state for over half a century, its 135 different national races and equally numerous dialects and languages renders language the main continual source of problems for its incomplete and problem-ridden nation-building process. Because successive post-colonial Myanmar governments based nation-building projects on the culture and history of the ethnic majority, Burman, many ethnic minority groups and observers have long accused the Burman-dominated post-colonial governments, especially the Socialist and current military governments, of Burmanizing the country's entire population. The adoption of the Burman language as the country's official language by successive governments and the suspension of minority language classes at pre-university public schools since the early 1970s were viewed by many as attempts to homogenize the population and establish a monolingual nation. Both scholars and minority nationalists have directly and indirectly suggested that the Burman-dominated language policy only benefited the regime and the Burmans, whereas ethnic minorities suffered from it.

While acknowledging the prevalence of Burman chauvinistic elements in the nation-building discourse and activities undertaken by post-colonial Myanmar governments, this paper intends to show that successive Myanmar governments did not try to establish a monolingual nation. Rather, the governments would usually allow ethnic minorities to undertake cultural activities, including the freedom to speak and write their own languages, as long as those activities were not related to political attempts to topple them or undermine their control of the country. In addition, to understand the complexities of the politics of language in Myanmar, one also ought to pay more attention to the politics of interaction between officials from the centre and local areas. During the Socialist and current military periods, local officials responsible for promoting minority cultures were not elected by local people but appointed by the central government. Since those officials were more interested in keeping their jobs than serving the minority peoples, most of them stayed away from minority cultural activities because they did not want to be associated with insurgent groups, who usually sought to promote minority cultures. Thus, the conspicuous absence of local officials willing to stand up for the interests of ethnic minorities contributed to the suspension of ethnic minority language classes in the country. This paper will also show that while the adoption of the Burman language as official language helped opponents of the regime to communicate with each other more efficiently and facilitated the various ethnic groups" sense of belonging to a united Myanmar, its institutionalization also generate some misunderstanding between the Government and ethnic minorities.[1]

LANGUAGE AND NATION-BUILDING IN MYANMAR: HISTORICAL BACKGROUND

Myanmar's present boundaries were only established after its annexation into the British Empire. The British absorbed much of Myanmar's frontier regions into its Empire because it considered these regions with tributary relations to the Myanmar kings as part of colonial Myanmar. Although the British ruled Myanmar proper — the area inhabited by the majority ethnic Burman, and the frontier areas, the regions inhabited by ethnic minorities — under two separate administrative systems, the British colonial administration adopted English as the official language throughout Myanmar. Indigenous people, however, were allowed to speak and study their respective languages. Christian missionaries that came with the colonial administration also invented written languages for the Kachin, Chin, Lahu and a few other ethnic minorities to facilitate their missionary activities.

Language was not a political issue until Burmese students at Rangoon University College were politically awoken by the 1920 University Act that adopted very strict and high admission standards, which included a high level of English language proficiency. Since most Burmese could not meet the requirements of the new University Act, university students organized protests against the university administration. Student leaders and other nationalist leaders collaborated to establish national colleges and schools that placed emphasis on the Burman language. Although most national schools that refused the colonial Government's financial assistance were closed down some three years later, the movement opened a new chapter for the Burman language by providing educated Burmans with the inspiration to invent a new literary style for the Burman language and to work for the introduction of an honors program in Burmese literature at Rangoon University.

The politics of language reached its zenith when a group of politically conscious and educated young people formed "Do Bama Asiayone" (DBA, Our Bama Association). The DBA noted in its first declaration:

> Bama pyi (the Bama country) is our country.
> Bama literature is our literature.
> Bama language is our language.
> Love our country.
> Praise our literature.
> Respect our language.[2]

Dubbing themselves *thakin* (Master), members of the DBA organized nationalist and anti-colonial activities throughout the country. The organization became a major nationalist organization when more and more politically conscious young people, including independence hero, Aung San and other future leaders of the country, joined its ranks. Although the DBA initially attracted mostly Burmans, far-sighted DBA leaders also tried to win the minds and hearts of ethnic and foreign minorities by declaring that an insult directed at any indigenous person was tantamount to insulting the entire indigenous population. DBA leaders were quoted as saying that if a Burman from Myitkyina (the capital city of Kachin state) were insulted, Burmans from Yay and Tavoy (cities in Mon State) would be insulted as well.

However, DBA leaders failed to convince most minority elites and nationalists that their organization was a united entity of various ethnicities. This was because the emergence of national consciousness was not confined to the Burmans, but to the ethnic minorities as well.[3] With the introduction of modern education and the availability of books on politics, many ethnic minorities also came to understand the power of nationalism. Probably due to the colonial administration's tradition of favouring ethnic minorities over Burmans, minority nationalists based their nationalist discourses on anti-Burmese stories which highlighted the suffering of their ancestors under the rule of the Burmese kings. Minority elites and nationalist leaders appeared to believe that their cooperation with the colonial administration engendered the antipathy of Burmans, especially those engaging in the struggle for independence. Minority elites and nationalists also believed that they and their people might be discriminated against by the Government if Burmans were to assume control of the country. Hence, when these minority elites and nationalists sought more political rights for their peoples in the 1930s and 1940s, they wanted the British Government to keep their areas separate from Myanmar proper.

A major problem in the DBA's nationalist activities was that while the organization claimed to represent all indigenous groups, it failed to develop a strong, convincing and all-encompassing Myanmar identity. Although it called for the improvement of the physical welfare of all indigenous groups, leading DBA members did not promote the culture of ethnic and religious minorities. DBA's nationalist discourses continued to focus on promoting Buddhism and the Burman language even though it had launched a campaign to mobilize ethnic minorities. Realizing this, many left-wing DBA leaders dropped Buddhism from their discourses and tried to mobilize religious and foreign minorities by appealing to their individual cultures and sensibilities. The traditional nationalist leaders and Buddhist monks, however, continued to emphasize Buddhism and the Burman language. Consequently, although it managed to recruit a number of Mon, Rakhine, Chin, Pa O, Indian and Chinese, the DBA was regarded as a predominantly Burman organization throughout the colonial period. When Burman nationalist leaders fought against the British with the help of the Japanese army in the Second World War, many Karen, Kachin and Chin soldiers from the colonial army maintained their loyalty to the British colonial administration by fighting the Burman Nationalist Army alongside British forces. When the British retreated to India, many minority soldiers remained in Myanmar, and this accentuated Burman distrust of minority peoples. This distrust was further compounded when some members of the Burman Nationalist Army killed a large number of Karen in a communal riot.

Therefore, when Burman nationalist leaders negotiated for the country's independence with the British Government, the Shan, Karen and Kayah indicated that they did not want to be a part of independent Myanmar. Many minority elites and nationalists begged the British Government to keep their areas under its rule (U Kyaw Win et al. 1990, pp. 52, 87). However, after a series of lengthy meetings with Burman nationalist leader Aung San at Pinlong in Shan State, ethnic leaders agreed to be a part of independent Myanmar on the condition that if they were unsatisfied with the Union, their regions would be allowed to secede from the Union ten years after Independence.

In the discussions leading up to the establishment of a constitution for an independent Myanmar, language became a major political issue between Burman and ethnic leaders. The first language-related issue encountered by the constitution drafters was on the issue of the official language (Maung Maung 1961, p. 204). When the Burman nationalists called for the Burman language to be designated the official language, it was easily resolved as none of the minority groups seriously took up the issue with the Burman nationalists. A Shan leader astutely noted that the minority leaders' acceptance of Burmese as the official language was due to their understanding of the necessity and practicality of having an official language through which all ethnic groups in the Union are able to effectively communicate with one another (Interview, 21 July 2003). He also noted that minority leaders accepted the replacement of English with Burmese partially because most ordinary people in the ethnic minorities did not speak English and also because Burmese was easier than English. A *thakin*, however, observed that some ethnic leaders were very anxious to maintain English as the official language as it was a neutral language. However, in spite of these sentiments, they did not block the designation of Burmese as the official language in part, because they wanted to devote their resources to other more important issues, and also because they believed all ethnic groups should know the language of the ethnic majority dominating the Union's politics (Interview, 11 July 2003).

The second and more important language-related issue emerged from the question as to which minority group should be granted statehood.[4] Aung San suggested that any ethnic group desirous of forming a separate state should possess, among other things, a language totally different from Burmese (Maung Maung 1961, pp. 167–70). Naturally, the ethnic groups pushing for the formation of their own separate state accordingly placed greater emphasis on the distinctiveness of their respective languages. For various reasons, the Constitution initially granted statehood to only the Shan and Kachin. The Constitution, however, guaranteed the right of all citizens to practise and promote their respective cultures and religions freely (Constitution of the Union of Burma 1947).

All in all, the Union of Myanmar did not emerge out of mutual trust and love between the Burmans and ethnic minorities. Ethnic minorities joined the predominantly Burman Union with the expectation that they would be considerably better off as a part of the Union than if they were independent from it. For ethnic minorities, especially ethnic elites and nationalists, keeping their own ethnic identity was more important than becoming "Myanmar". The central Government, on the other hand, wanted all citizens of Myanmar, regardless of ethnicity, to use Burmese as the lingua franca. This fundamental difference between minority nationalist leaders and Burman political leaders was to have a long-term impact on the nation-building process in post-colonial Myanmar.

LANGUAGE POLICY AND NATION-BUILDING IN PARLIAMENTARY MYANMAR[5] (1948–1962)

The parliamentary Government understood that unless it found a method to unify all the ethnic groups and give them a cause to feel as if they belonged to the larger predominantly Burman society, it would be extremely difficult to keep the newly independent country together. Aware of the ethnic minorities' growing nationalism, the Burman-dominated Anti-Fascist People's Freedom League (AFPFL) Government promised that it would not seek national unity by pressuring all of the country's inhabitants to accept and endorse a common culture. Prime Minister, U Nu, publicly declared that national unity would only emerge if the Government instituted a system that accommodated the cultural differences am ous ethnic groups and guaranteed the economic wellbeing of all ethnic groups.[6] One might, therefore, argue that the AFPFL Government tried to, or at least claimed to, establish unity in diversity.

The complex socio-political situation under which the AFPFL Government attempted to undertake nation-building activities should be taken into consideration. This is especially so given that a large majority of Burmans believed that independence and a Burman-dominated Government would alleviate and eliminate all their economic and social difficulties. While attempting to to meet the Burmans' expectations, the Government also had to deal with minority elites whose main fear was that a Burman-dominated Union would marginalize their status as leaders of their respective communities. Thus, the Government found that it had to contend with minority nationalists who were distrustful of the Burmans.[7]

The Government was prudent enough to comprehend that the ethnic minorities' distrust of Burman political leaders and their methods of dealing with ethnic insurgent groups would have a serious impact on the groups' perception of it. Therefore, when the Government took actions against minority insurgent groups, it tried to ensure that it did not antagonize those who were not involved in the movements. For instance, in order not to provoke and alienate the Karens who did not join the insurgent movement, U Nu labelled the Karen insurgent movement as the illegal activity of recalcitrant citizens. U Nu's high praise of the Karens who did not turn against the Government resulted in some ethnic Burmans dubbing him 'Karen Nu' (Pu Ga Lay 1949, p. 111). While it attempted to appease the law-abiding Karen, the State simultaneously sought to reassert its control of the country by launching military operations against insurgent groups. The defections of several battalions led the military to form militia groups to fight the insurgent groups. This arrangement was problematic because the militia was mainly comprised of unemployed thugs and bullies who did not care about winning the hearts and minds of minority peoples. Many militia groups and government soldiers reportedly looted and physically abused ethnic minorities they came across during military operations. Senior military and political leaders privately apologized to minority leaders for the abuses committed by government soldiers and requested them to be patient while the Government sought to discipline them.[8] U Nu and some political leaders also reasoned that it would be easier to win the hearts and minds of minorities if they were Buddhists and if they were to have a common language. The Government thus tried to promote the teaching and learning of the Burman language and Buddhist missionary work in minority areas (Kyawt Kyawt 2002, pp. 173–77).[9]

The teaching of Burmese in minority areas did not cause any major resentment among minority communities, as ethnic groups were allowed to teach their languages in pre-university level classes as well as to freely publish books, newspapers and magazines.[10] However, not all minority languages were taught at public schools in minority areas. Public schools in minority areas only taught the languages of major ethnic groups such as Shan, Karen, Chin, Kayah and Mon.[11] The languages of smaller ethnic groups were taught only in Buddhist monasteries and Christian churches. This was because some local state governments in minority areas dominated by major ethnic groups did not care for the promotion of the cultures of smaller groups. Therefore, politically conscious members of some smaller ethnic minority groups resented the elites of the dominant ethnic groups in their areas. For instance, the Red Shan group, who resides in Kachin State and speaks a Shan dialect, resented the Kachin state government and Kachin leaders for paying insufficient attention to the wellbeing of non-Kachin groups residing in the state (Interview, 1 October 2003).[12] In some areas where smaller ethnic groups outnumbered the dominant ethnic groups, state governments did not require public schools to teach the language of the dominant ethnic group, instead the public schools in these areas used Burmese as the medium of instruction.[13]

From this situation arises the question of "how did the promotion of the Burmese language and the Government's flexible language policy contribute to the creation of national consciousness?"[14] Many ethnic minorities welcomed the teaching of Burmese in their respective areas, for proficiency in Burmese was essential if they wanted to succeed in their professional lives and in business. Also, the teaching of Burmese in minority areas enabled the various ethnic groups to communicate with each other and to conduct business transactions more efficiently. A retired government official originally from Kachin state noted:

> I spoke only Shan until I started to study Burmese at school in the early 1950s. The village I grew up in was a multiethnic one. The residents of the village included Shan, Kachin, Chinese and Burmese. Most people in the village understood a little bit of each others' languages. We tried to communicate with each other through what little we knew of each other's languages. Of course, we often misunderstood each other. For important matters, leaders from different ethnic communities talked to each other through the people who knew both languages. When we were forced to study Burmese at schools, we all came to master the language quite quickly. We could then communicate with people from other ethnic groups more efficiently. Also, the knowledge of Burmese enabled us to read newspapers and books in Burmese. Not everybody liked to read books and newspapers in the past, but with an education in Burmese, more and more people came to read newspapers and books. As a result, more and more people came to understand what was going on in the region and in the country. (Interview, 12 October 2003)

Nevertheless, although the teaching of Burmese had helped the various ethnic groups to better understand one another, the relations between the Government and minority elites and nationalists continued to deteriorate. This was because while ethnic minorities were more interested in gaining benefits for themselves and their people than in preserving the Union, the Burman military and political leaders equated their primary duty with the preservation of the Union.[15] The major problem between ethnic minorities and the central Government thus was that the former wanted more political and economic rights and benefits from the Union than the central

Government would dispense.[16] Burman political leaders' practice of
dividing revenue for various ethnic regions according to the size of the
population did not endear them to the ethnic minorities or their leaders.
Since the majority of the population resided in Myanmar proper, the
budget allocated for Myanmar proper was always several times more
than the budget for minority states. Minority leaders also thought that
since minority areas were more underdeveloped than Myanmar proper,
the central Government ought to invest more in the development of
those areas. While the ethnic minorities were pressing for the
development of their regions, Burmans, too, wanted the Government to
build more schools and roads in their areas. The central Government,
however, did not possess the fiscal capacity to meet the demands of
both the Burman and ethnic minorities.

Electoral politics importantly also aggravated the already volatile
relationship between the Government and the minority leaders. Since no
political party was able to win majority seats in the parliament without
the support of the majority of Buddhist Burmans, major political parties
always placed emphasis on winning in the constituencies in Myanmar
proper. Political parties thus adopted policies that would help them obtain
the support of Burmans at the cost of the support of ethnic minorities. In
order to win the support of Buddhist monks and Buddhist Burmans,
Prime Minister U Nu promised to make Buddhism the state religion if he
won. When his party won with the support of Buddhist Burman votes,
U Nu had little choice but to keep his promise, which upset the ethnic
and religious minorities (Kyaw Yin Hlaing 2003a). Although U Nu tried
to assuage the situation by passing a law guaranteeing the rights of
religious minorities, the minority leaders, including Buddhist minorities,
conclude that the Burman-dominated central Government was prepared
to sacrifice the welfare of ethnic minorities in order to win the support
of their own people.[17] Hence, although the central State tried to improve
their relations with the ethnic minorities, it could not remove the ethnic
minorities' view that the central Government was the government of the
Burmans. A former Shan insurgent leader was observed to have said,

> If the Government wanted us to consider it *our* government, it
> had to take care of us, it must be actively involved in the promotion
> of our culture and languages. All post-colonial governments
> claimed that they wanted to help us develop our regions and our
> cultures. The problem is that they never matched their words and
> their deeds. Ethnic minorities, therefore, always referred to the

central Government as, *Bamar a-soe-ya* (the Burman Government) (Interview, 9 June 2003).

Indignant with the central Government, many young Karen, Kayah, Rakhine, Mon, Pa O, Palong and Kachin people went underground and fought against the central Government for the independence of their region. Conversely, ethnic minority leaders banded together to pressure the Government into granting them more autonomy and revenues. An interesting point here is that minority leaders of various ethnic groups communicated with each other in Burmese. A former member of the Shan State Army recalled:

> Most minority leaders in those days understood English but many of them were not comfortable discussing political matters in English. So, Shan, Kachin, Mon, Karen and Chin leaders communicated in Burmese. Since Burmese was the official language, all minority leaders were forced to speak it. I graduated from high school during the parliamentary days. I learned Burmese at school. After I joined the underground movement, I had to deal with members of BCP and KIA and we all talked to each other in Burmese (Interview, 7 June 2003).[18]

Prior to the declaration that rendered Burmese the official language, many minority leaders only spoke broken Burmese. However, when Burmese became the official language, all minority leaders were forced to speak it and over time, they came to master the language.

The knowledge of Burmese also allowed politically conscious ethnic minorities to better understand Burman chauvinistic views and the problems inherent in the nation-building activities undertaken by the State. Although Burman political leaders repeatedly noted that all indigenous ethnic groups residing in Myanmar are blood relations, they failed to define "Myanmarness" clearly. Many political leaders continued to use the nationalist discourses developed by the Do Bama Asiayone (DBA) during the colonial period. Since DBA's nationalist discourses were based on anti-colonialism, they were unsuitable or unifying the country in the post-colonial period. A lot of ethnic minorities who were on good terms with the colonial Government viewed such discourses as evidence of the Burman-dominated Government's hostility towards them. Even some politicians who understood the sensitive situation within the nation-building process often made comments and statements in their speeches (which were directed at the Burman audience) that upset minority elites.

As more and more ethnic minorities came to better understand Burmese, the reckless chauvinistic statements uttered by Burman political leaders began to impact negatively on the minorities' perception of the Government. A Mon community leader commented,

> In their political speeches to the Burmans, many Burman politicians liked to talk about how ancient Burman kings unified the country. The problem with this is that many ethnic minorities also had access to newspapers. Many ethnic minorities grew up learning that Burman kings were patronizing and were often very abusive towards their vessels. Burman leaders used anti-British discourses to instigate nationalistic sentiments among Burmans. Likewise, many minority leaders used anti-Burman discourses to instigate nationalism among their respective ethnic groups. For minority nationalists, Burmans were colonizers. Some minority leaders even used excerpts about Burman leaders' chauvinistic statements from newspapers as evidence that Burmans do not think much of us. The chauvinistic statements of Burman leaders offended many young people who understood Burmese. That is why, a lot of minority leaders who studied at Yangon and Mandalay universities in the 1950s and early 1960s joined the armed struggle against the Government (Interview, 23 October 2003).

In general, most ordinary ethnic minorities stayed out of politics. All twenty-five Shan, Mon, and Kachin interviewees who were between sixty and seventy-two years old noted that most ordinary ethnic minorities just wanted to live peacefully. However, due to the abusive manners of Burman soldiers and militia groups in their areas, many ethnic minorities came to see the central Government as the colonizer of their regions. Even members of smaller ethnic groups who had no quarrel with the dominant ethnic groups in their respective regions were disgusted with the soldiers of the central Government. Sixty-five-year-old Pa O recalled:

> Shan police and Shan Sawbwa never looted our property but a lot of Burman solders were really barbaric. We could not support the Government that sent such barbaric people to our region (Interview, 10 June 2003).

In 1961, minority leaders impatient with the central Government had a meeting to collectively pressure the Government to establish a true federal state. They also threatened to secede from the Union if the Government did not comply with their demands. Before minority leaders and Burman political leaders could reach an agreement, however, the military seized control of the country, claiming that it did so to prevent the disintegration of the Union.

In conclusion, declaring Burmese as the official state language by the Burman-dominated Government proved to be a double-edge sword. While it allowed the Government to communicate with minority peoples, the knowledge of Burmese permitted minority peoples to better understand the low opinion many Burman political leaders and traditional nationalists had of them. Furthermore, the Burman-dominated Government failed to develop a new nationalist discourse that would appeal to both the Burman majority and minority ethnic groups. In so doing, the Government failed to meet the demands and expectations of minority people; this led many minority leaders to use Burmese as a means in organizing anti-Government activities.

LANGUAGE AND NATION-BUILDING IN THE SOCIALIST PERIOD (1962–1988)

As a regime that came to power claiming it would prevent the disintegration of the Union, leaders of the Revolutionary Council (RC) repeatedly emphasized the importance of national unity and promised to institute a system that would serve the interests of all citizens of the country. A few months after it seized control of the country, the RC formed the Burma Socialist Program Party (BSPP) and announced that it would establish a socialist system called the "Burmese Way to Socialism". The RC's language policies proved to be more anti-colonial than its predecessor's; it maintained Burmese as the official language, but tried to do away with the use of English at the state level.

Within two years of seizing power, the RC closed down all missionary schools and announced its plan to make Burmese the only medium of instruction in all university and pre-university classes, except English language classes. The RC also planned to invent new Burmese alphabet-based scripts for languages that previously used Roman scripts. Although the latter plan was never implemented, Burmese became the only medium of instruction in most university and pre-university classes by the end of 1970. In contrast, the RC limited the teaching of minority languages only up to the second standard and publicly announced that minority groups could develop and promote their respective culture freely as long as their cultural activities did not negatively effect the national unity and the RC's socialist projects.[19]

As a result of the BSPP's rigorous nation-building activities, foreign observers of Burmese ethnic politics and minority nationalists accused the BSPP of "Burmanizing" the entire population. Many scholars and journalists claimed that "adherence to a minority cultural tradition is treated as tantamount to subversion of the nation and is branded as a mark of group inferiority within the nation" (Lehman 1967). Others argued that the Government only allowed ethnic minorities to practise their cultures if their practices were in line with the Burmese Way to Socialism, or viewed the promotion of Burman language and literature and the suspension of minority languages in public schools as evidence of the Socialist Government's attempt to "Burmanize" the entire population.

In reality, however, the Government cannot be said to be systematically forbidding ethnic minorities the practice of their respective customs and cultures. All ethnic groups were allowed to promote and develop their own cultures. The Socialist Government was not against the idea of ethnic minorities possessing multiethnic identities. In many minority areas, ethnic minorities were also allowed to resolve legal problems including rape, divorce and inheritance according to their respective customary laws and practices (Interview, 21 October 2003). Ethnic minorities enjoyed more cultural freedom than most scholars and minority nationalists would suggest. Indeed, traditional cultural activities of minority groups did not have to be in line with the Burmese Way to Socialism; as long as their traditional activities did not challenge the authority of the Government, minorities were allowed to organize cultural activities freely.

The problems of teaching minority languages were also more complex than many scholars and ethnic nationalists intimated. The 1966 Education Act required public schools in minority areas to teach minority languages up to second grade. The Ministry of Education published textbooks for Mon, Shan, Po Karen, Scot Karen, Chin and Kachin languages. Ethnic communities that wanted to teach their languages beyond the second standard were allowed to use classrooms in public schools before or after regular school hours. While it was indeed true that some schools in minority areas suspended the teaching of minority languages in1960s, nevertheless many schools in several minority areas continued to teach minority languages until the early 1980s. The Ministry of Education published textbooks for Kachin language courses until the early 1970s, for Shan and Po and Scot Karen language courses until the mid-1970s, Chin language courses until the late 1970s and Mon language course until the early 1980s.[20]

Given these diametrically opposing facts then, two questions could be raised: Why was the Socialist Government accused of "Burmanizing" the ethnic minorities?, and Why did some schools stop teaching minority languages when others continued to teach them? The answers to both questions lie in the complexities of the political system and the way in which the Socialist Government functioned. A retired senior BSPP official noted that some senior Socialist Government officials thought that the Burmese Way to Socialism would help the Government achieve national unification by encouraging all ethnic groups to transcend their ethnic nationalistic sentiments (Interview, 19 July 2003). Since the Government was more willing to work with the people who would endorse the Burmese Way to Socialism, the system would marginalize the ethnic nationalists.

Chauvinistic statements made by senior central state officials further compounded this situation. For example, BSPP chairman, U Ne Win, publicly stated that Burmans would have to help their backward minority brothers and sisters improve their living standards and the level of culture so that these other cultures will be comparable to that of the Burmans.[21] Also, like its predecessor, the Socialist Government did not define "Myanmarness" clearly and referred to the Burman cultural elements when promoting the Union of Myanmar. Infuriated by the political system and the way senior government officials engaged in nation-building activities, minority nationalists, especially insurgent leaders, began to develop anti-government discourses, which accused the Government of "Burmanizing" the entire population.

In theory, the Socialist Government was supposed to function under collective leadership. In practice, however, most of the State's power was concentrated in the hands of Party Chairman Ne Win. Known to the general public as Number-One-Gyi (Big Number One) or A-Pho-Gyi (Big Old Man), Ne Win had the power to appoint and dismiss, at his own discretion, state and party officials at all levels of administration. Although there were initially some officials who were genuinely interested in establishing a socialist system in the country, by the early 1970s, only those who were willing to please Ne Win remained in important positions. In other words, by the early 1970s, most senior government positions were filled with those who were more interested in securing and maximizing their self-interest than serving the interests of the public. In order to keep their jobs, many senior officials came to practise three *mas* — *ma-loke* (not doing any work), *ma-shote* (not getting involved in any complication) and *ma-pyoke* (not getting dismissed) as guiding principles in performing their duties. In turn, the senior officials appointed their loyal followers to positions in the division/state and township-level administrative units. Hence, although local administrative units were theoretically supposed to be staffed with people elected by the public, the elections, in reality, were merely ceremonial and most candidates nominated by senior government officials always won. Since they owed their jobs to senior government officials, most local state officials were more interested in impressing their patrons than serving the interests of the public (Kyaw Yin Hlaing 2003a, pp. 35–36).

As expected, most self-interested central and local state officials were unwilling to deal with controversial issues even if these deeds would benefit the public. For instance, in the late 1960s, a group of Shan university students tried to promote new Shan scripts and vocabularies invented by some Shan nationalists. Since the old Shan scripts were much closer to Burmese scripts, young educated Shan associated the invention of the new Shan with the Shan nationalist movement. However, based on their suspicions that the promoters of the new Shan scripts were linked to the Shan insurgents, the then members of the Shan State Council refused to accept the new Shan scripts. When some Shan language teachers started speculating whether they should teach new Shan at public schools, the Shan State Council decided to suspend the teaching of Shan language at public schools under their jurisdiction.

Some schools in Mon, Kachin, and Karen states stopped teaching minority languages when they could no longer find teachers capable of teaching both minority languages and other courses. This was because the Socialist Government, unlike its parliamentary predecessor, did not provide its Ministry of Education with a means of allocating budgets for public schools in minority areas to hire minority language teachers. The Ministry expected primary school teachers in the minority areas to follow the example of teachers in Myanmar proper and to teach all subjects. The People's Councils were responsible for helping schools to hire qualified teachers, however, local state officials, instead of locating and hiring qualified teachers, simply suspended minority language classes.[22] When they saw the suspension of minority languages in other schools, many teachers capable of teaching minority languages called for the teaching of minority languages to be suspended as well (Interview, 2 October 2003). This was because they did not want to handle the heavy workload of teaching more classes than they could manage. In some places, local authorities and teachers decided to suspend minority language classes, because students were unable to handle the workload. According to a former Socialist Government official, the irresponsibility of Socialist Government officials was the main reason for the suspension of the teaching of minority languages at public schools in minority areas.[23]

Nevertheless, since the 1966 Education Law allowed public schools in minority areas to teach minority languages up to second grade, there were public schools in minority areas that continued to teach minority languages until the early 1980s. Clearly, the teaching of minority languages at public schools in minority areas continued as long as local state officials were willing to work for it. The teaching of minority languages could sometimes be problematic as insurgent groups and ethnic nationalists hostile to the Socialist Government also tried to promote their languages or their own brand of their languages on their own. This made local state officials, who did not want to be implicated with any socio-political complications, reluctant to promote the teaching of minority languages in minority areas.[24] However, because by the beginning of the 1980s, the officials left in the various levels of the Socialist Government were predominantly those who chiefly abided by the three *ma* principles, most public schools in minority areas stopped teaching minority languages.

It would, however, be incorrect to assume that the teaching of minority languages was suspended throughout the country. Buddhist monasteries and Christian churches continued to offer minority language courses soon after public schools stopped offering them. People from some minority villages collectively hired language teachers to teach their children how to read and write their mother tongues. Moreover, public schools in Chin state, Palong and other remote areas continued to use their mother tongues as the medium of instruction.[25] In city areas, however, younger members of the ethnic minorities came to lose interest in learning how to read and write their own mother tongues as there was no incentive for them to do so. More generally, a growing disinterest in the study of their languages led to the suspension of teaching of minority languages in many monasteries in several minority areas. A Mon lecturer from Yangon University surmised that Mons in Mon state who could speak Mon only made up approximately 50 per cent of the population and only about 20 per cent knew how to write in Mon (Interview, 2 October 2003). A retired Shan politician also noted that only Shan people living in remote areas took the trouble of learning to write Shan (Interview, 28 July 2003). Both the Mon lecturer and retired Shan politician were united in their observations that young people from their respective states were more familiar with Burman history than their own ethnic histories. Thus, in contrast to those who grew up in the parliamentary period, these young ethnic minorities tend to associate themselves with the country more than their ethnic group.[26]

For ethnic nationalists, the central and local government organs were part of the same authoritarian state. Regardless of the true reason behind the cessation of minority language classes, the ethnic nationalists strongly believed that the Government was responsible for the public schools' suspension of minority languages classes. Furthermore, they also resented the Government for not rendering any assistance to them. Minority nationalist leaders blamed the Government for the illiteracy of the large majority of young ethnic minorities living in cities and its surrounding areas in their own languages. Unsurprisingly, schools opened in the insurgent areas, often referred to as "liberated areas" by insurgent groups and "black areas" by the Government, taught most courses in minority languages and Burmese was taught only as a foreign language. Insurgent leaders and teachers from those schools also tried to instill anti-Burmese sentiments into the minds of their young ethnic minority students by emphasizing the brutalities of Burman kings and soldiers in their history lessons. An NGO activist currently running teachers' training courses for ethnic minorities in Chiang Mai attests to this:

> Most ethnic minorities growing up in liberated areas were taught to view Burmans in a negative light. This is more so given the fact that most of them grew up experiencing the attacks of government forces. This explains why most of them only speak their own languages and are not fluent in Burmese. They have associated Burmans with danger and the military forces attacking them, as such, whenever they heard that Burmans were coming, they would run away. The paradoxical thing is, though, most minority leaders need to speak Burmese so as to enable them to directly communicate with other minority leaders (Interview, 7 June 2003).

Although it never stopped developing anti-colonial discourses, the Socialist Government's policy towards the English language changed when one of U Ne Win's daughters did not get into the Royal Medical School in England because of her poor English. English came to be re-emphasized as the language of modernization and re-introduced as a major medium of instruction both in high schools and universities. In fact, contrary to appearances, English did not cease to be a popular language throughout the socialist period. The young people in Myanmar, like many other young people in poor countries in the 1980s, were extremely keen on getting jobs in foreign countries, and to do so, they needed to have some working knowledge of English. The reintroduction of English as a medium of instruction at various levels of public schools, however, did not help young Burmese to improve their English because many lecturers were trained in Burmese and were ill-equipped to teach courses in English. Although the Government re-introduced English as a medium of instruction in the classroom as part of its modernization of the education system, people viewed the poor state of English proficiency among young people as evidence of the Socialist Government's failure to modernize the country.

All in all, the Socialist Government did not have a clear plan to "Burmanize" the entire population. In fact, some of the top ten most powerful Socialist Government officials were not Burmans; for example, the BSPP's powerful Assistant Secretary, Tin Oo, and the penultimate President of the socialist regime, Sein Lwin, were Mons. The Government's major problem was its officials' failure to represent the interests of both the majority Burmans and the ethnic minorities. These government officials were mainly interested in either keeping their jobs or getting promotion, and, consequently, the teaching of minority languages was suspended largely because the state officials were not willing to work for the interests of minority peoples. Even in the face of lack of state officials' support, the Socialist Government generally allowed minority groups to promote their languages and cultures freely, as long as they did not challenge its rule. Therefore, one may argue that during the socialist period, minority groups enjoyed a great deal of cultural freedom, but little political freedom.

LANGUAGE AND NATION-BUILDING IN THE SLORC/SPDC PERIOD (1988–)

The State Peace and Development Council (SPDC), at first known as the State Law and Order Restoration Council (SLORC), seized control of the Government in late 1988. Initially, the military leaders regarded all political opposition and insurgent groups as major opponents, but gradually came to perceive the major opposition party, the National League for Democracy (NLD), as more dangerous than the ethnic insurgent groups, precisely because the former wanted to take its place.[27] The Junta began to make peace with insurgent groups in order to consolidate its position vis-à-vis the NLD in 1989 and, by the close of 1997, it had made ceasefire agreements with seventeen insurgent groups. When making ceasefire agreements with insurgent groups, the Junta began to promote the idea that Myanmar was a multiethnic state with 135 different races and over 100 different languages. Some observers and minority nationalists concluded that the Government promoted such ideas to undermine the unity between different minority groups and to perpetuate Burman dominance.

Among the Junta's strategies to preserve the unity of the Union was to maintain Burmese as the official language. Due to past governments' successful efforts in promoting the teaching of Burmese in minority areas, most young people, and those in their fifties, spoke Burmese as fluently as Burmans. The Junta used Burmese as a means of transmitting its propaganda, which was designed to undermine its opponents and to convince the public, both the majority Burmans and ethnic minorities, that their lives would be better off only under military rule. Senior military officials and the Government-controlled media repeatedly noted that if the public did not cooperate with the military Government and lacked Union spirit, they would be responsible for Myanmar's absorption into any of the other foreign powers surrounding it.[28]

Like the Socialist Government, the Junta permitted both indigenous and foreign minority groups to freely promote the teaching and studying of their own languages. Ethnic minorities were further impelled to promote their own languages when the Junta held the National Convention in 1992 to draft a new constitution. Referring to the language requirement for statehood proposed by Aung San in 1947, many ethnic groups tried to emphasize the uniqueness of their languages when they presented their causes at the Convention (*Proposals Submitted at the National Convention* 1993). Since then, some minority groups have tried to revive their languages. For instance, the rare use of the Kachin state's Red Shan written language culminated in the ignorance of many Red Shan of the existence of their written language. Given the trend in promulgating ethnic languages, it was certainly no coincidence that a Red Shan cultural association wrote the history of Red Shan in its own language in the early 1990s (Interview, 12 October 2003). Although the National Convention has been stalled since 1996, minority political parties have continued to promote their languages in a more aggressive manner than they did in the 1970s and 1980s (Interviews, June 2003–October 2003).

In 1998, however, the Junta's National Education Promotion Program dropped the teaching of minority languages at pre-university level classes. This was because, a Ministry of Education official explained, the existence of many different ethnic minority groups with their own dialects and languages in each minority state and their constant pressures on the Government to introduce their language classes at public schools in their respective areas created many problems. It was also noted that public schools in minority areas lacked the capacity to teach the mother tongues of all the peoples residing within their jurisdiction. Subsequently, the Government decided to let the minority groups organize their ethnic minority language classes on their own. This led the local communities of many minority areas to hire language teachers to teach their students the written aspects of their languages.[29]

This phenomenon was not merely restricted to the ethnic villages. In Yangon, there were Minority Cultural Associations, especially, Mon and Shan Associations, offering courses in their languages. Also, university students could organize minority language courses at the universities,[30] so long as they obtained permission from their respective registrars to have a room for that purpose (Interview, 12 October 2003). But since 1996, after the Government had closed the universities for about three years, student associations became less active and accordingly stopped organizing language classes (Interview, 29 October 2003).

Regardless of its efforts, the Military Government remained very unpopular and was continually criticized by the opposition and minority groups for "Burmanizing" the entire population. The Government was not the only beneficiary from the widespread usage of the Burman language within the country. The predominance of Burmese made it easier for opposition groups to continue their dissemination of anti-government propaganda throughout the country; this usage of Burmese as a subversive anti-government tool had its roots in the socialist period. Thus, with the exception of the inhabitants of a few remote areas, Daw Aung San Suu Kyi and other NLD leaders were able to directly communicate with ethnic minorities when touring their areas. Also, many people from minority areas could read anti-government literature distributed by opposition groups and learn about developments, which the Government wanted to cover up, from the Burmese language programmes from BBC, VOA and RFA radio broadcasts.[31] Political opposition groups and foreign radio stations served as alternative sources of information, and their anti-military discourses undermined the Government's anti-colonialist and NLD discourses.

For all its enthusiastic promotion of Union spirit, the Military Government did not have a clear definition of "Myanmarness" other than the fact that Myanmar represented all the ethnic groups in the country. Similar to the parliamentary and socialist periods, there were a lot of overlaps between the "Myanmarness" and "Burmanness". Most cultural activities undertaken by the Junta under the label of promoting Myanmar culture focused mainly on Burman culture. For example, although the Government rewrote its interpretation of the historical wars between the Burman and Mon kings, public school history textbooks continued to emphasize the roles of the Burman kings who attempted to unify the country. To make matters worse, some senior military officers often expressed their desire to emulate the "mighty ancient Myanmar kings" in reunifying the Government. Many ethnic nationalists resented the teaching of such historical lessons as well as the fact that the Government did not provide any assistance to the teaching of minority languages.[32] Not surprisingly, ethnic nationalists responded by constructing anti-government discourses and disseminating them through the foreign media and the Internet.

The Government's intolerance of the opposition groups also engendered much misunderstanding of its language policy. Any group suspected of preaching anti-government sentiments was labelled by the Government as working towards the disintegration of the Union. In teaching their own language, ethnic minority groups also promoted ethnic nationalism and were occasionally critical of the Government. When the Government got wind of this "marked opposition", it would close such schools. For instance, in 1994 and 1998, the Government closed down some Mon schools run by the New Mon State Party. Mon nationalists and foreign observers alleged that the schools were closed for teaching their own ethnic languages. This allegation was not fully justified, for while the schools in the ethnic regions were closed down, the Mon Cultural Association in Yangon, and the Departments of Myanmar Language and Literature in the universities continued to offer courses on the Mon language. In reality, the Government was not bothered with the teaching of ethnic languages, but only proceeded to close down the schools because they feared that the schools might become the birth place of anti-government activists. When it was proven, after some meetings with the Mon leaders, that language was the only thing taught to the students, the Government permitted the Mon schools to reopen.

In most of the country, the absence of government support for minority languages and cultures and the promotion of Burmese contributed to the decline of minority languages and culture.[33] Furthermore, the success of the Government's education programme in teaching the peoples of Myanmar to be almost united in their loyalty to the country is quite evident. In other words, ethnic minorities, taught in Burmese as the medium of instruction and exposed to the Burman nationalist interpretation of Myanmar history, were likely to identify themselves with the defence of the nation. Nevertheless, when asked where their loyalties lie, with the Government or the country, none of them stated the Government. In contrast, ethnic minorities who grew up in the so-called "liberated" areas, controlled by insurgent groups, went through a different socialization process. Since they studied Burmese in their schools as a second language, they assumed that they need not master it. Many of them did not know how to speak, read and write Burmese very well and, in fact, they hated Burmans and considered Burmese as the language of the enemy. This could be attributed to their association of the Burman language with the brutality and violence of the "invading" Burman armies attacking them.[34]

However, it is interesting to note that the various ethnic insurgent groups would use Burmese as their common medium of negotiation. At Mesot, at the Thai-Myanmar border, the multiethnic front of the National Council for the Union of Myanmar (NCUB), which consists of Burman, Shan, Karen, Kachin, Rakhine and other ethnic groups, used Burmese as its chief mode of communication. Although they use Burmese in their discussions or for planning their anti-government activities, many of the ethnic nationalists and anti-Burman Government activists wanted to promote English as the official language. However, their plan to render English as the official language is problematic because most of the ethnic nationalists and anti-Burman Government activists speak better Burmese than English. Their desire to institute English as the official language stems from their belief that English, being a neutral language, will ensure that no one group will dominate politically or socially. The rationale is that if Burmese remains the national language, the ethnic Burmans will continue to have the upper hand in politics and all other sectors of society.

Ironically, in spite of its anti-colonial stance, in recent years, the Government has placed a great deal of emphasis on the importance of English, such that most departments in all universities have reverted to using English as a medium of instruction. However, in effecting this change, the Government failed to consider that most of the university teachers were trained in Burmese and thus unqualified to teach in English. The students, being not well versed in the language themselves, usually resorted to plagiarism in their term papers and thesis. Also, there were students who wrote their theses in Burmese before getting someone to translate their work into English. Despite the negative effects, the Government persisted in its promotion of English; for example, various government-sponsored civil society organizations, such as the Union Solidarity and Development Association (USDA) opened English language classes for its members.[35]

It can be surmised that the Junta carried out nation-building, activities as a part of its attempt to justify its continued rule of the country. It used the official language as a means of conveying its intent and propaganda. However, the Military Government does not enjoy sole control over the use of languages as a propaganda tool. Opposition groups also made use of the official language to disseminate anti-government discourses throughout the country. Similar to the Socialist Government, the Junta allowed minority groups to freely promote their languages and cultures as long as they did not challenge its rule. Nevertheless, due to its failure to support the promotion of minority cultures, the Junta was accused of "Burmanizing" the entire population.

CONCLUSION

Successive governments claimed that they instituted Burmese as the official language for the sake of better communication amongst the various ethnic groups. They also claimed that being an independent country, it is only natural that Myanmar uses one of its native languages as the official language, rather than a foreign language like English. Since the majority of the people are ethnic Burmans, the selection and implementation of Burmese as the official language seemed a natural choice. Until recently, most ethnic nationalists did not see the implementation of Burmese as the official language as a slight on the other languages and culture in the Union. However, they resented successive Myanmar governments for not sufficiently supporting their respective languages and cultures. There is a fundamental difference between ethnic nationalists and Burman political leaders on the matter of language politics and nation-building. While ethnic elites and nationalists believe that the Union should only last as long as it benefited them, the Burman political leaders appear to be obsessed with ancient Burman history and their grandiose thoughts of unifying the country.

Apart from their belief in themselves as the chief unifiers of the country, post-colonial Myanmar governments have neither a clear nation-building discourse nor a clear definition of "Myanmarness". Whenever they claimed that something was done for the sake of nation-building, it was usually a deploy to keep themselves in power. For example, they often used the official language as a propaganda tool. Since they were not popularly elected, the Socialist and current Military Governments had to organize popular activities to legitimize themselves. The promotion of Burman culture and language was clearly a means to pacify and gain the support of the majority Burman populace. Although it is true that the Government did not actively seek to promote minority cultures and languages, this oversight was more due to ignorant irresponsibility than governmental policy.[36]

The establishment of Burmese as the official language has helped to facilitate communication between the various ethnic groups. Indeed, Burmese played a crucial role in making the various ethnic groups feel that they are all fellow citizens belonging to the same country. With the exception of the first twenty years of the socialist period, successive Myanmar governments viewed English as a language of modernization. The current military government is actively trying to promote it, however, the present educational system is too weak to aid people in mastering the language. For the public, English is a language that could help them to get good jobs both within and outside the country. Due to their antipathy for the Burmans, many minority activists based in Thailand are keen to make English the official language of the country. While they believe in the necessity of linguistic centralization, they have no desire to be "linguistically subdued and culturally incorporated". This is extremely apparent in that many politically conscious and motivated minority nationalists have publicly stated that their languages need to be reinstated. In contrast, the NLD and other large political parties want to maintain Burmese as the official language. Given this situation, it is not preposterous to assume that language policy-making will be a controversial political issue for whoever comes to power in the future.

Notes

1. Before proceeding, it would indeed be prudent to clarify the usage of the terms: Myanmar, Burma, Burman and Burmese. While Burman usually refers to the ethnic majority "Bamar", Burmese and Myanmar can be said to be the name of the ethnic majority, the Burman language, and the term representing all citizens of the country or the name of the country. In order to avoid confusion, this paper will use Burman as the name for the ethnic majority, Burmese for the Burman language and Myanmar for the name of the country and all its citizens.
2. Committee for the Compilation of the History of Do-Ba-Ma-Asyayone, *Do-Ba-Ma-Asyayone Tha-Mai (History of Our Bama Organization)*, Vol. 1 (Sarpay Beikman, Yangon: 1976): 127.
3. In fact, the Karens formed the first organization bearing the name of an ethnic group.
4. The statehood is a federated state where an elected State Council enjoys some autonomy in administering its territory.
5. In modern Myanmar history, the period between 1948 and 1962 is known as the Parliamentary period, for the country in the British-style and system during that time.
6. U Nu also attended ethnic cultural festivals in order to show his endorsement

of different ethnic cultures (Nu 1954, p. 1). In trying to encourage various ethnic groups to respect and value each others' cultures, U Nu was recorded to have said at a Mon cultural conference, "Mon culture is not the sole concern of the Mons. It is also the concern of Burmans. Likewise, the term Burman culture is not the monopoly of Burman; it is also the property of the Mon people as well" (ibid., p. 3).

7. When the Government refused to grant Union Statehood to Karen, the Karen National Defense Organization (KNDO) launched an armed struggle against it, instigating the Karen battalions in the government army to join the KNDO's fight against the Government. Similarly, the Burman Communist Party (BCP) and some Kachin soldiers also went underground during this period. Following these incidents, the remnants of the KMT forces entered Eastern Shan state with the intention of using it as a stronghold against the communist government in China.

8. As retired Brigadier General Aung Gyi remarked, the Government blamed this misunderstanding between Burman soldiers and ethnic minorities on the soldiers' lack of discipline and the lack of a common language between the soldiers and ethnic minorities (Interview, 25 June 2002).

9. Although the Buddhist missionary work was aimed chiefly at the minorities practising animism, a large number of Christian minorities resented the Government's actions. They felt that the Government was seeking to marginalize non-Buddhist groups by refusing to help them.

10. There were reportedly more than ten minority language newspapers in circulation during the parliamentary period.

11. The language of a major ethnic group, Rakhine, was not taught separately as Rakhine uses the same alphabets as Burmese.

12. For example, some Pa O tribes in Shan state briefly rebelled against Sawbwas (Shan traditional rulers) (Yaunghwe 1987, p. 114). However, most small ethnic groups were on the whole too politically weak to turn against the dominance of their respective local governments.

13. For instance, public schools in the *In-daw-gyi* area of Kachin state did not offer Kachin language courses, because almost two-thirds of its students were non-Kachin.

14. Regardless of the Government's palpable promotion of Burmese, the Constitution also permitted the use of English in the country. The Government thus allowed missionary schools where English was the medium of instruction to continue its operations. In fact, English remained a popular language in the country. This was evident from the many English bureaucratic letters and memos. Likewise, many Indian and westernized Burmans continued to write letters to government officials in English. Many well-to-do Buddhist families, including those supporting the promotion of Burmese, continued to send their children to missionary schools so as to allow their children to master English. At universities, students could take their lessons in either

English or Burmese, but those who opted for classes where the medium of instruction was English were considered smarter than those who took classes in Burmese.

15. U Nu and many other Burman political and military leaders, including leaders of opposition parties, frequently discussed the importance of keeping the Union together. They overtly and indirectly said that under no circumstance would they allow the Union to disintegrate. This rationale later justified the military's seizure of the country in 1962; as will be discussed later, it took control of the country on the pretext that the country was on the verge of collapse.

16. A prominent Shan leader and the first president of independent Myanmar, Sao Shwe Thaik declared in Parliament that if he had known standardized education, health services and the economy in his state would remain poor under the Burman-dominated Government, he would not have signed the Panglong Agreement (Parliamentary Proceedings (CN), II, xx1, 821).

17. Apart from attending minority peoples' cultural festivals, most central state officials were rarely involved in the promotion of minority cultures. In contrast, they actively participated in the promotion of Burman culture and language.

18. Three retired members of Mon and Kachin insurgent movements revealed that they too communicated with people from other insurgent groups in Burmese.

19. The RC also tried to better understand the cultures of minority people by commissioning scholars and officials from the Ministry of Culture to conduct research into minority cultures. The Ministry of Culture also opened cultural museums for minority peoples' cultural artifacts at the capitals of minority states, so as to promote and conserve these minorities' cultures (Daw Mya Oo 2003, p. 71). The curators of the museums at minority capitals must not only be members of the dominant ethnic groups whose names the state bore, but also speakers of their respective ethnic languages. In 1965, the Socialist Government also established the Academy for Development of National Races to train teachers and socialist cadres for minority areas. The Academy's trainees were recruited from among the residents of minority areas.

20. Ten government officials and eight businessmen who went to primary school in Shan state in the early 1970s said that they studied Shan language at school. A retired administrative official from Shan state also confirmed Shan language was taught at schools in Shan state until the mid-1970s (Interview, 25 October 2003). Some college students from Chin and Mon states also remarked that some schools in their respective villages taught their respective minority languages until the mid-1980s. Three Mon tutors from Yangon University said that they studied the Mon language for four years in primary schools in their respective villages in the early 1980s

(Interview, 22 October 2003). They also remembered taking Mon language exams held by their respective township people's councils. One of them also remembered being conferred a certificate for passing the exam.

21. In reality, however, apart from making people from Naga tribes wear pants, especially when they attended the Union Day festival in Yangon, the Socialist Government did not forcibly change or eliminate any of their cultural practices. Traditionally, people from the Naga tribe rarely covered their private parts.

22. A retired schoolteacher from Shan state noted that the State Councils at minority areas ought to have sent more people to the Academy for the Development of National Races to train as teachers because most of the Academy's graduates wanted to become party cadres rather than teachers (Interview, 29 July 2003).

23. Many minority nationalists thought that it was U Ne Win who wanted the suspension of the teaching of minority languages at public schools in minority areas. If the central Government and U Ne Win wanted to suspend the teaching of minority languages in public schools, the suspension of all languages would take place at the same time. A retired senior government official noted that many senior government officials often gave "U Ne Win does not like it" answer whenever they did not want to deal with an issue raised by the public. Three retired education ministry officials did not recall receiving any orders suspending the teaching of minority languages. In reality, U Ne Win asked officials from the Ministries of Education and Culture to develop Burmese-Ethnic minority language dictionaries to foster better understanding between Burmans and ethnic minorities in 1981 (The Speeches of the BSPP Chairman 1985, pp. 39–48). However, due to its limited human resources and technical capacity, the Ministry of Culture has yet to implement Ne Win's instruction. However, developing Burmese-ethnic minority language dictionaries remains on the list of future projects the Ministry of Culture wishes to undertake.

24. A retired socialist government official confirmed the widespread notion that minority areas blessed with some righteous officials willing to promote local culture and customs tended to teach minority languages for longer periods of time than in places where the officials did not have much interest in preserving and promoting local culture and customs.

25. Many people from such areas only learned how to speak Burmese properly when they went to college in major cities.

26. It is worth noting at this juncture that most young ethnic Christian minorities continued to study the reading and writing of their mother tongues because their churches encouraged them to read the Bible in their own languages. Apparently, the socialist regime was insecure in its own legitimacy. It was intolerant of any challenges to its rule. When it suspected that private minority language classes had become venues for anti-government activists to get

together or that these classes were birthplaces for anti-government activists, the Government closed down these language courses and arrested the teachers (Interview, 15 October 2003).

27. The Military Government allowed a multiparty democratic election to be held in 1990, but it refused to hand over power to the winning party, the NLD.

28. The Military Government also used anti-colonial discourses in demonizing the NLD and its leader. Because NLD leader Daw Aung San Suu Kyi was married to a British academic, Dr. Michael Aris, the government media attacked her as a person who diluted the purity of the Burman race. This, by inference, implied that Daw Aung San Suu Kyi is injurious to the preservation of the Union.

29. Schools run by the ceasefire insurgent groups also offered minority language courses (Thein Lwin 2000).

30. However, while the Department of Myanmar Language and Literature at various public universities did not stop teaching Mon language in their honors classes, the University of the Development of National Races (upgraded from the Academy) continued to require its trainees to take a minority language course other than their own and Burmese.

31. I interviewed many people from more than forty ethnic minority group, and these people in their fifties and sixties, all recalled seeing people listening to the Burmese language programmes on the BBC and VOA broadcasts in the 1950s and 1960s in their native places. However, they all added that with the advent of the 1990s, many people living in minority areas have come to be regular listeners of Burmese language programmes on foreign radio broadcasts. They all noted that one of the reasons for the present number of ethnic minorities listening to radio broadcasts in Burmese is that, unlike in the 1950s, most ethnic minorities these days speak, read and write Burmese as well as the Burmans.

32. The fact that the Government discriminated against Christian and Muslim civil servants also undermined its attempt to win the support of minority people.

33. A random survey of some 300 people from the various minority groups showed 100 per cent of them were better acquainted with Burman history than their own ethnic histories. While all of them have read novels in Burmese, less than 5 per cent have read literature in their own languages regularly. Eighty per cent of them said that their best friends were Burman. In terms of music, 100 per cent listened to Burmese songs, 85 per cent listened to either Burmese or English songs, and only 10 per cent regularly listened to songs in their own languages. While almost 35 per cent of them could speak their own languages, only 20 per cent knew how to write in them. But all of them could read and write Burmese very well.

34. I spoke to five students from the Karen area and they told me that roughly

40 per cent of their compatriots did not know any Burmese, while the rest did know some Burmese. My other sources, an ex-Karen solider, informed me that about half the Karen population in the "so-called liberated area" could speak Burmese and the other half could not; however, he added that those who spoke Burmese fluently accounted for less than 5 per cent of the population in that area.

35. The Government also set new standards for the Romanization of place names within the country in 1989. This came when the name of the country in English was renamed Myanmar. The English names of several Burman cities also reverted to their Burmese names, Rangoon was now Yangon and Moulmein was now Mawlamying. Street names in Myanmar were also affected by this change. While this "renaming" project has been dubbed by some members of the opposition and the international community as the Military Government's method of Burmanizing the country, the truth is, this name changing or name reversion carried out by the Government hardly affected the locals, because locals had always referred to these places by their Burmese names. This name changing of locations was meant to affect the international community as a part of the Government's anti-colonial nation-building process. Thus, this is not the Government's method of Burmanizing the society.

36. However, the ethnic elites and nationalists consider the Socialist and current Military Governments' actions unacceptable and that the words of the Burman political leaders were nothing more than empty rhetoric. Amongst these ethnic elites and nationalists were certain factions who believed that their territories ought to be independent from the Union, as such, these ethnic nationalist and activists have formed insurgency groups to rebel against the Burman-dominated Military Government.

References

Allot, Anna. "Language Policy and Language Planning in Burma". In *Language Policy: Language Planning and Sociolinguistics in South-East Asia*, edited by David Bradley. Canberra: Department of Linguistics, Research School of Pacific Studies, Australia National University, 1985.

Burma Socialist Program Party. *Political Report to the Fourth Party Congress.* Yangon: BSPP Headquarters, 1981.

———. *Historic Speeches of the BSPP Chairman U Ne Win*, Vol. II. Yangon: BSPP Headquarters, 1985.

Callahan, Mary. "Language Policy in Modern Burma: Fashioning an Official Language, Marginalizing all Others", unpublished paper.

Chao Tzang Yawnghwe. *The Shan of Burma: Memoirs of a Shan Exile.* Singapore: Institute of Southeast Asian Studies, 1987.

Kyaw Yin Hlaing. "Reconsidering the Failure of the Burma Socialist Program

Party Government to Eradicate Internal Economic Impediments". *South East Asia Research* 11, no. 1 (2003*a*): 5–58.

———. "Plural Society Revisited: Misapprehension of Muslim Burmese by Buddhist Burmese". Paper presented at the 2003 APSA meeting, 2003*b*.

Kyaw Win, U, et al. *Nationalities Affairs and the 1947 Constitution*, Vol. 1. Yangon: Universities' Press, 1990.

Kyawt Kyawt Khine. "Nation-building in Myanmar (1948–62)". *Journal of Myanmar Academy of Arts and Sciences* 1, no. 1 (December 2002).

Lehman, F.K. "Ethnic Categories in Burma and the Theory of Social Systems". In *Southeast Asian Tribes, Minorities and Nations*, edited by Peter Kunstadter. Princeton: Princeton University Press, 1967.

Ministry of Culture. *Facts about the Department of Culture*. Yangon: nd.

Ministry of Education. *Hakha Chin Kindergarten Reader*. Yangon: Sarpay Beikman, 1979.

———. *Kachin First Grade Reader*. Yangon: Sarpay Beikman, 1972.

———. *Mon Kindergarten Reader*. Yangon: Sarpay Beikman, 1982.

———. *Po Karen Kindergarten Reader*. Yangon: Sarpay Beikman, 1976.

———. *Scot Karen Kindergarten Reader*. Yangon: Sarpay Beikman, 1975.

———. *Shan Kindergarten Reader*. Yangon: Sarpay Beikman, 1974.

———. *The Objectives of the Academy for the Development of National Races*. Yangon: Ministry of Education, nd.

Maung Maung. *Burma's Constitution*. The Hague: Martinus Nijhoff, 1961.

Mya Oo, Daw. "Tai-Yin-Tha-Yin-Kye-Mu-Thu-Thay-Tha-Na", [Research on Minority Cultures], *Yinkyemu* [Culture] 10 (2003): 69–78.

Nu, Thakin. *Towards Peace and Democracy*. Yangon: Government Printing House, 1949.

———. *From Peace to Stability*. Yangon: Government Printing House, 1951.

———. *Towards a Welfare State*. Yangon: Government Printing House, 1952.

Nu, U. *Burma Looks Ahead*. Yangon: Ministry of Information, 1953.

Pu Galay, U. *Thakin Nu's Revolution*. Yangon: Daw Tin Yee Press, 1949.

San Nyein and Mya Han. *Myanmar Politics in Transition (1962–1974)*, Vol. II. Yangon: Universities' Press, 1993.

San Nyein, U. and Dr. Myint Kyi. *Myanmar Politics*. Yangon: Universities' Press, 1991.

Scott, James. *Seeing like a State*. New Haven: Yale University Press, 1998.

Smith, Martin. *Burma: Insurgency and the Politics of Ethnicity*. London: Zed Books, 1999.

Stepan, Alfred. *Arguing Comparative Politics*. New York: Oxford University Press, 2001.

Thein Lwin. "The Teaching of Ethnic Language and the Role of Education in the Context of Mon Ethnic Nationality in Burma: Initial Report of the First Phase of the Study on the Thai-Burma Border, November 1999–February 2000". Available online at <http://www.students.ncl.ac.uk/thein.lwin>.

Others
A Brief Biography of Mon Leader U Chit Thaung.
Do-Ba-Ma Asyiayone Tha-Mai (History of We Bama Association), Vols. 1 & 2. Yangon: Sarpay Beikman, 1976.
Parliamentary Proceedings, Chamber of Nationalities, Vol. ii, xxl. August 1952.
Proposals submitted to the National Convention (9–14 August 1993). Yangon: News and Periodical Enterprise, 1993.
Pyi-Htaung-Su-Sait-Dut (Union spirit). Yangon: News and Periodical Enterprise, 2001.
Speeches given by the Chairman of the Myanmar Historical Commission, SPDC Secretary I General Khin Nyunt, Vols. 1 & 2.
Summary Report on Insurgency in Myanmar. Yangon: News and Periodical Enterprise, 1990.
University for the Development of National Races [a small booklet about the university].

8

The Positions of Non-Thai Languages in Thailand

Theraphan Luangthongkum

INTRODUCTION

Thailand is located in the middle of the Southeast Asian mainland, which is a region where a large number of ethnic groups and languages can be found. There are only a few Southeast Asian countries, but each country comprises several ethnic groups. As a result, both cultural diversity and linguistic diversity are natural. The governments and the authorities of each Southeast Asian country have to accept, or at least be aware of, this fact in order to set up appropriate policies at all levels if they would like to achieve their goals in whatever they are pursuing. Handling peoples who have different cultural backgrounds is not an easy task. Without a real understanding of their diverse minds, it would be impossible to maintain peace and national unity.

In the past, the hidden policy of the Royal Thai Government used to be "assimilation". Thus, the emphasis was on *Ekkalak* that is a coined word meaning "only one characteristic". The "Thai identity" was related to *Ekkalak Thai*, a cliché that could be heard and seen very often. Furthermore, the *Office of Ekkalak Thai* was established in order to make the policy become true and fruitful. One of the major duties of the *Ekkalak Thai Office* is to campaign for the national unity and security of Thailand on the basis of "one language and one culture in Thai society". When the Eighth National Socio-Economic Development Plan was launched in 1997, the concept of *Pahulak* or "pluralism", recommended by the National Security Council and reinforced by Thai academics, replaced the previous concept of *Ekkalak*. Cultural diversity has indeed become part of tourism promotion in Thailand. Consequently, linguists specializing in ethnic-minority languages are able to share this new mainstream thinking.

This paper will look into: (1) some aspects of Thailand's demographic characteristics, (2) the classification of the ethnic minorities, (3) sociolinguistic setting in Thailand, (4) the positions of Thai and regional Thai languages/dialects, and (5) the positions of the non-Thai languages, which will be the main focus of this paper.

DEMOGRAPHIC SKETCH

According to the *2000 Population and Housing Census*, the total population of Thailand is 61 million. It is noticeable that females outnumber males in all regions. Regarding the population distribution, 68.9 per cent live in non-municipal areas and the other 31.1 per cent live in municipalities. For those living in the municipal areas, 33.6 per cent live in Bangkok, the capital of Thailand. On the basis of population distribution, Thailand can be said to consist of five regions: the North, Central, Northeast, South and Bangkok. Comparing the population in these regions, the Northeast has the largest population (34.2 per cent), followed by the Central region (23.3 per cent), the North (18.8 per cent), the South (13.3 per cent) and Bangkok (10.4 per cent) respectively.

Nearly all of the people living in Thailand, i.e. 99.5 per cent, have Thai nationality, the rest (about 0.5 per cent) have other nationalities: Chinese (141,649), Indian (9,112), Nepalese (13,492), Pakistani (2,921), Bangladeshi (1,949), Sri Lankan (10,164), Vietnamese (8,336), Lao (29,137), Cambodian (18,718), Japanese (9,971), Korean (1,262), Filipinos (1,264), Burmese (108,540), Malaysian (1,290), Singaporean (803), Indonesian (549), American (4,411), Canadian (907), Australian (1,595), New Zealander (2,403), British (3,217), German (2,531), Portuguese (143), Dutch (406), French (1,343), Danish (437), Swedish (670), Swiss (997), Italian (658), Norwegian (805), other nationalities (55,727) and non-identified or unknown nationalities (288,841). Most Thais are Hinayana Buddhists (94.6 per cent), a few are Muslims (4.6 per cent), and the rest are Christians and others.

Regarding the average years of educational attainment, the results of the *2000 Population and Housing Census* indicate that the population aged fifteen and older have an average of 7.8 years of education. The average years of schooling in the municipal areas are much higher than that in non-municipal areas, i.e. 10.2 compared to 6.6 years. The population of Bangkok has the highest average years of schooling (11.9), followed by that of the Central region (8.0), the South (7.7), the Northeast (7.0) and the North (6.6), respectively.

Based on languages spoken in households, most of the over-five-year-old Thai population is monolingual. This means that they speak only Thai or a non-Thai language. Bilinguals and multilinguals are much less in number. The number of speakers in each category can be found in Table 8.1.[1]

CLASSIFICATION OF THE ETHNIC MINORITIES

Thailand's ethnic minorities are classified in different ways by official government bodies and/or academics in accordance with the purpose of

TABLE 8.1
Number of Monolingual and Bilingual/Multilingual Speakers

Language	Number of speakers
Only Thai/ Thai dialect	52,325,037
Thai and Non-Thai language(s)	3,218,970
Only Non-Thai language(s)	737,531
Non-Thai languages	3,956,727
English	48,202
Chinese	231,350
Japanese	38,565
Malay	1,202,911
Mon-Burmese	67,061
Khmer-Suai	1,291,024
Lao-Vietnamese	25,037
Tai	44,004
Lahu	70,058
Lisu	24,476
Akha	54,241
Khmu'	6,246
Lawa	31,583
Thin	2,317
Karen	317,968
Hmong (Miao)	112,686
Mien (Yao)	21,238
Haw (Chinese Muslim)	3,247
Indian	5,598
Others	33,481
Unknown	325,134

Source: Adapted from *The 2000 Population and Housing Census*.
<http://www.nso.go.th/thai/stat/stat_23/toc_3/3.2.2.1-1>.

the classification. For example, the National Security Council classifies ethnic minorities for political and security purposes, while linguists base their classification on academic principles.

The law classifies the ethnic minorities in Thailand into eighteen categories.[2] The official committees of the National Security Council and of the Ministry of Interior define so-called "ethnic minorities" as follows:

> ...ETHNIC MINORITIES mean the groups of people who do not have Thai citizenship. They are less in number than the owner of the country. Their cultures, customs and traditions differ among each other and from the national ones. They entered and stayed in Thailand in many different ways...
>
> (Population Registration Office 1999, p. 1)

Based on the above definition, the ethnic minorities of Thailand have been classified into eighteen categories, where each ethnic group can be identified broadly by the colours of their identification cards:

1. Vietnamese refugees (white with blue rim)
2. Former Kok Min Tang military officers and soldiers (white)
3. Haw refugees or Chinese Muslims from Yunnan (yellow)
4. "Independent Haw" or the relatives of Kok Min Tang military officers or soldiers (orange)
5. Former Malay-Chinese Communists (green)
6. Tai Lue from Sip Song Panna Autonomous Region in Yunnan (orange)
7. Lao refugees (pale blue with blue rim)
8. Nepalese refugees (green)
9. Displaced Burmese nationals: Mon, Karen, Shan, Wa, Burmese, etc. (pink)
10. Illegal immigrants from Myanmar (orange)
11. Burmese labourers (purple)
12. Displaced Burmese-born Thai (yellow with blue rim)
13. Highlanders or tribal peoples: Mon, Karen, Miao, Yao, Lahu, Akha, Thin, Lisu, Lua' and Khmu' (pale blue)
14. Cambodian-born Thai refugees from Kong island (green)
15. Illegal immigrants from Kampuchea (white with red rim)
16. Mla Bri or the Spirits of the Yellow Leaves (pale blue)
17. Highland communities (green with red rim)
18. Illegal foreign labourers from developing countries (special work-permit document issued by the Ministry of Labour and Social Welfare)

The most recent ethno-linguistic field survey done by Premsrirat et al. (2001) confirms the known information that approximately sixty languages (excluding foreign languages) are spoken in Thailand. The results of their findings are shown in various ways on many small maps.[3]

Genetic relationship is one of the criteria used by linguists for language classification. On this basis, it can be said that languages spoken by the sixty ethnic groups can be classified into five language families, namely: Tai-Kadai, Sino-Tibetan, Miao-Yao (Hmong-Mien), Austroasiatic (Mon-Khmer) and Austronesian. The distribution of the sixty languages[4] in the four geographical regions is illustrated in Tables 8.2–8.5. For each region, the numbers of provinces, inhabitants and languages including the percentage of speakers are given.

SOCIO-LINGUISTIC SETTING

As stated in the previous sections, the cultural-linguistic diversity in Thailand cannot be denied. However, it is amazing that Thailand has had

TABLE 8.2
Northern Region
(16 provinces, 13 million inhabitants, 34 languages)

Tai-Kadai *(92.5%)*	Sino-Tibetan *(5%)*	Hmong-Mien *(1.6%)*	Mon-Khmer *(0.9%)*
Tai Yuan (Khammueang)	Chinese	Miao	Dara-ang (Palaung)
TaiYa	Haw	Yao	Wa
Tai Yai	Karen		Lua'
Thai Loei	Jingphaw		Plang (Samtao)
Thai Klang (Central Thai)	Burmese		Lamet
Lue	Lisu		Khmu'
Yong	Lahu		Thin (Mal, Prai)
Khuen	Akha		Mla Bri
Song (Tai Dam)	Ugong		Mon (Raman)
Phuan	Mpi		
Lao Isan (Northeastern Thai)	Bisu		
Lao Lom			

Source: Compiled and adapted by Author from Premsrirat, Suwilai et al., 2001.

TABLE 8.3
Central Region
(27 provinces, 16 million inhabitants, 25 languages)

Tai-Kadai (99%)	Sino-Tibetan (0.3%)	Austronesian (0.01%)	Mon-Khmer (0.7%)
Thai Klang (Central Thai)	Chinese	Pattani Malay	Mon (Raman)
Thai Korat (Thai Boeng)	Karen		High Khmer
Tai Yuan (Khammueang)	Ugong		Suai (Kui, Kuai)
Lao Wiang	Burmese		Vietnamese (Kaew)
Lao Khrang			Khmu'
Lao Ngaew			Chong
Lao Tai			Kasong
Lao Isan (Northeastern Thai)			Samre
Song (Tai Dam)			Sa-och
Phuan			
Nyo			

Source: Compiled and adapted by Author from Premsrirat, Suwilai et al., 2001.

TABLE 8.4
Northeastern Region
(19 provinces, 22 million inhabitants, 20 languages)

Tai-Kadai (90%)	Mon-Khmer (10%)
Lao Isan (Northeastern Thai)	High Khmer
Nyo	Suai (Kui, Kuai)
Yoi	Nyoe
Kaloeng	Bru
Phu Thai	So
Phuan	Thavueng (So)
Thai Korat (Thai Boeng)	Vietnamese (Viet, Kaew)
Thai Loei	Nyah Kur (Chao Bon)
Thai Klang (Central Thai)	Mon (Raman)
Tai Dam (Song)	
Saek (Thraek)	

Source: Compiled and adapted by Author from Premsrirat, Suwilai et al., 2001.

TABLE 8.5
Southern Region
(14 provinces, 9 million inhabitants, 11 languages)

Tai-Kadai (96.5%)	Sino-Tibetan (3.3%)	Austronesian (0.2%)	Mon-Khmer (0.01%)
Thai Tai (Southern Thai)	Chinese	Malay (Yawi)	Sakai (Kensiw, Aslian)
Thai Tak Bai	Burmese	Urak Lawoi	Mon (Raman)
Thai Klang (Central Thai)		Moklen (Moken)	
Lao Isan (Northeastern Thai)			

Source: Compiled and adapted by Author from Premsrirat, Suwilai et al., 2001.

less political problems related to the ethnic-minority affairs than her neighbouring countries. While in the past there were less ethnic minorities in Thailand, the number of ethnic groups has been increasing recently due to wars and all kinds of political problems in the other mainland Southeast Asian countries, which share their borders with Thailand.

Suwannaphum or the "golden land" is similar to North America in a sense, i.e., a hotchpotch of heterogeneous population. One obvious difference is that the Suwannaphum kingdom is many thousand years older than the United States of America. Far back in the prehistoric period, different races began to mix because of historical circumstances, and the process has continued until the modern time. The peoples of Suwannaphum learned to be friendly, open-minded, tolerant and diplomatic since the dawn of Southeast Asian civilization. In spite of cultural-linguistic diversity, Thailand have never had serious racial problems. One of the reasons is that the Thai have never experienced bitterness caused by being under a colonial power; therefore, they are inclined to be friendly towards foreigners. Moreover, Hinayana Buddhism and the Royal Family also have made great contributions to peace in the nation and also in the region.

Linguistic diversity can be portrayed in terms of a language hierarchy parallel with a social hierarchy in Thai society. There is no competition among the languages because each language or language group has its role, function and status in Thai society as pointed out by Smalley (1994). The language hierarchy of Thailand consists of three layers from top to bottom: Standard Thai, regional Thai languages/dialects and minority languages. The minority languages can be classified into four sub-categories: Tai displaced languages,[5] town languages, marginal languages and enclave languages.

Standard Thai is the national or official language of Thailand. It is understood and used all over the country by literate people no matter what languages they speak at home. It is used as the medium of instruction in all Thai schools, starting from pre-school level or kindergarten. Standard Thai is also the language of mass media, such as newspapers, radio and television broadcasting, and so forth. There are a lot of loan words from Pali, Sanskrit, Khmer (Cambodian) and English in Standard Thai. Prescribing and maintaining the standard of usage are the major duties of the Royal Institute of Thailand. The Royal Institute Dictionary is the guide for proper use of words and expressions, especially in legal documents. Due to modernization and globalization, new learned words have been coined.

There are four regional Thai languages/dialects: Northern Thai (10 per cent), Central Thai (39 per cent), Northeastern Thai (28 per cent), and Southern Thai (9 per cent). This means that 86 per cent of the Thai population speaks one of the four regional dialects as their first language or mother tongue before learning to speak, read and write Standard Thai. Thus, the majority of the Thai population is bidialectal.

All of the minority languages are non-Thai and have the lowest status in the language hierarchy. Displaced Tai languages belonging to the Tai-Kadai language family are Lue, Yong, Tai Yai, Tai Khoen, Tai Ya, Lao Wiang, Lao Tai, Lao Khrang, Lao Ngaew, Song (Tai Dam), Phuan, Nyo, Yoi, Kaloeng, Saek. Several dialects of the Chinese language (Teochiew, Hokkien, Hainanese, Cantonese, Hakka) are regarded as town languages. Normally, they are used as a business or trade language among the Thai-Chinese. Punjabi, spoken by the Sikhs from the Punjab, who are in the textile business, and Vietnamese, spoken by the Vietnamese immigrants can be regarded as town languages. Most of the minority languages that form the biggest group are marginal languages. They are spoken in every geographical region: the North, Central, Northeast and South. High Khmer is the mother tongue of 1.2 million people in the southern area of the Northeast, while Malay (Pattani Malay) is the first language of 1.2 million Thai Muslims living in the five southernmost provinces of Thailand. Among the tribal languages that are also classified as marginal languages, 317,968 people in the North and in the West speak Karen. The enclave languages: Lua', Mpi, Bisu, Mla Bri, Nyah Kur, Ugong, Thavueng (So),

Chong and Samre, which are spoken in the remote areas, occupy the bottommost of the language hierarchy. Some of these enclave languages, such as Bisu, Samre, Kasong, etc., have only a few speakers and thus are facing extinction.

POSITIONS OF THE NON-THAI LANGUAGES

According to the *2000 Population and Housing Census*, the approximate number of non-Thai language speakers (monolingual, bilingual and multilingual) is 3,956,427. Some non-Thai languages, i.e. English, French, German, Spanish, Italian, Japanese, Mandarin Chinese, Korean, Standard Malay, Standard Burmese, Standard Cambodian, and Standard Lao, are regarded as foreign languages, thus they have no position in the language hierarchy. Classical and religious languages like Pali, Sanskrit and Arabic, even though non-Thai, are also not part of the language hierarchy. Foreign and religious languages have different status, due to their prestige value.

In order to discuss the positions of the non-Thai languages in Thai society, seven languages — English, Mandarin Chinese, Pali, Arabic, Chinese (Chaochou or Teochiew), Pattani Malay and Karen — will be selected as the representatives of the three categories: foreign languages, religious languages and minority languages.

English is taught as a foreign language in Thai schools and some private colleges and universities. Imported English textbooks and books in many academic fields and areas of studies are common. They can be found in the libraries of every institute of higher education. International programs for graduate studies in several fields, such as Business Administration, Economics, English as an International Language (EIL), etc., are very popular. International programmes on Southeast Asian Studies are also available. English newspapers and magazines are sold not only in bookstores, but also in small shops. A number of radio and television stations broadcast some of their programmes in the English language. Learning English is encouraged indirectly by the promotion of tourism and by the international meetings and conferences organized by both governmental offices and the private sector.

However, because of low salary, there are few English language teachers and instructors who are English native speakers. A lack of competent English language teachers in primary and secondary schools, especially in the countryside, has caused a disaster as far as English language teaching and learning in Thailand is concerned. It is very hard, even impossible, to discard the fossilized errors which have been carried on into the later stages of English language learning in high schools and colleges. British English, American English, Canadian English and Australian English are equally well accepted. Nevertheless, in first class universities, British English is preferred for classes such as English poetry, English literature of different periods, etc., which are normally taken by the English language and literature majors. Generally speaking, English language teaching and learning in Thailand may be regarded as a failure. After studying English for not less than twelve years, most of the graduates from Thai colleges and universities still cannot speak English well. However, in comparison with other language skills, their reading ability is quite good.

Serious English language teaching in Thailand started more than 150 years ago in the Court of Siam, during the Reign of King Rama IV, to serve the royal policy of "modernizing oneself" before "being modernized" by the help of colonial powers. Learning English became fashionable among the Siamese (Thai) aristocrats and then spread out from the high society to the commoners. Up until the present time, English has held a very prestigious position in the learned society of Thailand and this will undoubtedly continue. There is no chance for other foreign languages to replace English, and due to the fact that good students in liberal arts always want to major in English language and literature, the competition to get into an English language program is very high, especially in famous universities.

Mandarin Chinese has been taught in the so-called "Chinese schools" since the beginning of the Rattanakosin period (1782 to the present) to help educate the children of the Chinese immigrants living in Bangkok's Chinatown (Yaowarat) and other Chinese areas of Bangkok. These Chinese schools were not encouraged during the time of heavy communist infiltration into Southeast Asia. When diplomatic relations between Thailand and the People's Republic of China were renewed after the Cold War, the teaching and learning of Mandarin Chinese came back to life again. Because of the need to communicate, especially in business and trade with Chinese-speaking countries and regions, learning Mandarin Chinese has quickly boomed. Besides being taught properly in governmental high schools, vocational schools, colleges and universities, lessons in Mandarin Chinese are also offered by private tutors and organizations all over the country. Japanese used to be the second most popular foreign language taken by Thai students, but nowadays the popularity has shifted to Mandarin Chinese. More good jobs are available for graduates who know Mandarin Chinese and have good computer skills. Unlike English, the teaching and learning of

Mandarin Chinese started at the bottom (the commoners) and then has moved up to the top (the Royal Family). To promote a good relationship between Thailand and China, Her Royal Highness Princess Mahachakri Sirindhorn (HRH) visited China many times. HRH has learned not only to speak, but also to read and write Chinese, and her knowledge of Chinese poetry and calligraphy is well known and appreciated by both the Thai and the Chinese.

Pali and Arabic are learned in Thailand as the religious languages of the Buddhists and the Muslims respectively. The classical Pali language is privately taught at a number of Buddhist monasteries all over the country to help Thai Buddhist monks better understand the Buddhist sermons, precepts and scriptures, and also to pass the national Pali examinations in order to receive higher religious ranks. Moreover, it is also taught as a subject in the Oriental Languages Department of some state universities. Thai Buddhists pray in Pali, sometimes with a Thai translation. Pali is a dead language since it is not spoken, but it is used for religious purposes and has played a great role in Buddhist sacred rituals.

Classical Arabic is taught in mosques all over the country and in private Muslim schools and colleges in South Thailand to help Thai Muslims understand the Koran, the sacred book of the Muslims. Modern Arabic is part of a program in Islamic Studies, a subject which Muslim and non-Muslim students can take as their major or minor subject in some state universities in the South.

Chinese, as a town minority language, comprises five major varieties: Teochiew (Chaochou), Hokkien (Fukienese), Hainanese, Cantonese and Hakka. Most Thai Chinese speak Teochiew. Even though 40 per cent of the Thai population are descendants of former Chinese immigrants, the third and fourth generations generally do not speak the language anymore. According to the *2000 Population and Housing Census*, there are only 231,350 speakers of Chinese (the five varieties) at present. In fact, many wealthy and/or well-educated people in Thailand are Chinese descendants. Assimilation caused by mixed marriage has been very common. About 250 years ago, when a large number of Chinese from the southern parts of China started to migrate to Thailand, the Chinese migrants were only males. Due to the policy of the Chinese government at that time, their families had to be left behind in China to guarantee their return with wealth from overseas. Therefore, most of them married local women and never returned to their homeland. Not only people in business, but also the ruling elite and scientific elite of the country are Thai-born Chinese. The majority of the gambling terms, a lot of dish names and foodstuffs are Chinese loan words. Yaowarat, the Chinatown of Bangkok, is a famous place for exotic food and the gold trade.

Pattani Malay and Karen are chosen as the representatives of the marginal languages. The marginal languages of Thailand consist of languages spoken by the indigenous peoples in the four geographical regions of Thailand and those spoken by refugees and immigrants from neighbouring countries. Based on this classification, Pattani Malay, which is a variety of Malay, and Karen, which is a Tibeto-Burman language, can be regarded as two of the indigenous languages of Thailand. The Malay are the natives or local inhabitants of the five southernmost provinces of Thailand: Songkhla, Pattani, Yala, Narathiwat and Satun. Pattani Malay is spoken by 1,202,911 people who live not only in Pattani Province, but also in the other four southern provinces and some areas in Central Thailand. Most of the Malays in the south speak Pattani Malay at home and at schools when they are among friends. Some of them study Standard Malay as a foreign language at colleges and universities with a hope to further their graduate studies or to get better jobs in Malaysia.

The Karen live in the west of Thailand and the adjacent regions in Myanmar. They are the indigenous people of the remote mountainous areas of many provinces: Chiangrai, Chiangmai, Mae Hongson, Tak, Kanchanaburi, Ratchaburi and Phetchaburi. Because of political problems in Myanmar, a lot of the Christian and Buddhist Karen have migrated to Thailand. There are four sub-groups of the Karen: Sgaw Karen (Pagayaw), Pwo Karen (Pho, Kaphlow, Kaphlong), Bwe (Palaichi) and Thaungthu (Pa-O). The number of Karen speakers stated in the *2000 Population and Housing Census* is 317,968. Three kinds of scripts invented by missionaries working for different Christian missions have been used among the Karen, i.e. Burmese-based script, Roman-based script and Thai-based script. However, quite a few Karen are literate in their native language.

CONCLUSION AND DISCUSSION

Thailand is one of the Southeast Asian nations that has a heterogeneous population. On the basis of language spoken, the Thai population can be classified into sixty ethnic groups. In spite of heterogeneity, Thailand has never had serious racial problems that led to riots and wars,[6] even though some of the ethnic minorities, such as the Khmer (Cambodian) in the Northeast, the Malay in the South and the Karen in the North, have quite a large population. Even though there are different ways of life and religious beliefs (Buddhism, Islam, Christianity, Animism), peace and national unity was maintained. The important key word "assimilation" for national unity in the past has been changed to "diversity" in the present.

The linguistic scenario of Thailand is composed of three socio-linguistic layers from top to bottom: 1. Standard Thai (a variety of Central Thai), 2. regional Thai languages/dialects (Northern Thai, Central Thai, Northeastern Thai, Southern Thai), and 3. minority languages (High Khmer, Pattani Malay, Teochiew, Phuan, Mon, Karen, Hmong, Lahu, Akha, Lawa, etc.). The last layer which comprises a lot of non-Thai languages can be classified into four sub-categories: Tai displaced languages (e.g., Phuan), town languages (e.g., Teochiew), marginal languages (e.g., Pattani Malay), and enclave languages (e.g., Sakai).

Besides the languages within the language hierarchy previously mentioned, there are two more extra categories, i.e., modern foreign languages (e.g., English, French, German, Japanese, Mandarin Chinese, etc.) and classical-religious languages (Sanskrit, Pali, Arabic).

Among the modern foreign languages, English is the most popular and prestigious, followed by Mandarin Chinese and Japanese respectively. Pali is the religious language of the Thai Buddhists who are the majority of the country, whereas classical Arabic is that of the Thai Muslims. Pattani Malay, an indigenous language of the South, is spoken as the mother tongue of 1,202,911 Thai Muslims. Karen, an indigenous language of the North and the West, is the mother tongue of 317,968 highlanders. Without using complex parameters based on the function, role and status of each language, a clear picture of the positions of the non-Thai languages in Thailand cannot be successfully presented.

The emphasis on diversity in various aspects, which seems to be the right move of the Thai Government, will certainly bring a fruitful outcome in the near future, not only to Thailand, but also to the Southeast Asian region as a whole.

Notes

1. The reader should bear in mind that due to the weakness of the language questionnaire designed by the National Statistical Office, the figures in Table 8.1 do not reflect very well the reality. The information in Table 8.1 illustrates only a rough picture.
2. It used to be only eight: Hill Tribes, Haw, Displaced Burmese Nationals, Thai Muslims, Vietnamese Refugees, Refugees from Indo-China, and Illegal Immigrants from Cambodia (Burutphat 1983).
3. In 1977, Jerry W. Gainey and Theraphan L-Thongkum produced an

ethnolinguistic map of Thailand (2×3 feet) and handbook under the auspices of the Ford Foundation and the Office of State Universities of Thailand. The data collected from different sources were analyzed and synthesized before being plotted on a base map prepared by the Royal Map-Making Department. More information on the minority languages of Thailand can also be found in L-Thongkum (1985).

4. Linguistically, some of these languages are in fact dialects or varieties of other languages; for example, Yong is a variety of the Lue language spoken in Mueang Yong, Myanmar. Yong is classified as a separate language in order to comply with the belief of the native speakers.

5. Thai languages mean the Tai dialects/ languages spoken by the majority of Thailand. Those spoken by the members of the Tai race living in China, India, Myanmar, Laos and Vietnam are called "Tai languages". "Displaced Tai languages" are the ones spoken by the Tai immigrants and refugees from the neighbouring countries of Thailand.

6. Except perhaps for the periodic violence in the south.

References

Burutphat, Khachatphai. *Minority Groups in Thailand and National Security.* Bangkok: Phraephitthaya (in Thai), 1983.

Gainey, Jerry W. and Theraphan L-Thongkum. *The Language Map of Thailand and Handbook.* Bangkok: Indigenous Languages of Thailand Research Project, CIEL, Office of State Universties, 1977.

L-Thongkum, Theraphan. "Minority languages of Thailand". *Science of Language* 5 (1985): 29–74.

Population Registration Office. *Code and Regulations for the Ethnic Minority Affairs of Thailand.* Bangkok: Asaraksadindaen Publishing House, Department of Administration, Ministry of Interior (in Thai), 1999.

Premsrirat, Suwilai et al. *Ethnolinguistic Map of Thailand.* Bangkok: Kansatsana Publishing House, Department of Religion, Ministry of Education (in Thai), 2001.

Smalley, William A. *Linguistic Diversity and National Unity.* Chicago: The University of Chicago Press, 1994.

Statistical Data Book and Information Dissemination Division. *The 2000 Population and Housing Census.* Bangkok: National Statistic Office, Office of the Prime Minister (in Thai), 2001.

9

Vietnamese Language and Media Policy in the Service of Deterritorialized Nation-Building

Ashley Carruthers

LANGUAGE AND MEDIA POLICY FOR GLOBALIZATION

Until the mid to late 1990s, Vietnam's language and media policies were almost exclusively oriented towards issues of national unity, security and "territorialized" nation-building.[1] In more recent years, a consciousness of the need to re-tool language and media policy to face the challenges and seize the opportunities of globalization has emerged. A subset of this new policy direction is concerned with the Vietnamese diaspora, which the State estimates to number 2.7 million. This population is believed to reside in more than ninety countries, and eighty per cent of it is estimated to be located in developed nations (Politbureau 2004).

As part of a more general policy to engage the diaspora's economic and intellectual resources, Hanoi is currently in the process of implementing diaspora-specific media and language directives. These include a project to encourage and support Vietnamese language teaching in overseas Vietnamese communities, and renewed[2] attempts to project homeland print and broadcast media overseas. This latter initiative is being pursued by means of online versions of domestic newspapers and magazines, and satellite transmission and webcasting of a specially-packaged TV station, VTV4. These media initiatives have the twin goals of breaking the hegemony of anti-communist media producers in the diaspora, and fostering the maintenance and "updating" of the Vietnamese language overseas, especially among the younger generation(s). The ultimate aim of these policies is to create a sense of connectedness and nationalist affect in overseas Vietnamese communities, and thus to sustain links to the homeland across diasporic generations.

THE DIASPORA

The Vietnamese diaspora is made up principally of those who left as refugees during the Second Indochina War and its aftermath. In the United States alone, there were 1,122,528 Vietnam-born according to the 2000 Census. Other significant communities include those in Australia (154,830 in 2001), Canada (148,400 in 2001) and France (about 300,000). Overseas Vietnamese communities also exist in the former Eastern Bloc countries and in Vietnam's neighbours: Laos, Cambodia, Thailand and China. While political contradictions between the latter communities and Hanoi do exist, they are not significant, and these groups are typically considered to constitute a "loyal" diaspora. In the case of the refugee diaspora, however, considerable ideological differences remain.[3]

Many in the refugee diaspora continue to identify, at least symbolically, with the former Southern regime (the Republic of Vietnam or RVN) and oppose what they see as the illegitimate dictatorship of the Communist Party of Vietnam. Hanoi's attitude to this group remains ambivalent. On the one hand, it fears the destabilizing effect that committed anti-communists and democracy advocates in the diaspora may have on the nation. On the other, it appreciates the potentially enormous contribution this refugee diaspora could make to the project of national development. It is estimated that up to three billion U.S. dollars are now remitted each year from the diaspora to Vietnam, roughly equivalent to ten per cent of Vietnam's GDP, and constituting a major source of foreign exchange. In the first half of 2004, Ho Chi Minh City alone received some US$900 million in remittances, a total exceeding the amount of foreign direct investment in the city for the same period ("Viet Kieu Expected to Send Back $3 Bln", 2004). When one adds the cash and gold brought back by some 300,000 annually returning relatives, and the significant small to medium unofficial investments that overseas Vietnamese or Việt kiều[4] make in the names of their domestic relatives, the actual figure could be substantially higher. It is also estimated that there are some 300,000 tertiary educated Việt kiều who could provide much needed brainpower for Vietnam's national development. While admittedly the Việt kiều are not in control of a strongly developed diasporic economy such as that of the Overseas Chinese (Dorais 2001, p. 6), the resources sketched above are obviously of significance to the Vietnamese State.

DETERRITORIALIZED NATION-BUILDING

Vietnam is currently seeking to harness the nation-building potential of its overseas subjects through a set of policy initiatives that follows a logic of "deterritorialized nation-building" (Glick Schiller, Basch et al. 1994). Such strategies are emerging as important pillars of development policy for Third World nations with sizeable overseas populations. While policies differ significantly between nations, all forms of deterritorialized nation-building involve extending national belonging in one form or another to those who have left, despite the fact they may have taken out citizenship in and undergone social and cultural integration into second nations. Diasporic subjects might, for instance, be offered dual citizenship, "national" status, voting rights, special visa conditions and investment rights. As well as re-imagining citizenship in a more flexible mode, deterritorialized nation-building policies also necessarily make some movement towards re-defining the nation itself as an unbounded territorial, political, social, cultural and temporal entity. In such constructs, territoriality shifts from a literal to a symbolic sense, whereby diasporic "citizens" can be imagined to belong to a virtual national territory that exceeds the physical borders of the nation. Jean-Bertrand Aristide thus referred to Haitians abroad as the country's Dizyèm Depatman-an or "Tenth Department", Haiti being divided into nine administrative regions or "Departments" (Glick Schiller, Basch et al. 1994, p. 146). The concept of "Greater China" employs a similar sense of inclusive unbounded territoriality (Ong and Nonini 1997; Ong 1999; Yang 1999).

The goal of such strategic re-imaginings is, by and large, to "capture" the material, social and symbolic capital of diasporic populations for the nation-building endeavour. Through the diaspora-as-bridge, developing nations may seek such things as access to hard currency (through remittances and Foreign Direct Investment), knowledge and technology transfers, entry into overseas markets, and even political influence in host nations via ethnic community politics. I would assert that deterritorialized nation-building also necessarily involves the attempt to project governmentality beyond the national territory to try to discipline national subjects at a distance — despite the fact they are subject to the governmental power of host nations. This activity may be as subtle as the appeal to "remember one's roots", a gentle symbolic violence the Vietnamese State is fond of enacting on its overseas constituents. It should be noted that the State's power to discipline diasporic populations at a distance is necessarily relative and attenuated. Where such populations have access to permanent residency and citizenship in developed nations, as is the case with the Vietnamese refugee diaspora, the State will be less able to exercise transnational governmentality; where the diaspora is a transient labour diaspora, as in the case of the Philippines, the State will be in a stronger position. However, here we should keep in mind the failure of attempts in 1982 to force Filipino Overseas Contract Workers to remit fifty per cent of their earnings through Philippine banks, an initiative that was defeated primarily by means of grassroots political organizing by domestic workers and NGOs in Hong Kong (Gibson, Law et al. 2001, pp. 367–69).

REINCORPORATING THE VIỆT KIỀU

Prior to the Sixth Party Congress in 1986, post-war Vietnamese emigrants living in the developed world were generally read under the sign of the Western enemy, and referred to in official communications as Reactionaries [Kẻ Phản động] and Puppets [Nguy]. Hanoi's policy priorities vis-à-vis the refugee diaspora revolved around monitoring and defending against possible anti-regime activities. Việt kiều were permitted to remit money and send gifts to relatives during this "closed-door" period, but the regime envisaged no greater economic role for them than this. With the onset of economic reforms, however, Hanoi began to look towards the post-war diaspora as a source of capital for its programme of economic revitalization, and offered Việt kiều investors tax incentives and liberalized rules of business participation (Stern 1992, p. 16). Something of a backlash against these reforms occurred in 1989, when the re-emergence of security concerns in the context of events in Eastern Europe led to a return to a more cautious policy, and the Politburo acted to roll back some of reformer Nguyen Van Linh's more daring initiatives (Stern 1992, p. 19). Nevertheless, a fundamental shift in conceptualizing the role of the Việt kiều had occurred, and the State went on to grant more and more entitlements to them as the 1990s progressed. Milestones in this process have included: the liberalization of visa conditions; parity with domestic citizens on tariffs for transport, accommodation and other services (while foreigners had to pay higher prices for some goods and services under a two-tiered system); right to choose whether to invest under the domestic or foreign investment law; lower rates of tax on business profits; and limited rights to purchase land and houses.[5] The recently promulgated Resolution 36 on Việt kiều promises to continue in this vein, stressing the need for policy initiatives that will:

> Facilitate their return to visit their homeland, relatives and pay tribute to their ancestors; further streamline regulations on immigration, residence and travel of Việt kiều in Vietnam; quickly process applications for repatriation or return to work or live in

Vietnam for a limited period; continue to solve outstanding issues that involve Việt kiều such as house purchase in Vietnam, inheritance, marriage and family, adoption and so on; introduce a single price system for all Vietnamese, domestic and overseas alike (Politbureau 2004).[6]

Resolution 36 even appears to hold out the promise of limited political participation to Việt kiều, stating that it is a goal to "Put in place an appropriate mechanism for consultations with Việt kiều before the promulagation of legal documents and policies that concern them" (Politbureau 2004). Other issues highlighted include the need to facilitate Việt kiều wishing to do business and make investments in Vietnam, and encouraging the cooperation of Việt kiều professionals and intellectuals in local research and training. A concrete instance of this latter policy initiative is Vietnam's participation in the UNDP's Transfer of Knowledge Through Expatriate Nationals (TOKTEN) programme, now administered by the Committee on Overseas Vietnamese.[7]

Despite these encouraging signs, we should note that, as with all legislation in Vietnam, laws regarding Việt kiều are implemented irregularly and with much latitude for local non-compliance and obfuscation. There is much evidence that both institutional and informal discrimination against Việt kiều continues to be rife (Carruthers 2002; Long 2004). For their part, Việt kiều have tended to sidestep the legal investment channels that have been created for them by putting capital into property and small to medium enterprises under the names of their domestic relatives, a phenomenon referred to as đầu tư "chui" or "contraband" investment. Việt kiều small and medium investors have chosen this path because it makes more economic sense, and in many cases because of a desire to avoid (being seen to be) "collaborating" with the Hanoi regime. Those with Vietnamese community-based businesses in the U.S. quite rationally fear that these will be boycotted if it is known they are involved in official investment in Vietnam. Thus total unofficial Việt kiều investment in the country may be in the realm of tens of billions of dollars, while official Việt kiều FDI constitutes only a negligible proportion of total FDI.

As well as the promise of further rights and entitlements, signs of conservative opposition to the rehabilitation of the diaspora are in stark evidence in Politbureau Resolution 36, in which it is stated:

A number of Việt kiều, whether because they have not had the opportunity to come back to their homeland to see with their own eyes the achievements of Đổi mới, or because of their prejudices or sense of inferiority, don't fully understand the situation in the country. A small number [continue to] go against the interests of our nation, seek to destroy the country, and disrupt relations and cooperation between their country of residence and Vietnam (Politbureau 2004).

The controversial use of the terms thành kiến and mặc cảm, translated as "prejudice" and "sense of inferiority", seems unlikely to endear Việt kiều who remain sceptical about returning to participate in a State-defined project of national development. It is difficult to imagine the choice of a more insulting term than mặc cảm, which is often translated as "inferiority complex", but in Vietnamese means a strong sense of shame and unworthiness because of one's dishonourable and underhanded actions towards a person or community.

What kind of transnationalism is this, then? At present, I believe one can argue it is a reluctant and conservative one, born of the fact that Vietnam's structural position in the global economy obliges it to rely on its large and well-placed diaspora in the West, despite the fact that some in Hanoi continue to fear and suspect these former "enemies". Unsurprisingly, the form of transnational citizenship offered to Việt kiều is empty of political agency. The absence of political pluralism and the limited content of domestic citizenship in Vietnam, as well as the resolutely oppositional nature of public homeland politics in the diaspora, mean that there is no question of real political rights being extended to Việt kiều. Further, the Vietnamese State's capacity to exercise any sort of long-distance governmentality over former refugees in Western nations is negligible, due both to the stability of their residency in host nations and their ideological commitments.[8] Ditto its capacity to offer any real protection of their "cultural rights" in host nations that already enact liberal multicultural policies. These facts mean that Vietnamese deterritorialized nation-building policies towards the refugee diaspora have to date necessarily been limited to: (1) investment policies, designed to (conservatively) encourage Việt kiều FDI, remittances, tourism and knowledge transfer; and (2) symbolic policies, designed to foster feelings of enduring membership in and love for the homeland.[9] In other words, what has been offered is a limited form of market and symbolic "citizenship". Despite this relatively restricted definition of transnational citizenship, and a relationship that has waxed and waned, I concur with Long when she asserts that Việt kiều have played a "pivotal role" in

Vietnamese society in the transition period, and have increasingly been accepted as a "critical kinship link" to outside markets (2004, p. 70). Significantly, this participation has occurred in a largely grassroots and spontaneous manner rather than waiting for or following the channels set out in state policy.

METAPHORS OF INCORPORATION

As in conventional modes of nation-building, the dimension of affect is central to the processes of transnational nation-building. Diasporic investors and professionals are asked to "contribute" to the nation not simply in a self-interested or economic rationalist way, but rather to take risks and put up with lesser returns for the sake of love of their homeland. In order to make such a proposition palatable, discourses of transnation must successfully produce "homelands of identification" in which diasporic subjects can invest their desires. This process euphemizes the more exploitative dimensions of transnational nation-building, as well as suppressing the disjunctures between and within overseas and domestic populations.

The current "working definition" of the Vietnamese transnation came out of the Eighth Party Congress in 1996. There, it was resolved that "Việt kiều are an inseparable part of the community of the Vietnamese dân tộc" — dân tộc being translatable variously as race, nation or people. It was explained that the State seeks, through this recognition, to better "mobilise the strength of the entire dân tộc, including Vietnamese overseas, for the goal of a wealthy people, a strong country and a just and civilised society" (Tran 1997, p. 5). The final phrase of this formulation is of course the official slogan of contemporary Đổi mới Vietnam (Dân giàu, nước mạnh, xã hội công bằng, văn minh), a discursive attempt to steer through the contradictions of a socialist society with capitalist markets, and to colour the disjunctures of the Đổi mới reforms as an "extension" of the socialist revolution (Greenfield 1997, p. 124). Note that in this official formulation, the term "dân tộc" is used in preference to "nhân dân", which signifies a social (and socialist) collectivity rather than one based on ethnicity. Le Sy Giao notes that "in thought and feeling, when we speak of the community of inhabitants of Vietnam, using the concept of Dân tộc Việt Nam creates a closeness, an intertwining, a unity greater than the concept of Nhân dân Việt Nam" (Le 1999, p. 35).[10] Thus, ethnic and racial similarity are emphasized over ideological and historical differences, and Việt kiều are invited to participate in a warm sense of

Vietnamese communitas rather than a political community. Also significant is the fact that this metaphor is based on a temporal rather than spatial conceit. Fouron and Glick-Schiller note that such national projections revive "nineteenth century equations of race and nation in which a nation is understood as rooted in blood ties rather than in national territory" (Fouron and Glick Schiller 2001, p. 543). One might argue that this bracketing of the national territory as the absolute referent of nationness serves the purpose of symbolic inclusiveness well, since the idea of a global community of blood ties does not privilege Vietnam as the sole site in which legitimate Vietnamese identities can be formed. Neither does it claim a monopoly over the nationalist identifications of diasporic subjects, but accommodates their ties to host nations. One might add that such a metaphor is more palatable than one of spatial deterritorialization to Vietnamese war veterans and other patriots, given the price that Vietnam has paid in blood for the "salvation" of the national territory.

Other developments suggest that this de-centering of the nation is subject to oscillation in the discourse on Việt kiều. A recent shift in official terminology from "Việt kiều" to "Người Việt Nam ở Nước ngoài" parallels a Chinese shift from *huaqiao* to *haiwai huaren*. According to Nonini and Ong, with this move "China is reinstalled as primal source and centre, the Middle Kingdom, *fons et origo* of 'Chinese culture'" (Nonini and Ong 1997, p. 9). Similarly, we might point to the Vietnamese State's attempt to regain its position as the absolute referent of Vietnamese nationhood and culture, thus displacing the defunct RVN as the locus of diasporic nationalism. Finally, we should note that the above are all metaphors that assume an almost perfect degree of racial homogeneity, and put forward a self-evident definition of a Việt kiều. Those belonging to ethnic minorities, those of mixed ancestry, and those claiming a cultural membership of the nation are ambiguously positioned, if not excluded outright.

LANGUAGE TEACHING

The maintenance of Vietnamese language and culture falls within the scope of deterritorialized nation-building insofar as the second generation (born overseas) will only be "useful" to Vietnam if its members retain a sense of Vietnamese cultural identity rather than assimilating. As stated in Resolution 36, the Politbureau does not believe that sufficient "means of maintaining Vietnamese culture and tradition" are in place in the diaspora, and considers that "there are difficulties around the preservation of the Vietnamese language and national character in the young generation" (Politbureau 2004). We might read this as anxiety about the deracination of Việt kiều in Western host nations, combined with the fear that they are undergoing an "inappropriate" acculturation at the hands of anti-communist cultural pedagogues.

While plans to send language teachers to diasporic communities have been mooted for many years, in 2004 a concrete project to send language teachers from Vietnam to work overseas "where it is possible" was launched (Politbureau 2004). It is envisaged that this will initially mean sending teachers to neighbouring countries including Thailand, Laos and Cambodia ("Hội nghị phổ biến...", 2004). Also involved is a project of "cultural exchange", including running summer schools in Vietnam for Việt kiều youth to undertake intensive language study,[11] as well as the production of language materials, including textbooks and CD-roms. Transnational media are seen as important vehicles for making these learning materials available, and virtually all of the online domestic magazines and newspapers already have links to a "learn Vietnamese" page, which may include practice dialogues and even sound files. At present, the content of these online courses tends to be extremely limited, formulaic and generally uncompelling, and it makes no concessions whatsoever to the diasporic context and differences between homeland and Việt kiều usage. The Politbureau has targeted these materials for improvement.

The "Supporting Vietnamese language teaching and learning for Việt kiều" project reportedly has a duration of four years (2004–2008) and a US$500,000 budget, which is to be used for research into the Vietnamese language teaching situation in the diaspora, building syllabi, publishing, and organizing and supporting classes in community and cultural centres and associations (Prime Minister, 2004). It appears this project is indeed being implemented, although there is reportedly some difficulty in spending the money, as any SRV-funded language school that was set up in a Western diasporic context would immediately be boycotted and picketed. Anecdotal evidence suggests officials have approached Vietnamese nationals working as academics overseas to offer them financial and other support to develop syllabi and set up classes. It is envisaged that such teaching would offer: (1) "neutral" language-learning materials, in order to "update" the "old-fashioned" Vietnamese spoken in overseas communities; (2) a level of professionalism in a community teaching context, where language instructors are often not trained or qualified; and (3) a forum free of the homeland politics that is a feature of community-organized "Saturday schools". Interest in this topic in Vietnam is reflected by the fact that newspaper editors are petitioning Vietnamese citizens working overseas with some knowledge of Vietnamese language teaching in their locales to write reports on the Việt kiều language situation. Hence the appearance of a long interview with former Ambassador to Belgium, Tôn Nữ Thị Ninh, in VnExpress.net. Tôn warns:

> If the State doesn't create favourable conditions for teaching Vietnamese to Việt kiều, two things will happen. The first is the next generation will lose their Vietnamese roots entirely, and know nothing about the culture and language of the place they were born. The second is that now in many places, reactionary elements organise Vietnamese classes. A number of Việt kiều parents who don't want their children to lose Vietnamese resign themselves to shutting their eyes and let their children go to these classes only to have politics brought in ("Người Việt ở nước ngoài được hỗ trợ học tiếng Việt", 2004).

The spectre of the failure of linguistic maintenance across generations is of significant concern to Vietnam, since this could lead to the "loss" of the second generation of Việt kiều who, not speaking the language, would not consider themselves to have any special relationship with Vietnam. However, the difficulty in delivering SRV-funded language tuition in diasporic contexts means that for the moment, electronic delivery (via the internet and satellite TV) remains the most feasible way of offering "homeland-friendly" language tuition materials.

TRANSNATIONAL MEDIA

It seems clear that Hanoi sees diasporic anti-communist elites as its enemies in the endeavour to woo the Việt kiều. The State is well aware that anti-regime elites control the diasporic media and community organizations,[12] and is addressing the problem of how to reduce their influence, particularly on those recently arrived as economic or family reunion migrants. Indeed, there is evidence that Vietnam sees itself as being in struggle with elites in the diaspora not only for influence over the Việt kiều "masses" in the Western countries, but also for the loyalty of the communities in the former Soviet bloc. As discussed above, the State has quite consciously cast itself as the defender of communal rights of Việt kiều, most particularly, the right to extranational loyalty to the homeland, and also to more basic rights such as those of linguistic and cultural maintenance. In this it seeks to usurp the role of anti-communist diasporic elites as the guarantors of these communal rights in the host nations (see, for instance Tran 1997, p. 3; Nguyen 1998, pp. 267–68; Politbureau 2004).[13] While diasporic elites stress the "naturalness" of the anti-communist orthodoxy and promote essentialist representations of a unified refugee diaspora, homeland scholars represent the anti-communist element as a small but powerful minority that has self-interestedly seized control of diasporic media and community organizations. The picture most frequently drawn here is of an exploitative elite, drawn strictly from the military and administration of the old regime, foisting its outmoded Cold War politics on a silent majority of homeland patriots that does not identify with this exile identity (Pham 1997, p. 298; Tran 1997, pp. 157–81). Homeland scholarship usually emphasizes the disunity and internal contradictions of the diaspora, authors stressing that those departing Vietnam left at many different times and for many different reasons, and thus have diverse orientations to the homeland.

In order to address the near hegemony of anti-communist producers in the diasporic media, the State has sought to bring into being a "loyal" transnational media. This political function is, understandably, not spelt out in policy documents and press releases. Rather, the function of transnational media is typically described in apolitical terms: to further the use of the Vietnamese language outside the country; to encourage cultural maintenance and foster patriotic feelings towards the homeland; to inform Việt kiều of the "realities" of life in contemporary Vietnam; and to provide them information on laws, policies and other issues that affect them. State-managed[14] Vietnam Television (VTV) has introduced a new channel, VTV4, specially packaged for satellite broadcast to Việt kiều communities in Asia, Europe, Australia and North America.[15] Those possessing the appropriate satellite dishes could receive around eight hours of programming a day as a free-to-air broadcast until 15 May 2005, and since then have been able to enjoy the channel twenty-four hours a day. VTV4 carries a mix of programming from the other three VTV stations, including leisure, sports, children's, music and game shows.[16] In addition, VTV4 airs programmes made specifically for overseas broadcast, such as the vox pop shows *Tin tức cộng đồng* [Community Information] and *Trả lời khán giả VTV4* [Audience Responses], which visit Việt kiều communities in Asia and Europe, but reportedly never in North America or Australia. Other programmes include news broadcasts in Vietnamese, French and English; informational shows such as *Việt Nam hôm nay* [Vietnam Today], which covers topics such as retiring and investing in Vietnam; and shows that encourage Việt kiều tourism to Vietnam by dwelling on the nation's beautiful scenery. Some programmes broadcast on VTV4 have English subtitling, particularly dramas. While having a more narrowly defined brief than domestic television stations in Vietnam, programming on VTV4 is to some extent at least a reflection of the local media environment, which is characterized on the one hand by a frank commercialism and sometimes surprising cosmopolitanism, and on the other by continuing State control and tedious parochialism. Pettus has recently gone so far as to argue that the press in Vietnam constitutes "a new, liberalized space of public discourse" that shares some characteristics of the public sphere as defined by Mayfair Yang in the Chinese context, i.e. as a process of struggle to define a space independent of the State, market and family (Pettus 2003).

At present, screening VTV4 in public contexts such as restaurants and cafes in the refugee diaspora is difficult if not impossible, and few are willing to speak out publicly to admit they watch the broadcasts, much less enjoy them. On the part of those who do not dismiss the channel outright as a tool of communist propaganda, there is a mixed response, which certainly includes the perception that it serves the ideological and information needs of the Party and Government rather than the entertainment needs of Việt kiều audiences. Swiss Vietnamese commentator Hồ Thị Minh notes that her feelings of excitement and fascination on first seeing VTV4 quickly gave way to tedium and disappointment. She complains of the heavy ideological overtones of the programme *Việt Nam qua Con mắt Người Nước ngoài* [Vietnam through Overseas Eyes], in which "'Việt kiều who love their country', are affectionate towards the regime, and support the State, are put up on the VTV4 screen for display and used as 'decoys' to lure 'Việt kiều' back to invest and co-operate with the regime. These 'decoys' ... have been carefully chosen and coached so they know to say what the Party wants" (Ho 2004). Hồ's comments about other programmes reveal a highly oppositional and even paranoid mode of interpretation. She claims that films shown on VTV4, such as *Khi đàn chim trở về* [When the Flock Returns] and *Phia sau một cái chết* [The Other Side of a Death], which air issues of corruption and the inadequacies of Vietnam's legal system, are not in fact evidence of liberalization and media diversity in Vietnam, despite their appearance. Rather, her explanation is that these films are not in fact seen in Vietnam, and are made only to be shown on VTV4 to convince the overseas audience that there is freedom of speech in Vietnam, that the regime is open, and that it can face the truth of corruption. Such readings demonstrate both the resolutely oppositional nature of the subject position occupied by this Việt kiều viewer, as well as her incapacity to correctly "read" the VTV4 media text in relation to its context of production (Vietnamese reporters have been exposing low- to mid-level official corruption since the advent of Đổi mới, and the partial marketization of the media has encouraged the reporting of salacious "social facts" to satisfy viewers' curiosity for the macabre and seamy side of Vietnamese life (Marr 1998; Tran 2002)). We should note this oppositional mode of viewing does not preclude some genuine satisfaction of viewer desire, especially in terms of the nostalgia factor associated with the presentation of Vietnamese scenery and cultural events. Indeed, the author's intimate knowledge of programming — she names some eleven shows! — belies her antagonistic stance.

The public attitude of the Vietnamese community in Australia towards the transnationalization of Vietnamese media was vividly demonstrated in early 2004, when multicultural broadcaster SBS began to screen VTV4 news broadcasts as part of a relaunch of its WorldWatch programme. Screened early every morning, WorldWatch is intended to provide migrant audiences in Australia with native language news services. It re-broadcasts news programmes produced by national networks in China, France, Italy, Spain, Indonesia, United Arab Emirates, the Philippines and a number of other nations.[17] On the completion of a new SBS satellite dish capable of receiving Thaicom 3, one of the satellites on which VTV4 is broadcast, SBS management decided the time was right to include a Vietnamese language news bulletin on the programme. Management was aware of the backlash this would provoke in the Vietnamese Australian community, but committed to what they saw as SBS's charter of providing a Vietnamese language news broadcast for Australia's significant Vietnamese-speaking population (Interview with SBS management, 31 August 2004).[18] SBS's initial approaches to VTV were ignored, and WorldWatch had to take the expedient of using TV Canal France International, which was collaborating with VTV on a Diện Biện Phủ anniversary broadcast, as a go-between. Once communications had been established, SBS reports VTV was "keen but reserved", and their impression was that VTV executives did not want to be seen as "pushing" the re-broadcast of their Thời sự [Current Events] programme.[19]

The Vietnamese community's reaction was dramatic. Callers deluged SBS's 1800 feedback number, one person ringing twenty-three times. The Vietnamese Community in Australia's (VCA) campaign website forwarded to SBS messages from some 30,000 petitioners, the large majority coming from the United States (demonstrating the global diasporic dimension of this event). Thousands protested outside SBS's studios in Sydney and Melbourne, prompting VCA Head Trung Doan to call this the "single biggest event in the 28-year history of the community in Australia". So many travelled to the protests by train that Cabramatta railway station sold out of tickets and had to let people travel free ("Behind the Vietnamese Siege of SBS", 2004). Shocked by the scale of the protests, criticized by conservative talkback radio hosts and newspaper columnists, and pressured by both major political parties, SBS's management decided to indefinitely "suspend" the broadcasts. SBS predicts that it will not be possible to attempt to broadcast a domestic Vietnamese news service again for another ten years. For their part, Vietnamese community leaders complained that an existing written undertaking by SBS to consult with community was not honoured, and that the programme had been announced only one day before it aired. They suggested that a Vietnamese language news programme be sourced from Saigon Broadcasting in California, an option not acceptable to WorldWatch. VTV's reaction to the suspension of broadcasts was "regretful but resigned", and no further contact has taken place between them and SBS since they called to break the news about the cancellation.[20] Intriguingly, at the time of the protests, the SEA Games in Hanoi and the war in Iraq were both under way. *Thời sự*'s broadcasts were notable at this time for their celebration of the novel spectacle of a modern, global sporting event taking place in Vietnam, and their bland and even pro-United States reporting of the Iraq invasion, the vision for which was taken from BBC World. The fact that the protestors labelled this "communist propaganda" speaks not a little of the ironies of the post-Cold War world order. *Thời sự* reportedly attracted up to 28,000 viewers in its two months on air ("Behind the Vietnamese Siege of SBS", 2004), and it is a safe bet that many in the protesting crowds were watching the broadcasts, if only to be informed about what they were protesting against. Not all in the Vietnamese Australian community opposed the broadcasts, and some privately lament the loss of this brief flowering of diversity in the Vietnamese language media sphere in Australia.[21]

For those without the inclination or means to invest in an A$2,000 satellite dish, VTV4 is now accessible relatively cheaply on a DTH (Direct-to-Home) platform offered by Taiwanese company Pacific Media.[22] This supplier reportedly captures the signal for VTV4, as well as domestic Vietnamese stations VTV3 and HTV7, from the Thaicom 3 satellite, and then rebroadcasts them in an encoded form via Asat 4. Subscribers in Australia pay a third party supplier A$550 for a sixty-five cm roof-mounted dish and set-top decoder, and then A$328 per year after an initial six-month free service. One of the two suppliers operating on Pacific Media's behalf in Sydney, a Vietnamese-Australian former refugee of very marked and independent opinions, told me that he had installed around fifty of the dishes in the six months the service had been available (Interview, 3 October 2005). I was able to spend a number of evenings viewing Pacific Media's Vietnamese service with the Nguyễn family in Marrickville in Sydney's inner west, an area that is associated with more recently arrived "economic refugees" from Vietnam's north. The members of the extended Nguyễn family fit this profile, having departed from a town a few kilometres from the Chinese border by boat in the late 1980s after enduring a long period in a New Economic Zone (NEZ). This family has an enormous plasma television in its living room, which is so often full of family members, friends, visitors and card-players (not to mention anthropologists) that at times it feels like a quasi-public space. The first time a huge image of Hồ Chí Minh loomed up on the screen to the accompaniment of rousing revolutionary music I was more than a little disoriented, but the assembled company took this apparition entirely in its stride. On any given evening, the members and friends of the Nguyễns watched a succession of programmes including domestic soccer, music, drama and the more interesting of the "social information" documentaries with obvious pleasure. When I mentioned that some overseas Vietnamese critics had found the VTV4 broadcasts boring, Mrs Nguyễn irately barked "What boring?!" [Chán gì?!] at me. Particularly memorable was viewing the second instalment of the two-part telemovie Bố ơi! [Dear Father!], a drama about the travails of a man who sells boiling water for tea on the grounds of a Ho Chi Minh City hospital. Everyone in the room but me seemed to have seen the first part of the movie, and they filled me in as they emoted along with the man's harsh struggle for everyday economic survival, and admired his touching devotion to his sick daughter. Never did the TV-side conversation stray into the realm of politics, either in a "loyal" or critical mode. The elder members of the Nguyễn family certainly had their gripes with the Government for the way they had been relocated and forced to endure difficult conditions in the NEZ, but in general, they related to the nation in an apolitical mode, simply proud of Vietnam and its rapid economic development, and nostalgic for the pleasures of their seaside home town just below China.

A long-time informant who has recently migrated from Ho Chi Minh City to California as the spouse of a former refugee reported that she was struck by how many people seemed to be aware of VTV4 and its content. While her own household did not have a satellite dish, she was able to watch VTV over the Internet. For this young woman, who was experiencing considerable difficulty fitting into the Vietnamese community in Little Saigon, watching VTV and reading *Tuổi Trẻ* were important daily rituals that eased the pain of migration (communication by Yahoo Chat, 1 August 2005). Other evidence of viewing in the United States can be found on the websites of companies such as Sadoun Satellite Sales and Eman Technology, which both host Vietnamese television fora. There, one can find technical advice about how to configure equipment to receive VTV4, complaints about the "boring" nature of broadcasts, advice about when is the best time to watch, and even requests to be told how a certain film ended! The VietSatellite company, which is proudly located in Little Saigon and carries images of local Vietnam war commemorations on its homepage, gives instructions about how to tune into VTV4 using its ASIA satellite system. Admittedly, however, among viewers happy to publicly announce their pleasure in watching VTV4, we find few who identify with a "refugee" identity, and more Vietnamese citizens studying overseas, recent migrants, and those in non-Western parts of the diaspora. In *Tuổi Trẻ Online*, viewers in Russia, Iran and Belgium report tuning into VTV4 for information and, more importantly, to get in touch with the spirit of Tết in distant Vietnam (Ngô Văn Long 2004, Nguyễn Thị Thục 2004, Quế Viên 2004).

CONCLUSION

To date, commercial music and music video are the only fields of domestic media production to have produced genuinely and popularly transnational Vietnamese texts, programmes and celebrities (Carruthers 2001; Valverde 2003). After music, the main contenders are online newspapers such as *Vnexpress.net* and *Tuổi Trẻ*, which bring more of the diversity and topicality of the domestic press environment to overseas readers, and are frequently scoured for articles by diasporic newspaper editors (many of whom unscrupulously cut and paste them without crediting the source). In addition, the "unmediated" field of Internet chat is emerging as an exciting frontier of grassroots transnational communications between those in Vietnam and their counterparts in the diaspora (Valverde 2002). By contrast, it seems clear at the present moment that VTV4 is failing in its mission as a public or official transnational broadcaster, dedicated to informing and educating Việt kiều, and promoting a sense of enduring membership in and loyalty to the homeland. However, its persistent presence on the periphery of the diasporic mediasphere is significant in itself, and one can predict that over time this will create a familiarizing and naturalizing effect. While efforts have been made to keep VTV4 news broadcasts neutral, the station's ideological function is still marked, especially for those committed to an anti-communist or pro-democracy homeland politics. In my opinion, VTV4 would need to improve its production values, let go of a significant amount of its ideological function, and concede more to the influence of market forces and their orientation towards audience desire to increase its appeal to overseas viewers. Finally, the only way a Vietnamese transnational broadcaster will genuinely engage diasporic audiences is by moving towards a public sphere model which would permit some form of Việt kiều social, cultural and even political self-representation — although this last suggestion must remain unthinkable to Hanoi at the present juncture.

Notes

1. In a 1993 publication on language policy, the biggest issue is that of minority languages, and there is no reference to globalization or foreign languages in Vietnam (Viện ngôn ngữ học 1993). A 2002 publication on the same topic addresses the issues of transcribing foreign words in Vietnamese and maintaining the "purity" of the langauage (Viện ngôn ngữ học 2002).
2. First broadcast internationally in 1945, radio station The Voice of Vietnam (VOV) was Vietnam's first "transnational" medium, but predated de-territorialized nation-building as imaginary and policy, and carried a narrowly defined propaganda function. VOV remains infinitely more important as a domestic rather than international medium, because of still imperfect TV access in rural and especially remote Vietnam (Nguyen 1998). VOV6 currently broadcasts internationally on short and medium wave in twelve languages (including Vietnamese), and is also available as a webcast.
3. Socialist Republic of Vietnam (SRV) diaspora scholar Tran Trong Dang Dan regards the Australian and North American communities as "extremely anti-communist", while he sees the Western European communities as being more politically diverse (Tran 1997, p. 147) Of over 2,000 publications having anticommunist content surveyed by Tran, 60 per cent originated in the United States, Canada and Australia, while only 35 per cent originated in over ten Western European nations (Tran 1997, p. 147).
4. In some overseas Vietnamese contexts, the term Việt kiều ["distant" Vietnamese] remains a sensitive one. In the recent past it carried negative

connotations of "national betrayal" in Vietnam, although this is arguably no longer the case. Compared to the official term Người Việt Nam ở Nước ngoài [Overseas Vietnamese], Việt kiều simply sounds somewhat informal. Nevertheless, some in the diaspora see the term as an undesirably homeland-centric way of defining overseas Vietnamese identity, and prefer alternative phrases. It has been my observation that Vietnamese Australians typically do not refer to themselves as Việt kiều while in Australia, but may well do so while in Vietnam. See Hoa (2000) for a discussion of the history of the term.

5. This last issue is of special importance to that significant number of Việt kiều who are interested in having houses in their homeland for both sentimental and economic reasons. Currently, the right to purchase houses is limited to those who return for long-term investment or who have made significant cultural, educational or other professional contributions to the nation. At the time of writing, the National Assembly is debating a liberal new provision that would allow Việt kiều to buy houses in Vietnam after remaining in the country for three consecutive months.

6. This quotation is taken from the official English version of Resolution 36. Here, and below, I have corrected it where its wording is ambiguous, having referred to the Vietnamese original.

7. See <http://www.tokten-vn.org.vn/>.

8. In contradistinction to Vietnamese citizens working as temporary migrant labourers in Asia and the Pacific, who remain more susceptible to State control.

9. These categories are styled after Levitt and de la Dehesa (2003).

10. This distinction is comparable to that in Chinese between *renmin* (denoting a political community) and *minzu* (denoting an ethnic nation).

11. In 2004 a Summer Camp for overseas Vietnamese youth was successfully organized by the Central Committee of the Ho Chi Minh Communist Youth Union, the Ministry of Foreign Affairs and the Committee for Overseas Vietnamese.

12. On the politics of overseas Vietnamese media, see Cunningham and Nguyen (2000), Carruthers (2001) and Valverde (2003).

13. Such "policies of introversion" (Levitt and de la Dehesa 2003, pp. 588–89), concerned with defending the security and rights of overseas communities, are more realistically directed at vulnerable Vietnamese diasporas in countries such as Cambodia, Laos and Thailand, and new migrant labour diasporas in East and Southeast Asia and the Pacific. They may safely be interpreted as rhetorical gestures when applied to the refugee diaspora in the West.

14. Broadcast media continue to be directly managed by the State in Vietnam. All other media forms belong to mass, social and professional organizations (Nguyen 1998, p. 66).

15. VTV4 began to broadcast over North America via the Telstar-5 satellite in

2000. It can also be seen in Vietnam on commercial Community Area Television packages.

16. Examples include: Vào bếp với những ngươi nổi tiếng [Celebrity Kitchen], Nữ sinh và tương lai [lit. "Female Student and the Future"], Đường lên đỉnh Olympia [The Road to Olympia] and Chiếc nón ký diệu [The Magic Hat]; and cultural programmes such as Việt Nam - Đất nước - Con người [Vietnam – Land – People], Văn học nghệ thuật [Literature and Art], and Phim truyện và ca nhạc [Film and Music].

17. SBS also broadcasts two hours of Vietnamese radio programming per day. These programmes are locally produced and share the anti-communist homeland politics of other diasporic media.

18. This interview was conducted with a senior SBS manager who was centrally involved in the events described. I have withheld his name here, at his own request, owing to the sensitivity of the issue.

19. Forrester reports that VTV4 was "trying to secure re-broadcast of programmes through SBS in Australia" in 1998, and at the same time trying to secure cable access in the United States for free re-broadcast of its programmes in regions with concentrations of Vietnamese-Americans (Forrester 1998, p. 80).

20. Nguyễn Chiến Thắng, Vice-president of the Committee on Overseas Vietnamese, notes that "Looking at the total picture … the SBS affair was only a small spot, and is not representative of the aspirations of the whole community. But what's important is that we don't give up, and that we continue to think about more appropriate ways of reaching out to satisfy the desires of our compatriots" (Cẩm Hà 2004).

21. *Trái Tim Việt Nam Online*, an overseas Vietnamese students' website, hosted a discussion headed "SBS should broadcast VTV4 because:" (<http://www.ttvnol.com/Oz/341499.ttvn>).

22. See <www.pacific-media.net>.

References

"Behind the Vietnamese Siege of SBS". *The Age Online*, 20 December 2004.

Cẩm Hà. "Mẫu số chung luôn là nặng nghĩa nước tình quê" [The common denominator is always deep love of homeland]. *Tuổi Trẻ Online*, 1 January 2004.

Carruthers, Ashley. "National Identity, Diasporic Anxiety and Music Video Culture in Vietnam". In *House of Glass: Culture, Modernity, and the State in Southeast Asia*, edited by S. Yao, pp. 119–49 (Singapore: Institute of Southeast Asian Studies, 2001).

———. "The Accumulation of National Belonging in Transnational Fields: Ways of Being at Home in Vietnam". In *Identities: Global Studies in Culture and Power* 9, no. 4 (2002): 423–44.

Cunningham, Stuart and Tina Nguyen. "Popular Media of the Vietnamese Diaspora". In *Floating Lives: The Media and Asian Diasporas*, edited by S. Cunningham and J. Sinclair, pp. 91–128. St Lucia, Qld: University of Queensland Press, 2000.

Dorais, Louis-Jacques. "Defining the Việt kiều", in *Diaspora* 10, no. 1 (2001): 3–27.

Forrester, Jan. "Instant Noodle Propaganda: Vietnam Television in the Late 1990s". In *The Mass Media in Vietnam*, edited by D.G. Marr, pp. 78–90. Canberra: Department of Political and Social Change, Research School of Pacific and Asian Studies, The Australian National University, 1998.

Fouron, Georges Eugene and Nina Glick Schiller. " 'All in the Family': Gender, Transnational Migration, and the Nation-State". In *Identities: Global Studies in Culture and Power* 7, no. 4 (2001): 539–82.

Gibson, Katherine, Lisa Law, et al. "Beyond Heroes and Victims: Filipina Contract Migrants, Economic Activism and Class Transformations". *International Feminist Journal of Politics* 3, no. 3 (2001): 365–86.

Glick Schiller, Nina, Linda Basch, et al., eds. *Nations Unbound: Transnational Projects, Postcolonial Predicaments and Deterritorialized Nation-States*. Langhorne, PA: Gordon and Breach, 1994.

Greenfield, Gerard. "Fragmented Visions of Asia's Next Tiger: Vietnam in the Pacific Century". In *The Rise of East Asia: Critical Visions of the Pacific Century*, edited by M.T. Berger and D.H. Borer, pp. 124–47. London and New York: Routledge, 1997.

Hạ Anh. "Trở ngại nào, khi đào tạo bằng tiếng Anh" [Obstacles to training in English]. *Vietnamnet*, 14 January 2004.

Hồ Thị Minh. "Cảm nghĩ sau khi xem VTV4" [Feelings on Watching VTV4]. *Việt Luận Online*, 17 August 2004.

Hoa, Diep Dinh. "An Apple Cannot Fall Far From the Apple Tree: The Role of Education in Immigrant Societies in the Prevention of National Division". Paper presented at the Immigrant Societies and Modern Education conference. Singapore: Tan Kah Kee Society and National University of Singapore, 2000.

"Hội nghị phổ biến và quán triệt nghị quyết 36 của Bộ Chính trị về công tác đối với người Việt Nam ở nước ngoài" [Conference Popularising and Explicating Politbureau Resolution 36 on Việt kiều]. *Quê Hương Online*, July 2004, p. 285.

Le, Sy Giao. "Xung quanh việc sử dụng khái niệm dân tộc ở Việt Nam" [Around the use of the concept dân tộc in Vietnam]". *Thông Tin Lý Luận* 261 (1999): 34–36.

Levitt, Peggy and Rafael de la Dehesa. "Transnational migration and the redefinition of the state: Variations and explanations". *Ethnic and Racial Studies* 26, no. 4 (2003): 587–611.

Long, Lynellyn D. "Viet Kieu on a fast track back?", in *Coming Home?*

Refugees, Migrants and Those Who Stayed Behind, edited by L.D. Long and E. Oxfeld, pp. 65–89. Philadelphia: University of Pennsylvania Press, 2004.

Marr, David G. "Introduction". In *The Mass Media in Vietnam*, edited by D.G. Marr, pp. 1–26. Canberra: Department of Political and Social Change, Research School of Pacific and Asian Studies, The Australian National University, 1998.

Ngô Văn Long. "Đổi hộ chiếu ở Matxcơva: Cũng mất 'phí dịch vụ" [Changing passport in Moscow: also incurs service fee]. *Tuổi Trẻ Online*, 24 March 2004.

"Người Việt ở nước ngoài được hỗ trợ học tiếng Việt" [Việt kiều receive help to study Vietnamese]. *Tuổi Trẻ Online*, 25 March 2004.

Nguyen, Dy Nien. "Tôi mong rằng sẽ có một bước chuyển lớn trong cộng đồng Người Việt Nam ở Nước ngoài" [I hope there will be a big change in the Việt kiều community]". *Quê Hương Online*, December 1998, p. 67.

Nguyen, Long. "Voice of Vietnam Radio: Past, Present and Future Prospects". In *The Mass Media in Vietnam*, edited by D.G. Marr, pp. 64–77. Canberra, Department of Political and Social Change, Research School of Pacific and Asian Studies, The Australian National University, 1998.

Nguyễn Thị Thục. "Trước giờ giao thừa" [Before new year's eve]. *Tuổi Trẻ Online*, 21 January 2004.

Ong, Aihwa. *Flexible Citizenship: The Cultural Logics of Transnationality*. Durham, N.C.: Duke University Press, 1999.

Ong, Aihwa and Donald Nonini. *Ungrounded Empires: The Cultural Politics of Modern Chinese Transnationalism*. New York: Routledge, 1997.

Pettus, Ashley. *Between Sacrifice and Desire: National Identity and the Governing of Femininity in Vietnam*. New York & London: Routledge, 2003.

Pham, Xuan Nam. Đổi Mới chính sách xã hội: luận cứ và giải pháp [Đổi mới social policy: foundations and solutions]. Hà Nội: Nhà Xuất Bản Chính Trị Quốc Gia, 1997.

Politbureau. *Resolution No 36 - NQ/TU*, 26 March 2004 by the Politbureau on Việt kiều Affairs.

Prime Minister. Quyết định của Thủ tướng Chính phủ số 281/QĐ-TTg ngày 22 tháng 3 năm 2004 về việc phê duyệt Đề án Hỗ trợ việc dạy và học tiếng Việt cho người Việt Nam ở nước ngoài [Prime Minister's decision 281/QĐ-TTg 22 March 2004 on implementing project to support language teaching for Việt kiều].

Quế Viên. "Ăn Tết Nguyên đàn ở chốn hanh khô" [Tết in a hot and dry place]. *Tuổi Trẻ Online*, 16 January 2004.

Stern, Lewis M. "The Return of the Prodigal Sons: The Party and the Viet Kieu". *Indochina Report*, 1992, p. 31.

Tran, Huu Phuc Tien. "Vietnamese Media in Transition: The Boon, Curse and Controversy of Market Economics". In *Media Fortunes, Changing Times:*

ASEAN States in Transition, edited by R.H.-K. Heng, pp. 231–48 (Singapore: Institute of Southeast Asian Studies, 2002).

Tran, Trong Dang Dan. *Người Việt Nam ở Nước ngoài [Overseas Vietnamese]*. Hà Nội: Nhà Xuất Bản Chính Trị Quốc Gia, 1997.

Valverde, Caroline Kieu Linh. "Making Transnational Viet Nam: Vietnamese American Community — Viet Nam Linkages through Money, Music and Modems". Unpublished Ph.D. thesis, University of California, Berkeley, 2002.

Valverde, Caroline Kieu Linh. "Making Vietnamese Music Transnational: Sounds of Home, Resistance and Change". *Amerasia Journal* 29, no. 1 (2003): 29–49.

Viện ngôn ngữ học. *Những vấn đề chính sách ngôn ngữ ở Việt Nam [Issues in language policy in Vietnam]*. Hà Nội: Nhà xuất bản khoa học xã hội, 1993.

Viện ngôn ngữ học. *Cảnh huống và chính sách ngôn ngữ ở Việt Nam [Language context and policy in Vietnam]*. Hà Nội: Nhà xuất bản khoa học xã hội, 2002.

"Viet Kieu Expected to Send Back $3 Bln". *Vietnam Investment Review Online*, 2–8 August 2004.

Yang, Mayfair Mei-hui. *Spaces of Their Own: Women's Public Sphere in Transnational China*. Minneapolis: University of Minnesota Press, 1999.

Websites

Ngươi Viễn Xứ, <www.nguoivienxu.vietnamnet.vn>.

Tuổi Trẻ Online, <www.tuoitre.com.vn>.

Việt Luận Online, <www.vietluan.com.au>.

"Vietnamese TV Forum", *Eman Technology website*, <www.emantechnology.com/forumhome.asp>.

Vietnamnet, <www.vnn.vn>.

VietSatellite, <www.vietsatellite.com/home.htm>.

VTV4 Forum, *Sadoun Satellite Sales website*, <www.sadoun.net/>.

Index

Suwarsih Djojopuspito, 61
Swettenham, Frank, 142
syair, 53

T
Tai-Kadai language family, 188
Talib Report, 129, 130
Tagalog
national language of Philippines,
17
Tagalog-based Filipino, 8, 26
Tagalog-speaking elites, 30
Tamil language
difficulties in creating Tamil elite,
103
Singapore, use in, 90
Tan Kah Kee, 78
Tan Lark Sye, 78
textbooks
Myanmar, 162
Philippines, 14
Thailand, 189
Thai academics, 181
Thai identity, 181
Thai languages, 194
regional dialects, 188
Thai Muslims, 193
Thai population
diverse numbers of ethnic groups,
192
thakin, 152, 154
Thailand
Arabic language, 189
average years of educational
attainment, 182
Central Region, 186
classification of ethnic minorities,
183
cultural diversity, 181
Displaced Burmese Nationals,
193
Eighth National Socio-Economic
Development Plan, 181

English language, 189
English language teachers, 189
Hill Tribes, 193
illegal immigrants from
Cambodia, 193
importance of assimilation, 193
Karen language, 189
Mandarin Chinese, 189
minority languages, 188, 193
non-Thai languages, position of,
181–94
Northeastern Region, 186
Pali language, 189
Pattani Malay language, 189
population, 182
Population and Housing Census
(2000), 182, 191
refugees from Indo-China, 193
socio-linguistic setting, 185
Southern region, 187
Teochiew, 189
textbooks, 189
Vietnamese refugees, 193
threatened languages, 96
Tunku Abdul Rahman, 118, 141
twinning programs
Malaysia, 146
Tydings McDuffie Law, 11

U
U Ne Win, 163, 176
U Nu, 155, 156, 158, 175
UNDP Transfer of Knowledge
Through Expatriate Nationals,
199
Unfederated Malay States, 119
Union of Myanmar, 154, 157, 164
Union Solidarity and Development
Association (USDA), 171
United Chinese School Teachers'
Association (UCSTA), 144
United Malay National Organization
(UMNO), 124

www.ingramcontent.com/pod-product-compliance
Lightning Source LLC
Chambersburg PA
CBHW021542260326
41914CB00001B/131